ALASKA
ASCENTS

ALASKA
ASCENTS

▲

WORLD-CLASS
MOUNTAINEERS
TELL THEIR
STORIES

▼

Edited by Bill Sherwonit

Alaska Northwest Books™

Anchorage ▲ Seattle ▲ Portland

Acknowledgments

First and foremost, I would like to thank the writers for their stories of Alaska's great peaks and all those who permitted those stories to be reprinted in this anthology. I'm also immeasurably indebted to Tom Meacham, who gave me access to his mountaineering library and assisted my search for pioneering ascents of Alaska's mountains; and to Mirella Tenderini, who so graciously helped when my search for copyright permissions led me (via phone and fax) to Italy.

Special thanks to Fred Beckey, for writing the foreword to this book; to Bradford Washburn, for his insights and vast knowledge of Alaska's mountaineering history; to Rodman Wilson, for access to his collection of American Alpine Journals; to Neil O'Donnell, who led me to Dora Keen's story; and to Ellen Wheat, who helped to inspire this anthology and then offered guidance, encouragement, and her considerable editing and organization skills as it was being pieced together. I would also like to thank production editor Kris Fulsaas, map-maker Debbie Newell, and Dulcy Boehle for her help proofreading.

I'm also grateful to those who provided photos, to everyone who gave me suggestions and assistance as this anthology took shape, and, above all, to Mike Howerton, who introduced me to Denali and inspired my first mountaineering story about Alaska's great peaks. I dedicate this book to Mike.

Copyright © 1996 by Bill Sherwonit

Library of Congress Cataloging-in-Publication Data:
Alaska ascents : world-class mountaineers tell their stories / [compiled] by Bill
     Sherwonit.
          p.   cm.
        Includes bibliographical references and index.
        ISBN 0-88240-479-2
        1. Mountaineering—Alaska.   I. Sherwonit, Bill, 1950–
    GV199.42.A4A526   1996   96-3021
    796.5'22'09798—dc20   CIP

Editor: Ellen Harkins Wheat   Designer: Constance Bollen   Map: Debbie Newell

PHOTOS: FRONT COVER/PAGE 1: *Climbers traversing the Matanuska Glacier on their approach to Catalog Peak, a spur peak in the Mount Marcus Baker area, Chugach Range.* Photo by Joel W. Rogers. **BACK COVER/PAGE 129:** *Climbers descend Denali, Alaska Range.* Photo by Bill Sherwonit. **PAGE 21:** *East Ridge, Mount St. Elias, St. Elias Range.* Photo by John Bauman. **PAGE 117:** *Mount Marcus Baker (Mount St. Agnes), Chugach Range.* Photo by Bradford Washburn. **PAGE 267:** *The Arrigetch Peaks, Brooks Range.* Photo by Bill Sherwonit. **PAGE 296:** *The author at 17,200 feet, West Buttress, Mount McKinley.* Photo by Bill Sherwonit.

Alaska Northwest Books™
An imprint of Graphic Arts Center Publishing Company
Editorial office: 2208 NW Market Street, Suite 300, Seattle, WA 98107
Catalog and order dept.: P.O. Box 10306, Portland, OR 97210
800-452-3032

Printed on acid-and elemental-chlorine-free paper in the United States of America

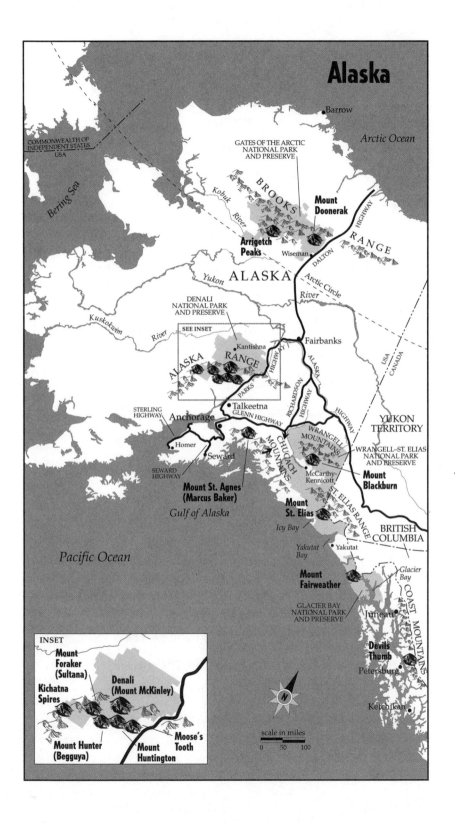

Alaska

Arctic Ocean

Bering Sea

Pacific Ocean

Gulf of Alaska

COMMONWEALTH OF INDEPENDENT STATES
USA

Barrow

GATES OF THE ARCTIC
NATIONAL PARK
AND PRESERVE

BROOKS

Mount
Doonerak

RANGE

Kobuk River

Arrigetch
Peaks

Wiseman

DALTON

HIGHWAY

Yukon

ALASKA

Arctic Circle

River

Kuskokwim

River

DENALI
NATIONAL PARK
AND PRESERVE

SEE INSET

Kantishna

ALASKA RANGE

HIGHWAY

PARKS

Fairbanks

ALASKA

RICHARDSON

HIGHWAY

USA
CANADA

STERLING
HIGHWAY

Anchorage

Talkeetna

GLENN HIGHWAY

Homer

Seward

SEWARD
HIGHWAY

Mount St. Agnes
(Marcus Baker)

CHUGACH

MOUNTAINS

WRANGELL
MOUNTAINS

McCarthy-
Kennicott

HIGHWAY

YUKON
TERRITORY

WRANGELL–ST. ELIAS
NATIONAL PARK
AND PRESERVE

Mount
Blackburn

Mount
St. Elias

ST. ELIAS RANGE

BRITISH
COLUMBIA

Icy Bay

Yakutat
Bay

Yakutat

Glacier
Bay

Mount
Fairweather

GLACIER BAY
NATIONAL PARK
AND PRESERVE

COAST

MOUNTAINS

Juneau

Devils
Thumb

Petersburg

Ketchikan

N

scale in miles
0   50   100

INSET

Mount
Foraker
(Sultana)

Kichatna
Spires

Denali
(Mount McKinley)

Moose's
Tooth

Mount Hunter
(Begguya)

Mount
Huntington

Contents

PART IV
The Brooks Range – 267

Foreword

– FRED BECKEY –

THE DELAY IN EXPLORING Alaska was in part due to the reluctance of the U.S. military to take up this monumental task, a delay that indirectly kept Americans from doing any serious mountaineering there until after the turn of the century—well after alpine climbing took place in Canada, Mexico, and the remainder of the United States. Long presumed to be the highest peak in North America was not Denali but the graceful St. Elias, sighted by Vitus Bering on July 17, 1741, during the Russian "discovery" of America. Not surprisingly, the first serious expeditions were those to Mount St. Elias, notably the brilliant and largely forgotten efforts of Israel C. Russell, who in the 1890s twice came close to reaching the summit. Russell's pioneering led to the heralded victory of the brother of the Italian king—Prince Luigi Amadeo di Savoia, duke of the Abruzzi, in 1897—and conducted on a grand style (the guided expedition included bedsteads for sleeping on the lower glacier).

Early European explorers saw only the coastal mountains of Alaska, where St. Elias, Fairweather, and other great ice-clad giants form the world's highest coastal range and generate the continent's largest expanse of glaciers. In stark contrast to the jumbled rivalry of peaks in the Alaska Range and in the Alaska Panhandle, the colossal St. Elias Mountains stand solitary or in compact, isolated groups.

The Alaska boundary, which bisects a mountain wilderness that must be seen to be appreciated, is a legacy of British Captain George Vancouver's charts, which depicted a continuous chain trending around all heads of the ocean inlets. Later explorations prove that these features had no real existence, and that there was only a "sea of mountains" amid glaciers that are a reminder of the Ice Ages. It was in these boundary ice-fields that both American and Canadian surveyors early in the century wrote a largely unsung chapter in the history of North American mountaineering. Where a clash of environments, with moist Pacific air thrust across the alpine coastal ranges, produced the Stikine and Juneau

Icefields, these intrepid surveyors spent twelve seasons laying out the Alaska–Canada boundary.

An 1862 gold rush led to the exploration of the great Stikine River, which later that century became a favored route into the Klondike. The mighty silt-laden river route led to the region's first serious cragging, that of John Muir in 1879. In his book *Alaska Days with John Muir*, the Reverend S. Hall Young cast the roaming environmentalist as moving in a "deer lope" as he "began to slide up that mountain . . . a sure instinct for the easiest way . . . a serpent-glide up the steep; eye, hand and foot all connected dynamically."

Most alpine undertakings in Alaska do not involve cragging, but represent committing teamwork, often involving a certain risk. Mountaineering here represents a grand human adventure in one of the most diverse regions imaginable. What the dean of the Alaska mountain expeditions, Brad Washburn, once wrote about Denali, "McKinley is always a serious proposition," can be equally valid elsewhere in the state. A proven method of minimizing problems is careful planning and preparation. Boyd Everett, who wrote *The Organization of an Alaskan Expedition*, epitomized preparedness, and he ran his expeditions like a general.

The variety of Alaskan ascents range from simple glacier hikes to the most terrifying ice route on Mount Huntington or a committing rock wall in the Kichatna Spires. Alaskan climbing, with some notable exceptions, seldom requires great athletic skill; gallantry can usually be obtained easier in other lands. And while technical skill and physical strength are absolute requirements for certain routes, good judgment and perseverance are equally important, and often more so.

Becoming marooned by storms and threatened by avalanches are hazards that may be encountered in most of the world's alpine mountain ranges. But in Alaska it is the crossing of glaciers that can provide a special catalog of horrors. All glaciers are not created equal: some are classified as temperate, others polar. Alaska has both, and some have internal characteristics of both types. Negotiating the countless stretchmarks on a large Alaskan glacier is often the most vexing and frightening aspect of a mountain adventure.

Denali, the centerpiece of the great Alaska Range, has become the focus of climbing expeditions to the state. But as Bill Sherwonit's anthology chronicles, this range includes not only internationally famous McKinley, but a marvelous cast of alluring attendant peaks—including

Foraker, Hunter, Huntington, the Moose's Tooth, and Cathedral Spires. In other compass directions are the Brooks Range, the Chugach Range, the Wrangell and St. Elias Mountains, and the Coast Mountains of Southeast Alaska. This collection of writings recalls especially noteworthy accomplishments in Alaska's mountain ranges. It is a thoughtful vision into the past. In the Great Land, the future for similar accomplishments is equally grand.

Giving Voice to Alaska's Great Peaks

– BILL SHERWONIT –

SEVERAL YEARS AGO I BEGAN work on an Alaska mountaineering book that would include climbing stories from all of the state's major mountain ranges. But in talking to climbers and researching Alaska's mountaineering literature, I found myself pulled more and more toward Denali—or Mount McKinley, as North America's highest peak remains officially named. There were so many compelling stories about the mountain, most of them unknown except within the climbing community; in just a few weeks, I found enough information to fill several volumes. And so I narrowed the scope of my writing to "The High One."

Since its publication in 1990, *To the Top of Denali* has been joined by at least five other books on McKinley, including three by past and present world-class mountaineers: a Bradford Washburn–David Roberts collaboration, and others by Jon Waterman and Fred Beckey. By Washburn's count—and no one has kept better track than he—more than twenty books have been written about Denali expeditions; many others have included one or more chapters on the peak. Given the mountain's status, and its tug on both climbers and authors, more are sure to follow.

In this book I return to my original idea and give voice to many of Alaska's great peaks, and the people—not always mountaineers—who've explored and climbed them. This anthology serves up a representative sampling of Alaska climbing literature past and present, from mountain ranges across the state. Included here are stories of Alaska's most highly acclaimed ascents, written by many of America's most celebrated climbers of the past half century.

Though Denali and its Alaska Range neighbors are the best known of Alaska's mountains, and the ones most highly prized and frequently written about by contemporary mountaineers, the state's climbing history began hundreds of miles to the south and east, along Alaska's

Gulf Coast in what are now called the St. Elias Mountains. That's where European explorers first sighted and described the state's great snow and ice mountains. And it's where the continent's tallest mountain was thought to be—Mount St. Elias. Climbing teams came in the late 1800s to capture that prize, and only in the early 1900s (after St. Elias had been ascended) did mountaineers shift their attention to the Alaska Range, where a peak newly named McKinley had become recognized as North America's highest.

Denali (I, like many Alaskans, prefer the Native name to McKinley, which honors Ohio politician William McKinley, who in his lifetime had no connection to the great peak) proved a magnet for mountaineering parties from 1903 until 1913, when it too was climbed. But for the next few decades, many of the state's milestone ascents were done in Alaska's Wrangell, St. Elias, and Coast Ranges, on high coastal mountains that grabbed climbers' attention and were comparatively easy to reach, in an era when foot, dogsled, and boat travel offered the primary access to the state's ranges.

The focus of Alaska mountaineering would change dramatically, and forever, in 1951, when bush pilot (and mountaineer) Terris Moore dropped a group of Denali mountaineers—Bradford Washburn among them—on the previously unexplored Kahiltna Glacier south of the peak. The use of airplanes was nothing new. In fact the first glacier landings had occurred on Denali's northern flanks in 1932, when Fairbanks pilots Joe Crosson and Jerry Jones delivered five climbers and their equipment to the Muldrow Glacier. By the 1940s, planes had been used to assist major climbing expeditions in nearly all of Alaska's major mountain ranges, both to air-drop supplies and to land people and gear near the bases of peaks to be climbed. Most major Wrangell–St. Elias expeditions in the past half century have used the expertise of such "glacier pilots" as Bob Reeve, Jack Wilson, and Mike Ivers.

But this 1951 air-supported expedition, more than any other, opened Denali to mountaineers, by making its easiest climbing route, the West Buttress, accessible to fly-in expeditions—and eventually, to the masses. It wasn't long before "Denali Flyers"—bush pilots based in the town of Talkeetna, gateway to the Alaska Range—were regularly flying mountaineers into and out of other Alaska Range peaks as well. In Denali's alpine neighborhood are several mountains considered among the most challenging and beautiful in North America: Hunter, Foraker, Moose's

Tooth, Mount Huntington, the Kichatna Spires. With the long and time-consuming overland approaches of earlier pioneering expeditions now replaced by half-hour or hour-long plane flights, mountaineers could go lighter and faster and focus their attention on the peaks themselves; the "getting there" was dependent only on flyable weather. Summerlong expeditions were replaced by month- or even weeklong trips and, in some cases, by one- or two-day alpine ascents.

Explorers gave way to rock- and ice-climbing specialists, who came in increasing numbers from around the country, and eventually from around the world, to take on the alpine challenges posed by ever more difficult walls and ridges. With Denali serving as its centerpiece, the Alaska Range became the state's most charismatic climbing ground, and one of the easiest to reach.

Beyond the Alaska Range, many of the state's other great peaks—Fairweather, St. Elias, Devils Thumb, Marcus Baker, Blackburn, the Arrigetch, to name a few—have continued to demand difficult approaches and complex expedition logistics even in this fly-in era. Coastal mountains are often plagued by even stormier weather than the Alaska Range, and some high peaks are ignored because their rock is difficult or dangerous to climb. Even St. Elias, once the grand prize of Alaska mountaineering, now attracts little attention. Some years, no one attempts the mountain, while on Denali more than a thousand try. Largely this has to do with St. Elias's weather; it's among the stormiest mountains in the world. But it also has to do with long, Himalayan-like approaches, even with airplane access, and the fact that most of its routes are highly avalanche prone.

It's therefore no surprise that while the Alaska Range has inspired hundreds of climbing stories, the state's other mountains have generated few, especially in the past forty years. The selections in this anthology reflect the Alaska Range's overwhelming appeal: more than half the pieces are from this one mountain range.

Beyond the climbing challenges that mountain ridges and walls present, mountaineers in Alaska face several variables that add to each peak's difficulty. There are the huge ice fields and miles-long, heavily crevassed glaciers to be negotiated, glaciers that are orders of magnitude larger than anything in the Lower 48; one is larger than the state of Rhode Island. On many of the great peaks there are the ever-present dangers of hanging glaciers, icefalls, and avalanches. And there are frequent and long-lasting subarctic and coastal storms unimaginable in more temperate climates. Accompanied by winds of more than 100 mph, mountain blizzards may dump five, ten, or even twenty feet of snow; Alaska's climbing literature is filled with stories of expeditions turned back from the summit by ferocious storms that last for days. There's also the subarctic cold; nighttime temperatures on the higher peaks may drop to –20° or –30°F even in summer. And the northerly latitude accentuates oxygen deprivation at high elevations. As Jon Waterman has explained in his book *High Alaska*, "A grading system [to denote degree of difficulty] that is unique to Alaska is needed because of the severe storms, the cold, the altitude, and the extensive cornicing. Conditions can change radically from day to day. . . ."

The anthology is divided into four geographical sections: (1) the St. Elias, Wrangell, and Coast Ranges; (2) the Chugach Range; (3) Denali and the Alaska Range; and (4) the Brooks Range. Within each section, the mountains are generally presented in the order in which they were climbed, though that rule is bent in the Alaska Range.

Located in the state's southeastern corner, the St. Elias, Wrangell, and Coast Ranges were the earliest groups of mountains to be seen, described, explored, and eventually climbed by white Euro-American adventurers and, later, mountaineers. (Alaska's indigenous Native groups have tended to revere the state's great peaks from afar, using them as points of reference and, in some instances, treating them as holy places, rather than something to be conquered. Only after non-Native pioneers—with their passion for discovery, exploration, and conquest—learned of the high mountains' existence did people attempt to unravel their secrets or climb to their tops.)

The anthology's first selection (in Part I) recounts the historic ascent of Mount St. Elias, a coastal mountain along the Alaska–Canada border. Once believed to be the continent's highest peak, St. Elias lured a half-dozen expeditions in the late nineteenth century. But with its successful ascent in 1897—and, perhaps more critically, the discovery that Denali was even higher—interest in the mountain waned dramatically. In this century only a few hundred climbers have attempted St. Elias, the world's highest coastal mountain and fourth-tallest peak in North America, largely because the mountain, even with air travel, has a long and dangerous approach and is notoriously battered by frequent coastal storms. Organized and led by Italian adventurer Prince Luigi Amadeo di Savoia, called the Duke of the Abruzzi, the 1897 ascent of St. Elias is considered among the most remarkable climbs ever done in North America. And the account of that expedition, written by team doctor and scientist Filippo de Filippi, is similarly considered one of the great mountaineering epics. Published in 1900 and out of print for decades, the American version of *The Ascent of Mount St. Elias* is now a collector's item.

The St. Elias Mountains of Alaska and Canada are the highest coastal mountains in the world, and they contain two of the continent's four tallest peaks (18,008-foot Mount St. Elias and the Yukon's 19,850-foot Mount Logan). Together with the Wrangell Mountains immediately to the northwest, they comprise what alpine guide Bob Jacobs calls "North America's mountain kingdom." Within the bounds of these two great ranges are nine of the continent's sixteen highest peaks and its largest sub-polar ice field, the Bagley, which feeds a system of gigantic glaciers. Three Wrangell peaks rise above 14,000 feet and two above 16,000: 16,523-foot Mount Blackburn and 16,237-foot Mount Sanford. But little, besides climbing reports or small articles in *The American Alpine Journal,* has been written about them or their neighbors. The best, by far, is the account written by Dora Keen, a world traveler and adventure seeker from the East Coast of the United States. Though not well known, Keen's magazine account of her 1912 ascent of Blackburn is an insightful and engaging tale of early twentieth-century mountaineering in Alaska.

Some 270 miles southeast of Mount Blackburn and 150 miles from Mount St. Elias, within Glacier Bay National Park, is another coastal mountain that in this century has arguably generated more climbing interest than any Alaskan peak outside the Alaska Range. One of the boundary peaks that mark the Alaska–Canada border, 15,300-foot Mount Fairweather began luring climbing teams in the mid-1920s, and was successfully ascended in 1931—decades before most of the Alaska Range giants were even attempted. Included here is Paddy Sherman's account of a 1958 expedition up Fairweather. A Canadian climber and journalist who's ascended several of North and South America's highest peaks, Sherman led a team to Fairweather's top to celebrate British Columbia's centennial.

Even farther down Alaska's coast, the St. Elias Mountains give way to the Coast Mountains, where in 1977 mountaineering author Jon Krakauer climbed another boundary peak, the Devils Thumb, a granite tower with Yosemite-like walls. Krakauer has climbed in several countries and throughout much of Alaska; his ascent of the Thumb is one of the great solo sagas in North America mountaineering history. More than a decade would pass before he finally wrote of his obsession with this 9,077-foot peak and put it in his book *Eiger Dreams.*

West of the Wrangell–St. Elias mountains is another coastal range, the Chugach Mountains (Part II). Arcing more than 300 miles from Cook Inlet almost to the Canadian border, the Chugach is Alaska's second-highest coastal range. But its mountains aren't especially grand, by Alaskan standards; the tallest Chugach peak, Mount Marcus Baker, is 13,176 feet high. And its rocks are largely crumbly metamorphics, known among climbers as "Chugach crud." The most notable story to be inspired by this range is Bradford Washburn's account of the first ascent, in 1938, of Marcus Baker, then named Mount St. Agnes. One of the most active climbers in Alaska from the 1930s through the 1950s, Washburn is known throughout the world for his mountaineering, mapmaking, and photographic talents. In Alaska he's best known as "Mr. McKinley," but he participated in major expeditions to a dozen peaks. Besides documenting the Mount St. Agnes expedition in typical Washburn depth, this famous New Englander presents a detailed picture of Alaska mountaineering in the 1930s.

Part III, the Alaska Range, begins with Denali. Among the many historic ascents of the mountain, I have chosen four milestone climbs that have, over the years, attained legendary stature. The first of those is the 1910 Sourdough expedition, in which four gold miners climbed the mountain's 19,470-foot North Peak, to challenge the claims of explorer Frederick Cook. Next is Hudson Stuck's account of the mountain's first successful ascent in 1913. An Episcopal missionary who'd come north to work with Alaska's Natives, he described his historic expedition in *The Ascent of Denali.*

The third Denali story is taken from Riccardo Cassin's *Fifty Years of Alpinism.* It documents an Italian team's ascent of the mountain's supposedly impossible south face in 1961. Considered one of Europe's foremost alpinists, Cassin was the driving force behind what many mountaineers still consider one of the greatest climbs ever done in Alaska.

The last of the included Denali accounts is an excerpt from Art Davidson's *Minus 148°: The Winter Ascent of Mt. McKinley.* Now a world-traveling author and Anchorage businessman, Davidson participated in numerous Alaskan expeditions during his climbing prime in the 1960s, but the one that achieved the greatest notoriety was the 1967 Denali expedition, in which a team of eight climbers became the first to walk the mountain's slopes—and reach its top—in winter.

Among Denali's satellite peaks are several of Alaska's highest and most alluring mountains. The Alaska Range accounts for one-tenth of Steve Roper and Allen Steck's *Fifty Classic Climbs of North America*—and some would argue that the range is underrepresented in their book. As a group, the range's big-walled and steep-sided granite mountains have inspired some of the most harrowing ascents and engaging accounts of Alaska's mountains. Among the most heralded is David Roberts' *The Mountain of My Fear*. Written in the late 1960s, this story about the first ascent of 12,240-foot Mount Huntington's West Face—in Roberts' words, "a magnificent wall of sheer rock"—has been widely praised as one of the most brilliant pieces of American mountaineering literature ever written, by a man who's been recognized as one of the nation's finest mountaineers and climbing authors.

That Huntington would inspire such writing seems only right: many within the climbing community call it Alaska's most beautiful mountain. Others would argue that such an honor should go to the Moose's Tooth. Located ten miles east of Huntington, overlooking the Alaska Range's "Great Gorge," this 10,335-foot granite monolith has entranced some of North America's most talented big-wall climbers, including Terrance "Mugs" Stump and Jim "The Bird" Bridwell. Their 1981 alpine-style ascent of the Moose's Tooth East Face was one of the most audacious climbs ever done in Alaska. And Bridwell's account, "The Dance of the Woo Li Masters," is a classic in its own right, the perfect match for his and Stump's climbing style.

Even more amazing was John Mallon Waterman's 1978 solo ascent of Mount Hunter, the Alaska Range's third-highest mountain and, in many climbers' view, the most difficult 14,000-foot peak in North America. Waterman's 145-day assault on 14,570-foot Hunter still has climbers shaking their heads. Some consider it a brilliant accomplishment; others merely see it as bizarre. Waterman wrote a short expedition account for the *American Alpine Journal*, but what's included here is a profile of "Johnny" by another Waterman well known in America's mountaineering circles: Jon. Excerpted from *In the Shadow of Denali*, Jon Waterman's essay not only describes Johnny's notorious "vendetta" with Hunter, but paints haunting portraits of two Watermans, Jon and Johnny, both intimately connected with the Alaska Range.

Another Hunter classic is Fred Beckey's account of his landmark ascent of the mountain's West Ridge with Heinrich Harrer and Henry Meybohm. Beckey arguably has been North America's most prolific mountaineer over the past half century. Though most intimately connected to the Pacific Northwest's Cascade Range, he's climbed dozens of Alaska's mountains, many of them first ascents. And no other mountaineer has maintained a longer active climbing connection to Alaska than Beckey, who first visited in the 1940s. Of his many Alaskan escapades, Beckey's "triple" ascents of Denali, Deborah, and Hunter in 1954 remain his best known and most highly applauded. In this collection is an essay on the Hunter ascent taken from his 1993 book, *Mount McKinley: Icy Crown of North America*.

A third Hunter expedition described in this section is Michael Kennedy and George Lowe's first ascent of the Northwest Face in 1977. But that climb was merely the warm-up for an even more ambitious undertaking: an attempt on Alaska's third-highest peak, 17,400-foot Mount Foraker, via a route that's been compared in both beauty and difficulty to Denali's Cassin Ridge. The pair's success on both Hunter and Foraker—traditionally known to Native Alaskans as Begguya and Sultana, Denali's Child and Wife—is told in an understated but vivid narrative by Kennedy, the editor of *Climbing* magazine.

The other Alaska Range piece concerns a group of dazzling granite towers that climbers somehow overlooked until the 1960s. The Kichatna Spires have attracted many of the country's premier big-wall climbers, including Yosemite legend Royal Robbins. Considered the premier rock climber of the 1960s and early 1970s, Robbins offers his unique perspective in "Californians in Alaska."

Part IV features Alaska's northernmost mountain range. Stretching east–west across the state, the Brooks Range, like the Chugach, has little to offer most hard-core mountaineers seeking great heights or granite walls or ridges; its mountains, for the most part, are comparatively gentle and easy to climb. A notable exception is the Arrigetch Peaks, steep-sided and big-walled granite spires up to 8,000 feet high. Unclimbed until the 1960s, the Arrigetch attracted a series of expeditions once word began to spread, and by 1970 the summits of all had been reached. The account given here is one by David Roberts, taken from his book *Moments of Doubt*.

More than 100 miles northeast of the Arrigetch is a "towering, black, unscalable-looking giant," which forestry scientist, wilderness advocate and Brooks Range explorer Robert Marshall named Doonerak in 1929. Though it later proved to be an easy ascent for experienced mountaineers, Doonerak was unclimbable for Marshall and his companions. Not a mountaineering tale in the usual sense, Marshall's account of his expedition to the mountain and attempts to ascend the peak—taken from his celebrated book *Arctic Wilderness*—is in its own right an Alaska classic.

From Filippi and Keen to Roberts and Krakauer, the storytellers in this anthology powerfully present the nature of Alaska's high peaks. These are remote and often dangerously wild places that most of us will never reach or even hope to visit. Yet it's also clear that they're enthralling, beautiful, inspirational. And they're places where many of the world's great mountaineers have pushed the limits of what's possible. In the telling of these stories, we also learn about the people who are drawn to mountaintops, who find challenge, hope, connection, triumph, and sometimes tragedy in Alaska's high places. Besides offering a sampler of Alaska's greatest mountaineering feats and literature, this anthology should tantalize the reader to wonder about those thousands of Alaska mountains that remain unclimbed or even untried, and that continue to offer great challenges not only for the ambitious climber but for the writer as well.

Part I

THE
ST. ELIAS,
WRANGELL,
AND
COAST
RANGES

The Ascent of Mount St. Elias

— Filippo de Filippi —

On July 16, 1741, Danish explorer Vitus Bering and his St. Peter crew, on an expedition for Russian czar Peter the Great, spotted "high snow-covered mountains . . . among them a high volcano" on their northern horizon. Not only did this North Pacific sighting mark their "discovery" of Alaska, it was also the first recorded observation of a starkly elegant mountain that would, for many years, be considered the continent's highest. Four days later, Bering anchored his ship off a point of land that he named Cape St. Elias, to honor the day's patron saint. The mountain, however, remained unnamed until 1778, when English captain James Cook took Bering's lead and identified it as Mount St. Elias on his charts.

In the late 1800s, St. Elias's reputation as the continent's tallest mountain lured a series of expeditions. The first, led by adventurer Frederick Schwatka and sponsored by the New York Times *in 1886, reached only 7,200 feet. Two years later, an English party led by W. H. Topham reached 11,600 feet before retreating. Then, in 1890 and again in 1891, University of Michigan professor Israel Russell took scientific teams to St. Elias; his second expedition reached 14,500 feet before being stopped by storms. Russell*

*determined the mountain's height to be 18,100 feet, remarkably close to what
is now the accepted altitude, 18,008.*

*Six years later, in 1897, an Italian team guided by Russell's maps and
notes would become the first to ascend a major Alaska mountain. The expedition's leader: Prince Luigi Amadeo di Savoia, Duke of the Abruzzi, brother of
the king of Italy. Though only twenty-four, and blessed with only moderate
climbing skills, the duke had been trained in the military, loved adventure, and
by all accounts was a naturally charismatic leader. Following Russell's suggestions, the Italians put their base camp near the Malaspina Glacier. On July
1, the duke, his nine team members, and several American porters began hauling gear to St. Elias's northern flanks. By July 28 they'd established a camp at
12,280 feet, along what is now called the Abruzzi Ridge; three days later all
ten climbers reached the summit. The duke went on to lead other major mountaineering expeditions in Europe, Asia, and Africa. St. Elias, meanwhile,
would lose its "tallest" status and, therefore, much of its allure. Not until 1946
would another team reach its summit.*

The following excerpts are from The Ascent of Mount St. Elias, *written
by Abruzzi team physician and scientist Filippo de Filippi. Considered an enduring favorite in mountaineering literature, it was published in Italian, English,
and German. An American edition translated by Linda Villari with the author's
supervision was published in 1900 by Frederick A. Stokes and Co. in New York.*

VII: Newton Glacier

ON JULY 16TH WE STRUCK our tents at Sledge Camp and set out to climb the
Newton Glacier, dividing our party into several caravans, each of which
started as soon as the loads were packed. We had spent one night only in
this camp, and had worked very hard to get everything in readiness for
the start. We were impatient to make our way up this last valley, from the
top of which we expected to obtain a complete view of Mount St. Elias
from base to summit.

The Agassiz Glacier pours down from its basin in a very broken state,
and its surface becomes still more chaotic as it flows past the terminal cascade of the Newton. The two glaciers do not fuse at once in a single mass
at their point of junction; for some distance the Newton séracs stand out

from the surface of the Agassiz in the shape of huge blocks of hard snow, scattered between the crevasses, or half buried in them, now stretching across them like a bridge, or again poised on the very brink, often at so sharp an angle that one expects them to fall at any moment. To reach the foot of the ice-fall at the western end, we have to walk for a while over this rugged tangle of the Agassiz, threading labyrinths of ice-blocks and cautiously crossing snow-bridges, over numerous crevasses, often half filled with water.

We gained the Newton plateau in the same way that we had mounted the terminal ice-fall of the Seward; namely, by a tongue of snow and ice wedged between the rocks and séracs. This gully, however, is double the height of that on the Seward (about 600 feet), and is split halfway up by three or four wide crevasses, with edges of live ice, placed almost vertically one above the other. To cross these with our loads was an unpleasant bit of work, but neither difficult nor dangerous. The snow in the gully was studded with stones and boulders fallen from the perpendicular rock-wall 1,000 feet in height, which bounds it on the left, and is furrowed with innumerable vertical grooves, surmounted at the top by a glacier, of which the edge is visible.

On reaching the top of this couloir we turned to the right towards the centre of the Newton Glacier.

The upper valley was filled with mist, and we could see nothing in front of us, excepting another huge fall of séracs, extending across the whole width of the glacier and apparently barricading the valley. In little more than half an hour we had traversed the plateau and cast off our loads almost at the foot of the second ice-fall, 14,485 feet above the sea.

The leading characteristic of all the great glaciers of this region—namely their division into terraces connected by ice-falls—is more obvious in the Newton than in any of the others. Here the foot of the terminal ice-fall is at 3,740 feet above the sea, while the basin from which it flows is at 8,661 feet. The difference of level is owing almost entirely to the three tremendous drops, between which the glacier forms three plateaux. The lowest of these, just above the terminal cascade, is 745 feet higher than the Agassiz; the second terrace is 1,875 feet above the first, while the topmost is at a level of 2,201 feet above the second. Thus the ice-falls increase in height as the valley rises. The lowest, however, has the most precipitous drop, and the ice is so broken that it might perhaps be impossible to climb it in the centre; the second is less steep, and subdivided by a short stretch of comparatively level, though still broken ice. The highest of the three is steeper and shorter than the middle one. The surface of the intermediate terraces is undulating and full of crevasses; but the uppermost of these is the widest and steepest. In fact, the two lower plateaux are almost level, and at certain points their slope is actually reversed.

The glacier runs through a deep valley, the head of which is closed by a steep ice-wall rising to the col between Mount St. Elias and Mount Newton. On either side it is bounded by two buttresses of Mount St. Elias, with a medium height of about 10,000 feet. Of these the one to the north is the more picturesque. To the blunt, flattened summit of Mount Newton succeeds a long series of slender pinnacles and dizzy ice-peaks, reaching heights of 12,000 to 13,000 feet, and connected by sharp ridges, variously twisted and curved, falling at every angle on all sides, and edged with huge cornices of snow. The chain extends as far as Mount Behring, keeping the same height throughout its length. A short ridge juts out from the latter summit, and, barring the base of the valley, compels the Newton Glacier, running from west to east, to change its direction during the last part of its course towards the Agassiz, so that its terminal cascade faces due south. The southern buttress of the valley, starting from the eastern crest of Mount St. Elias, forms two fine peaks— one of ice, the other of rock; then running down to the mouth of the vale, makes a turn to the south-west, and forms the western wall of the Agassiz Glacier. This mountain barrier separates the Newton and Agassiz from the Libbey Glacier, which pours down into the Malaspina from the south-east flank of St. Elias. Both sides of the valley throughout its length are precipitous and deeply covered with snow; even where the cliffs are vertical or overhanging the frequent snow-falls leave them sprinkled with white patches. Numerous glaciers, piled into séracs, cling to the steep rocks, as though suspended over the valley, and some end suddenly in a vertical white wall at the edge of the precipice. Of the many peaks crowning the valley, not one seems accessible from it; throughout this vast range of mountains one looks in vain for some point of vantage whence a reasonably secure route to the top may be descried. The sole exception is the short extent of cliff that bars the head of the valley and leads to the base of the northern ridge of Mount St. Elias, although at too great a distance for us to decide as to its safety from avalanches.

The Newton Glacier is about eight miles in length. It took us thirteen days to reach the upper end. We encamped six times on the way, and our average march was a little over a mile and a half. We had to contend almost constantly with persistent and dense snow-falls, which lasted entire days, enveloping us in a blinding cloud that made our surroundings strangely vague. It was heavy walking through the powdery snow, in which we often sank to our hips, while we had to grope our way patiently among the great blocks of ice, over snow-bridges, often insecure, and amid the incessant roar of avalanches and stone-falls which thundered down from morning till night on the margins of the glacier.

The Newton was no less inhospitable to us than it had been to our predecessor, Russell, for we had only three fine days out of the thirteen. It is hard to say whether these interminable snow-falls are owing to the general climatic conditions of the region or to local characteristics related with the direction of the valley, its altitude, etc. Mr. Russell maintains that there is more bad weather on the summits than on the frozen plateaux at the base of the chains. Mr. Topham, on the other hand, asserts that there is often a whole day of rain on the sea-shore when the sky is perfectly clear over the peak of Mount St. Elias. We ourselves observed that the sky always cleared first round the summits, and we found less fresh snow on the *col* and crest of Mount St. Elias than down in the valley. We also frequently noticed heavy fogs entirely covering the levels of the Malaspina Glacier and its banks when all the high valleys were in sunshine under a clear sky; while a comparison of the meteorological observations taken by Mr. Hendriksen, the missionary at Yakutat, with those taken simultaneously by ourselves on the mountain, shows that there is more mist and cloud at low than at high levels.

In spite of persistent bad weather, our days on the Newton Glacier were neither monotonous nor wearisome. The scenery revealed such wealth of colour and form, that every day, in all sorts of weather, some novelty was seen, some endless succession of unexpected views. The glacier is usually blue—and of deeper blue in mist than in sunshine—not greenish, as on Alpine ice-fields. This colouring pervades the air, and is caught and reflected by the mist, until everything is bathed in a transparent azure. The effect is so constant and so marked, although in varying degrees of intensity, that this might appropriately be named the Blue Valley.

Probably the tint is owed to the enormous quantity of snow that covers the ice everywhere, even in the deepest crevasses. During our first evening on the Newton, we saw a strange and beautiful spectacle. About 6:30 P.M. the dense fogs which had masked the valley all day lifted a little, clearing away from the glacier and its precipitous rock-walls, and all the head of the valley appeared of such a deep indigo tint, that it was impossible to distinguish which was ice, sky, or rock. Little by little this colour spread, growing gradually fainter and fainter, and tinging with blue, one after another, every ice-fall and sérac of the Newton, and the mountains on either hand, with their glaciers, until everything was bathed in an azure haze.

The portage of all our belongings, from the Agassiz up to the Newton, was only completed on the following day (17th July). An icy cold rain, mixed with sleet, was pouring down. The guides had returned to Sledge Camp to fetch the baggage left behind there the previous day. H.R.H. [His Royal Highness, the Duke of the Abruzzi] and Lieutenant Cagni had gone to fetch a few loads which had been brought up to the top of the ice-fall, and deposited on the snow. Two hours later, on their return to camp, great excitement was caused by the news that they had sighted four men climbing the Agassiz Glacier in the direction of the last camp, where our guides still remained. Evidently the strangers must be a portion of Mr. Bryant's caravan [a second St. Elias climbing party]. More than once we had felt surprise at finding no trace of the expedition that was supposed to be in advance of us, and had divined, what was really the fact, that it had ascended the Agassiz instead of the Seward Glacier, following the route taken by Mr. Russell in 1891. At about 6 o'clock P.M., during a downpour of rain, our guides appeared at last with a letter from Mr. Bryant. The progress of his caravan had been much delayed by the illness of one of the porters, and the consequent loss of his services and those of the comrade detailed to look after him. After climbing the Agassiz to within a mile or two of the Newton ice-fall, Mr. Bryant had decided to abandon the ascent. Having descried two tents left at the foot of the fall, he had gone up there to inform H.R.H. or some member of his party that he withdrew from the attempt on Mount St. Elias, and wished him every success. After giving this letter to our men and taking a short rest, Mr. Bryant started down the glacier with his party. We had missed, by a few hours, our one chance of meeting the only other men besides ourselves on the vast icy desert.

The lower plateau of the Newton was the last place where we had rain; higher up it was always snow. Accordingly, the limit of rainfalls in the St. Elias region may be assigned to the altitude of 4,400 to 4,500 feet.

The remaining portion of the plateau to be crossed before reaching the second ice-fall is seamed with huge furrows, and has several little tarns; before long, the glacier slopes upwards more steeply, and beyond some wide crevasses, we come to the séracs of this second cascade. Whether from special atmospheric conditions, or from the greater extent of snow-field, those optical illusions which are common to all glaciers were manifested on a most unusual scale. We found ourselves climbing in and out of troughs of varying depths between rugged ice-waves, almost without visual perception of them. In fact, we only realized their existence by periodically losing sight of the party ahead, or when, on turning to look back, we found our view of the glacier was shut out by some incline we had descended unawares.

The first half of the ice-fall is easy to climb. In some parts of it, the séracs lie in rows, divided by wide furrows, which form a direct and easy path between snow-walls rising to about thirty-five feet. But the numerous crevasses compelled us to perform more gymnastic exercises than were desirable with our heavy loads. At last, however, we emerged from one of these icy corridors on to the comparatively flat stretch of ice that divides the second cascade into two parts. It is seamed by numerous torrents flowing between high banks of snow, and scattered with round masses of ice, among which lurk limpid pools of blue water. H.R.H. decided to encamp on the margin of one of these lakelets, in a hollow sheltered by snow-slopes. Our march had taken two hours and a half.

A drizzle of sleet went on the whole of the 18th July; but the 19th being a splendid day, we took advantage of it to carry up our baggage as far as the lake. In the evening, Ingraham and five porters appeared with fresh supplies, so H.R.H. detained them to give us their assistance in moving our camp farther on. Excited by the view of Mount St. Elias, now apparently very near, and anxious about the uncertain weather, we decided to lighten our loads by leaving the iron bedsteads behind.

We started all together the next morning, under a clouded sky and in oppressively sultry weather. We were soon among the séracs and our route became very picturesque; but unluckily the varied details of the scene proved so many hindrances to our progress. We were always either clambering up or scrambling down, or squeezing through chilly ice passages, in the depths of narrow crevasses, where there was barely room for our loads, under dripping snow-cornices. In the faint, glimmering light we could just discern cavernous vaults, enclosing blue pools of half-frozen water. Beyond these passages, the view was bounded on all sides by thousands of white-crested séracs, forming so tangled a labyrinth that it seemed impossible to find a way through it. Before long, the fog closed about us more densely, and a shout from the front warned us that it was useless to try to thread all these intricacies in a blinding mist, and we were thus obliged to halt half-way up the ice-fall, on the scanty level of a sérac, barely affording room for our tents. The Americans soon started off on their return journey; while after a hasty meal, we sought refuge under the hospitable canvas to escape from the unspeakable melancholy of this waste of ice shrouded in cold grey wet mist. For three whole days we were detained in this camp, in the most obstinately bad weather it is possible to conceive. The resolutely hostile mountain was meeting its invaders in a manner worthy of its fame. Snow began to fall heavily on the night of our arrival, and on leaving our tents early the next morning (21st July), we found that the drifts had completely buried stoves, utensils, instruments, and numerous miscellaneous objects, left out on the previous evening. After a long and patient search, we succeeded in recovering all our belongings, and carefully gathered them together to avoid losses which might entail serious inconvenience.

The appearance of our camp was now entirely changed. The sides of the tents had caved in under the weight of the snow, the very pegs were capped with big white heaps, and even the ropes were covered with a thick layer of frost. Notwithstanding the waterproof qualities claimed for our canvas roofs, the water was dripping through inside, and we had to clear off the snow and tighten the ropes, to try to put a stop to this very inconvenient leakage. Armed with axes and cooking utensils, we set to work to dig trenches round the tents, and get rid of the accumulated snow. But it was falling so fast and so thickly, that almost incessant labour was needed to prevent everything from being buried. In a very short time there was a bank three feet high round the tents.

Through the faintly rose-tinted mist one could discern on all sides the vague outlines of piled séracs, bowed down, as it were, by their heavy load; while around the camp the ice sloped steeply downwards to invisible depths. Steadily, ceaselessly, the noiseless white flakes fell. From time to time the roar of an avalanche broke the oppressive silence. A flight of stray birds, doomed perhaps to perish of exhaustion on the ice, fluttered through the mist, and for a moment turned our thoughts to green woodlands and the stir of life.

Fortunately, bad weather in Alaska is usually calm weather. Snow and rain are seldom accompanied by storms of wind. We never saw, either in the horizon or about the peaks, the dark, rounded thunder-clouds which mean storms, nor even a single flash of lightning. All night and throughout the following day the snow-fall continued. Only towards evening, on the 23rd of July, had we a few hours' respite. The thick fog-curtain lifted gradually here and there; first, the near séracs emerged, then peaks appeared for a moment, soon to be hidden again behind drifting mists, while now and then blue sky showed between the clouds. There were continual, fleeting glimpses of mountain crests, lighted by an increasingly clear and brilliant radiance, a succession of pictures appearing and disappearing as the mists floated this way or that, until at last the whole valley lay revealed. The layers of mist, dividing séracs, cliffs, and crests into a series of terraces one above the other, added to the grandeur of the scene. Delicate mist-wreaths clung to the higher rocks, torn into fringes, and driven hither and thither by the breeze. All around us were ridges of ice, and the infinitely various and grotesque humps formed by the séracs, laden with fresh snow. The fleecy burden softens every curve, and rounds every angle and edge of the fissures, so that these Alaskan séracs have a very different aspect from those of our Alps, which are real polyhedrons of ice, hard and angular in form, with smooth surfaces of cleavage.

Soon the whole valley wakes to life in the sunshine, and avalanches thunder on all sides. Enormous masses of stones, ice, and snow hurtle down from the lofty cliffs, with prolonged rumblings, with explosions and sharp volleys as of musketry, repeated by multitudinous echoes. The snow-avalanches are the most beautiful of all. Their descent lasts whole minutes as they slide down giddy slopes, leaping from cliff to cliff in dazzling white cascades, with a dull, continuous roar, testifying to the enormous weight and velocity of the moving mass. The entire aspect of the mountain walls is sensibly changed; glittering ice-needles, and tangled cross lines of fracture break the uniform whiteness of the huge mass of snow. Innumerable furrows appear traced on every slope, hitherto absolutely smooth and even.

The sun sinks slowly until it touches the peak of Mount St. Elias, then, after seemingly lingering a while, slowly sets, shedding a dazzling light over the whole valley. The air is clear as crystal. Peaks of rock and ice, slender ridges fringed with snow-cornices, furrowed cliffs, worn by the incessant fall of stones and by the great avalanches of ice, all stand out, every detail defined with extraordinary clearness. The temperature has sunk below zero, and silence reigns once more. In its frozen immobility the valley is a symbol of eternal duration, serene and unchangeable.

At nightfall the mist settled down again, and peaks, precipices, and ice-falls were enveloped in a shroud of increasing thickness. Fresh masses of vapour rose from below, spreading in every direction, choking every opening of the glacier, every hollow of its flanks, until by 9 o'clock P.M. we were again imprisoned in the damp chill of the grey fog.

We had not been inactive during these days. On the 21st the guides went down to Sledge Camp and brought up fresh supplies; on the 22nd, in spite of the bad weather, H.R.H. pushed forward at the head of a caravan, and found a track to the second plateau; and on the 23rd, the first loads of stores were transported thither, during a short interval of sunshine.

On the morning of July 24th, two caravans set out in a heavy snow-storm, to carry up a good part of the camp material, and were back by 11 o'clock; two hours later we started all together with the final loads. The snow was still falling thickly, and the refraction of the white mist was blinding. It was impossible to realize the inclination of the slopes. We walked like somnambulists, mistaking shallow depressions for bottomless gulfs, and scraping elbows and packs against walls of snow close beside us which we thought to be flat! Climbing séracs or marching along their edges, we appeared to one another as shadowy giants on giddy heights and impossible slopes, plunging apparently into space at every step. One curious phenomenon caused by refraction was that while we could fairly distinguish the outlines of séracs about 150 feet distant, we could see nothing that was close to us; and the illusion was so complete that the leading guide occasionally sounded with his axe to ascertain if his next step would fall on the snow or into empty space.

Thus, clambering over some blocks, and skirting others, scarcely conscious of the way, we reached the second plateau. The deep track marked out in the early morning was already snowed over; but the guides showed marvellous ability in re-discovering and following up the trail. The leader of the first party groped about with his feet for the beaten track beneath the snow; outside that track one sank in to the waist, and all progress was impossible; while even on it the snow lay more than knee-deep. We were divided into three parties, leading by turns, for the guide in advance had to work so hard pushing his way through the snow that he could only do short spells.

During one of our brief halts, a guide made the valley echo with the typical, long-drawn mountain cry. His voice had the strangest effect, breaking the silence of the peaks. An answering cry came from Sella, who had remained in the place selected in the early morning for the next camp; and although we were still over forty-five minutes' march from him, his voice was as strong and distinct as though he were only fifty paces off. Soon afterwards, the tents already pitched at the new camp came into sight, and it seemed extraordinary they should be visible at that distance through the mist. It is impossible to judge the extent of one's field of vision in a mist, unless there is some dark object on the snow to direct the eye. Both snow and air give exactly the same impression of uniformly diffused white light. Seeing is no less hard than in the dark. Steering is also very difficult, as we proved when we tried again to sight the tents after having turned our eyes elsewhere; sometimes, looking in every direction, it took us a full minute to discover them, although they were plainly in sight.

At last, about 5:30, we came up with Sella. A little gusty wind had now risen, which drove the snow straight in our faces, and we felt very cold. Hurrying on to the camp, we pitched the remaining tents on firm foundations of snow, formed by treading it down thoroughly. Before long we were all dining together under canvas. We were cheerful in spite of the weather, for our confidence in the success of the expedition was unshaken. The slightest lifting of the mist sufficed to dispel whatever doubt the inclemency of the weather and the continual fall of fresh snow might have awakened. Complicated wagers passed between us as to the height of Mount St. Elias, the result of our ascent, and even as to the day and hour of attaining the summit. We sat talking on into the evening by the faint light of our little Alpine lanterns. By this time there were as much as four hours of real night, and the few candles packed with the provisions came into use. The snow fell on the tents with a slight crackling sound. To prevent it from caking, we gave the canvas an occasional shake from inside.

As the accumulation of new-fallen snow must have already effaced every sign of our track, we began to feel rather anxious for our Americans, who would be on the Newton Glacier by now. Accordingly, on the morning of the 25th July, H.R.H. sent three guides back to meet them, and put them in the right way if necessary, while at the same time another party went on ahead to explore the third ice-fall.

The weather showed signs of improvement, with alternations of sleet, mist, and sun. The latter was still pale and hazy, but grew stronger and brighter every day. After being so long wrapped in fog, we now had broken glimpses of the scenery about us. We were not encamped in the middle of the glacier, but near its right edge, close to the southern buttress of the valley. This spur, projecting from the east side of Mount St. Elias, first runs up into a fine peak that is an exact copy, much reduced, of the great summit; and then curves round, clasping a considerable basin surmounted by an ice-peak tipped by a daring white pinnacle that darts up into the sky like an obelisk. This basin, which descends to the second plateau of the Newton, contains a glacier which scales the walls that encircle it, and covers them completely throughout their height. H.R.H. gave it the name of the Savoy Glacier.

The guides sent back by H.R.H. to seek the porters remained absent two entire days, and only returned to camp early on the 27th, a little ahead of the American party. They had found the latter just preparing to go back, after vain attempts to find their way. Besides provisions, they brought us a welcome, though unexpected, packet of letters from Italy, which had come to Yakutat by a coasting vessel, and, thanks to Mr. Hendriksen, had been conveyed by Indians to an appointed place on the Malaspina coast. The weather now cleared up splendidly, and our anxieties vanished. Early in the afternoon we struck camp and all set off, leaving behind one of the Whymper tents, one stove, the cooking utensils, and some more articles of clothing.

Our march was a short but very fatiguing one, owing to the bad state of the snow. It brought us over the foot of the third ice-fall to the real séracs, where the steepest part of the ascent begins. On the previous day a party had gone without loads to beat a track through the snow, taking two hours to cover 250 feet of road, and had been followed by a second party with part of the baggage. Nevertheless, we found it hard and unpleasant work to struggle along in deep, uneven ruts, which often gave way under our weight. The next camp was pitched at 7,431 feet, on a narrow strip of snow between a wide crevasse and a sheer cliff of sérac about 60 feet in height. Fringes of snow were continually breaking off from the narrow cornice at the upper edge of the sérac and slipping down on to our tent-flaps with a rustling as of silk. Our camp was now reduced to three tents: one for the guides, one for our party of four, and the small Mummery tent occupied by H.R.H.

The following day, 28th of July, we carried up everything in two journeys to the highest plateau of the Newton Glacier at the top of the valley.

By skirting to the right, round the sérac overhanging the camp, we managed to climb the mass, and going on to its farthest edge found a deep crevasse nearly 100 feet wide yawning at our feet. Fortunately, a narrow snow-ridge projected from the sérac on which we stood, and slanted down across the great fissure to the opposite and lower edge. We cautiously ventured on to this slender causeway, taking care to place our feet exactly in the centre, since both sides were precipitous and covered with loose snow that broke away at the slightest touch. The passage effected, we made our way over masses of ice connected by shaky bridges of almost loose snow, most of which were either broken or incomplete. All of us broke through more than once, but by careful use of the rope no accident occurred. Through the great holes with jagged margins produced by these stumbles, we saw mysterious azure caverns deep below, of the most marvellous blue ever created by snow, with a sheen like watered silk, and brilliant, almost metallic reflections. At last we emerged from this labyrinth of ice-blocks at the head of the ice-fall in the great upper basin of the Newton. At this point the glacier has an undulating surface, and we found it so loaded with snow that the crevasses, if there were any, were all hidden. This basin is two miles in width and about three in length, and is overhung by the walls of Mount St. Elias, of the col, and of Mount Newton.

Turning towards the middle of the plateau, we pitched our camp within a mile of the outlet of the basin, out of reach of the avalanches threatening to fall on every side. We were now at 8,661 feet above sea level.

Directly over us rose the vast pyramid of Mount St. Elias, which had a bulky, flattened aspect, seen thus foreshortened. The almost rectilinear north-northeastern ridge sloped at a moderate angle, broken here and there by séracs which did not look formidable; half-way up and a little below three groups of black crags broke the pure snow-line, while above these the arête rose without interruption to a huge buttress of ice, beyond which was the rounded dome of the peak. The wall rising to the col was rather steep. Save for a triangular rock-island exactly in the middle, it was entirely covered with snow; above, and to the right of this cliff, the slope was broken up into séracs; but towards the left it showed smooth, and looked easy of ascent, although not quite free from danger of avalanches of ice and stones from the north-east flank of Mount St. Elias.

On the 29th of July, three guides started ahead to pick out the way and cut steps up the wall of the col. H.R.H., with a small party, returned down to our preceding camp to bring up provisions. The light mists which had floated all day about the mountain sides and peaks melted away in the cool of the evening, and a cloudless night began.

VIII: The Ascent of Mount St. Elias

Called up at 1 o'clock A.M. (July 30th), we set about preparing for the penultimate stage of the ascent. The col between Mount Newton and St. Elias was to be climbed that day. Thence we hoped, by the long north-east ridge, to win the great peak on the following morning. So confident were we now of success that hope amounted almost to certainty. The supplies to be taken with us had been most carefully chosen, and comprised the following articles:

Two Whymper tents, ten sleeping bags, rations for two and a half days, one petroleum cooking stove, one spirit lamp, meteorological instruments, the smaller of Sella's photographic machines, Gonella's small camera, and a few extra flannels.

We started at 4 o'clock, divided into three parties, along the route marked out by the guides, who had prepared a track right up to the col on the previous day. It was a bright, cold morning, with a perfectly clear sky. The snow was firm enough in the beaten track, but loose everywhere else, and covered with a thin crust of ice that gave under our feet. The strip of plateau, extending for about two miles and a half ahead to the flank of the col, lies at the very foot of the north-east face of St. Elias. This face is rocky at the steeper parts, but showed almost everywhere a coating of ice overlapping its precipices that threatened us with formidable avalanches. The condition of the snow warned us of this danger, seeing that for a stretch of over one mile it was no longer loose, but hardened avalanche snow, which crackled under the nails of our shoes, and was thickly sprinkled with sérac fragments fallen from a height of over 3,000 feet. Fortunately for us, most of the accumulated fresh snow had already come down during the past three days of fine weather, and the rest of it had had time to harden a little; but what chiefly served to keep the ice safely bound to the precipitous rocks was the intense cold of early morning.

After about an hour's march, the slope of the glacier gradually began to increase, and we soon reached the foot of the cliff where the real ascent begins. The wall rises in a series of somewhat steep slopes, separated by great transversal crevasses, and varying from 400 to 600 feet in height. We zig-zagged obliquely up these snow-slopes, the surface of which was pretty good for long stretches, where the guides had found it necessary to cut steps on the previous day. The first crevasse immediately beneath the isolated rock that projects from the middle of the wall cost us some trouble, and nearly half an hour's labour. The first two caravans crossed it easily enough by a snow-bridge, but this broke down when attempted by Sella, the leader of the third rope. After searching vainly for some solid foothold on the snow-vault, the third party finally managed to reach the other side by leaping boldly across the gap in the bridge. But the last guide unluckily dropped his jacket as he jumped, and had to be let down to a good depth in the fissure to recover it.

Keeping to the left of the rocks, we then mounted to the second crevasse, which cuts straight across the steep incline in such a way that its upper edge overlaps the lower one like a roof, leaving an interval of about seven feet. At a short distance, however, along the lower side, we discovered a point where the edges drew a little closer together. By mounting on a guide's shoulders, we managed to get safely across, and our loads were hauled up after us. Another snow-slope, a last and easily negotiated crevasse, and then, at about 10 o'clock A.M., we landed on the top of the col.

Our tents were pitched a little beneath the crest, on the east side, facing the Newton Glacier, 12,297 feet above the sea, and 3,636 feet higher than our previous camp. H.R.H. named the col after I. C. Russell, who was the first to conquer it, in 1891.

As soon as we reached the col, we turned eager glances to the new region revealed to us towards the north-west. At our feet we beheld a very extensive level glacier, covered with snow, and with no signs of crevasses; but its eastern and western boundaries were hidden from us by the mountains at either side. Beyond the portion fronting us lay an interminable stretch of snow and ice, an infinite series of low mountain chains bristling with numberless jagged, sharp-pointed, and precipitous peaks, where rocks and ice-fields were closely intermingled. Towards the horizon we had a confused view of some very high ranges. We realized that from the summit we should see the whole of this region more distinctly mapped out.

The view to the north was blocked by Mount Newton, which now took the shape of a sharp-pointed snow-cone. Just to its left, and farther back, we discerned the pinnacled rock forming the western extremity of the Logan chain. From Mount Newton an irregular ridge runs down to the col, edged, to the north, by a bulky snow-cornice, and cut by deep indentations forming the heads of the gullies of stones and ice which score the mountain side towards Newton Glacier. The great ridge of Mount St. Elias is of wholly dissimilar structure, for being so wide it resembles a *slope,* and cannot be easily identified with the even, straight crest seen from below. Viewed from the col, it appears to be broken by projections of varying steepness, amongst which three distinct clusters of rocks rise above the snow; while the wide, rounded summit seems to soar upwards at a short distance from the last group of crags, and apparently very little higher; whereas, from the valley below, these rocks seemed to stand about midway between the col and the summit of the mountain.

Beneath the Newton and St. Elias ridges the mountain sides become precipitous. Masses of snow, ice, and rock, set loose by the first rays of the morning sun, thunder and hurtle down into the valley with a roar which reaches us distinctly, raising clouds of pulverized ice in their descent.

More than 3,000 feet below us the spacious Newton Valley descends to the east. At this distance the ice-cascades, with their piled séracs, seem mere tracts of rugged, wrinkled glacier between the smooth, level plateaux. We identify all the peaks around us, and in the depth beneath, the white, flat stretch of the Malaspina Glacier, bounded by its black lines of forest and marginal moraine. Beyond, and more than 62 miles off, lies the blue expanse of Yakutat Bay.

The afternoon hours pass rapidly and almost unheeded, and the pure cold evening is an omen of splendid weather for the morrow. North-wards all is cold shade under a steel blue sky, but the rest of the horizon is orange red. Little by little Mount Augusta crimsons like a fiery volcano. The thermometer is at 18° Fahr., and a chill north-west wind drives us to our tents. Lying down closely packed in these narrow shelters, we try to get some rest to fit us for the last and most serious effort; but most of us are too excited by the thought of the morrow's task to be able to sleep.

At midnight we all turn out, and swallow a bowl of hot coffee before packing the loads. These consist of one day's rations, a small spirit stove, a mercurial barometer, two aneroids, a hygrometer, spirit and mercurial thermometer, and photographic apparatus. The night is perfectly clear and still; Venus shines serenely over the summit of Mount Newton. The temperature stands at 18° Fahr. We are roped in three separate parties.

H.R.H., Lieutenant Cagni, the two guides Petigax and Maquignaz are on the first rope; Gonella with Croux and Botta on the second; Sella and myself with Pellissier on the third. We are too excited to talk. We feel that we are on the very point of realizing the hope which has sustained us through prolonged days of toil and through the painful anxiety which, during the last stages, kept us questioning the barometer or the direction of the wind every few minutes.

The crest of the ridge where it reaches the col forms an ice-cliff, which we skirt on the right. The powdery surface snow is very unequally distributed, here and there leaving uncovered the harder layer beneath, in which steps have to be cut by the first guide. Petigax and Maquignaz go on in front, each taking the lead for half an hour in turn, and we all mount rapidly at a steady pace.

On reaching the top of the cliff, we cross to the east flank of the ridge running down to Newton Valley, where the snow is firmer, being more exposed to the sun. The surface is uneven and ribbed, reminding us of winter snow-slopes in the Alps.

After about an hour's climb, we come to the first rocks, which are formed of black splinters of diorite, round which we soon make our way through the snow. A little higher up, while skirting a fissured hump of ice, blasts of frozen north wind drive the powdery snow against our faces. Far above us, the summit is gilded by the first rays of the sun, and gradually the great golden disk rises to the right of Mount Newton. As we climb higher, this summit rapidly sinks, and before long we see its peak beneath us, while behind it, and more than twenty miles off, rises the south flank of the Logan chain. Towards 5 o'clock A.M. we reached the last crags, and speedily surmounted them.

Our ascent was favoured by completely calm weather, and an ideal temperature, unusual in the high mountains, neither inconveniently cold nor oppressively hot. At 6:30, H.R.H. called a short halt; we breakfasted and were off again in half an hour. Soon the aneroids proved that we had reached the altitude of Mont Blanc (about 15,700 feet), and some of our party began to feel the diminished pressure in the shape of palpitation and difficult breathing, which although too slight to impede progress, yet sufficed to suggest that some of us might be prevented from reaching the summit.

At 8 o'clock Cagni arranged his instruments and took meteorological observations. We were now at an altitude of over 16,500 feet; and the temperature was 16° to 17° Fahr. There was an extraordinarily fine view to the east. The peak of Mount Augusta, although now beneath our level, preserved its daring grandeur of outline. But the Logan chain to the north was the most majestic of all. On our right stretched the vast, precipitous north crest of St. Elias, all rocky save the upper portion, which was covered with snow. About midway it is broken by a towering crag, at whose feet a small glacier descends from the ridge. Around us there was nothing but dazzling snow, its whiteness just softened by faint opalescent tinges of colour.

The observations being duly registered, we resume our way up the tiring, monotonous slope. Less than 1,600 feet now separate us from the summit, but they will cost us more labour than the 4,200 already won. Almost all of us are suffering more or less from the rarefaction of the air, some being attacked by headache, others by serious difficulty of breathing and general exhaustion. H.R.H. slackens the pace of his caravan, and sometimes calls a halt, to wait for those who have fallen in the rear. He is determined to keep us all together, knowing the sense of discouragement felt by any one left behind by the rest of the party. The ascent is very monotonous on the whole and perfectly easy, leading either over the great rounded hump of the crest, or along its eastern flank. Luckily there is only a thin stratum of loose snow, so that one barely sinks into it ankle-deep; while now and again we strike a belt of hard snow in which the leading guide has to cut steps with a few strokes of his axe.

Before long we all experience these alternations of hope and disappointment which are typical symptoms of over-fatigue. Every slope ahead seems as though it must be the last; every ice pinnacle is mistaken for the great gendarme near the top of the crest which we had discerned from below. Even the guides make strange blunders regarding the extent of slope still to be won.

Our rate of progress is now of the slowest. We climb for ten minutes, and then rest for five or six. One or two of us lie down panting on the snow; some sit or crouch, while others take their rest standing, and lean on their ice-axes. H.R.H., Sella, and two of the guides are the only persons showing no signs of distress. Gonella suffers from headache; Cagni, myself, and Botta have to fight against the drowsiness which comes over us at every halt. The two remaining guides have slight symptoms of mountain sickness.

Our legs seem heavy as lead. Every step requires a distinct effort of the will, and we get on by dint of certain devices familiar to all who have made ascents when tired out—leaning both hands on the knees, or planting the axe in the snow ahead and dragging the body up by it, while at every step we pause for breath. Still, we manage to climb somehow; we are spurred on by excitement, and our nerves are strung to the highest pitch.

At last, after untold disappointments, a little after 11 o'clock, a sharp ice pinnacle soared above us, and to the right of it and somewhat higher, the ample curve of a snow-dome. For some minutes past no one had spoken a word. Suddenly we all exclaimed: "The summit!" Only an ice-slope about 150 feet high had still to be surmounted. It was steep, and in our exhausted condition we had to attack it in a slanting direction, resting for breath every few steps. On reaching the top of this incline, we again came to a halt. Before us rose gently towards the west a slope which, in the dazzling light, appeared to be of vast extent. We had actually passed from the crest to the eastern limit of the terminal dome, and scarcely realized that we were so near to the summit.

The leading caravan started ahead, the two others lagged about 150 feet behind. Suddenly we saw the leading guides, Petigax and Maquignaz, move aside to make way for the Prince. They were within a few paces of the top. H.R.H. stepped forward, and was the first to plant his foot on the summit. We hastened breathlessly to join in his triumphant hurrah!

Every trace of fatigue disappeared in the joy of success. This moment was the reward of our thirty-eight days of labour and hardship.

It was the 31st of July, a quarter to 12 noon. A few minutes later, H.R.H. hoisted our little tricolour flag on an ice-axe, and we nine gathered round him to join in his hearty shout for Italy and the king. Then we all pressed the hand of the Prince, who had so skilfully led the expedition, and had maintained our courage and strength to the last by the force of his inspiring example.

Our excitement was of short duration. Once our object attained, we experienced the inevitable reaction after so many months devoted to the pursuit of one idea. Nevertheless, it was needful to pull ourselves together, and set to work taking observations. It was the most favourable hour for them. At mid-day, Mr. Hendriksen, at Yakutat, always registered the indications given by the meteorological instruments we had left in his charge. Therefore it was most important that simultaneous observations should be noted on the summit of St. Elias. The Fortin barometer marked a pressure of 15 inches 2 lines. With the due corrections and rectifications, it indicated an altitude of 18,090 feet, which very nearly agreed with the angular calculation made by Mr. Russell in 1891, fixing the height at 18,100 feet. All preceding calculations had proved discordant and untrustworthy. Only one gave an approximately correct result; namely, that made by the Italian navigator Malaspina in 1792, fixing the altitude of Mount St. Elias at 17,847 feet.

We had risen 5,793 feet from the col to the summit. The ascent had occupied ten hours and a half; but we must deduct from this the thirty minutes spent over lunch, and another half-hour devoted to meteorological observations. During the first five hours we had climbed 3,400 feet, at an average rate of 680 feet per hour; and 2,400 feet in the last four hours and a half, at an average rate of about 600 feet an hour.

The summit of Mount St. Elias consists of a spacious plateau stretching, with a slight inclination, from south-east to north-west. The highest point stands north, and forms a raised platform about 40 square yards in extent. The temperature in the sun stood at 10° Fahr.; there was no wind, but a light breeze sufficed to chill us. We found some shelter a few yards from the top, and without leaving the terminal dome. Here we sat down to take some refreshment, trying to overcome the repugnance to food induced by fatigue and mountain sickness.

Beneath us, on every side, lay an indescribable panorama, glittering in the intense mid-day light. Only the Malaspina Glacier and the sea were covered by a low-hanging curtain of fog; in every other direction the horizon was perfectly clear. The enormous extent of snow-fields, glaciers, and mountains revealed to our sight, surpassed all imagination.

Those majestic peaks which two days before towered above us, while we were painfully struggling through the snows of Newton Glacier, now lay at our feet. We traced along the valleys the long course we had followed, while memory recalled difficulties and obstacles now lost in the distance. Often had we turned longing glances from the depths towards this small ledge outlined against the sky, as if imploring encouragement from the lofty summit!

The peak of Mount Augusta, still imposing, although nearly 4,000 feet below us, now assumed the form of a huge pyramid, turning a rocky face southwards, but covered, on the north side, with ice that spreads up to the terminal cupola. Beyond the Seward Glacier soars Mount Cook; and to the left of this another and more remote snow-summit, that must be either Mount Hubbard or Mount Irving, but which of the two it is hard to decide. From the sea of mist shrouding the Malaspina Glacier, the higher peaks of the Samovar and Hitchcock chains thrust up like isolated rocks. Lastly, in the far distance, to the south-east, we distinguish the summit of Mount Fairweather.

About twenty miles away to the north, and running parallel with the Newton-Augusta range, we see the vast chain of Mount Logan, the sole competitor disputing the supremacy of Mount St. Elias. The lengthy crest constituting its summit rises gradually from west to east, in an almost uninterrupted arête, without depressions or deep cols, broken only by a few rocky pinnacles and ice-domes, and reaching its greatest height in a snow-peak at the eastern extremity. After this point the crest makes a sudden dip, running on in a series of lesser heights, which, after bounding the north side of Seward Glacier, turn in a wide curve towards Mount Cook, and are then blocked from view by Mount Augusta. Likewise, to the west, the crest falls rapidly, and ends in a series of short spurs among the lower hills.

The southern face of the chain, which is in full view from base to summit, is about 10,000 feet high, and extremely wild and picturesque. Throughout the whole extent it is composed of precipitous crags, intersected by piled glaciers, having the aspect of avalanches suddenly checked in their career down the very steep incline, and frozen fast to the rocks. Short, low spurs start from the base of the great wall, and project into the Seward Glacier; while the numerous ice fields filling the intervening hollows cover the foot of the chain, and run up it in wedges here and there to a considerable height.

The space lying between Mount Logan and the Newton–Augusta chain forms the basin from which the Seward Glacier takes its origin, and its size is duly proportioned to the great ice-stream issuing from it. From the western extremity of Mount Logan starts a ridge stretching farther south than the others, apparently running into the Newton–Augusta chain, thus closing the Seward basin on the west, and separating it from another huge glacier that spreads to the feet of Russell Col, and of the north and north-west flanks of St. Elias. This glacier, of even greater extent than the Seward, forms a vast snow-level showing no fissures on its surface. We could trace its course for a long distance westward, without being able to determine how and where it comes to an end. The ridge which appears to divide it from the Seward is certainly very low, and seems to run uninterruptedly between the two glaciers, but it cannot be traced very clearly from the summit of St. Elias. As to the new glacier now discovered, the absence of crevasses, and the difficulty of distinguishing the real trend of smooth slopes of snow from a lofty post, made it impossible to form any decided opinion as to the direction of this new current of ice—whether it finally issued to the west or the north. Its course seemed to us to lie at about the same level as the second plateau of the Newton; *i.e.*, at from 6,400 to 6,500 feet. H.R.H. gave it the name of "Columbus Glacier."

The whole north-west region to the left of Mount Logan is an unexplored waste of glaciers and mountains, a vast zone bristling with sharp peaks and crags, rugged and precipitous to the south, snow-covered to the north, and surrounded by vast snow-fields free from crevasses, and connected with each other by the snowy cols of the mountain chains. The medium altitude of the snow-fields is about 7,000 feet, that of the mountains from 9,000 to 10,000 feet. No words can express the desolation of this immeasurable waste of ice, which Russell has compared with the ice-sheet that covers Greenland. No smallest trace of vegetation can be discerned on it, no running water, no lake. It might be a tract of primitive chaos untouched by the harmonizing forces of nature. Surveying this strange scene, we realized for the first time that we were close to the limits of the mysterious Polar world. Such is the region forming the north-west boundary of the Columbus Glacier. Numerous tributaries pour into the latter from the lower hills; and the most considerable of these affluents, running into the Columbus on the immediate left of Mount Logan, was named by H.R.H. after Quintino Sella, the illustrious pioneer of Italian Alpinism.

On the far horizon, somewhere between fifty and one hundred miles off, a broad summit towered up behind the western corner of Mount Logan, which was ascertained by the compass to be at 328°. H.R.H. named this peak "Lucania," in remembrance of the ship that had brought us to America. West of this new peak, at about the same distance and due north of St. Elias, we descried another great mountain at 326°, which we believed to be identical with the peak christened Mount Bear by Russell in 1891. Finally, to the north-west, some 200 miles off, a conical peak soared up at 311°, apparently of even greater height than the other two. This was christened the "Bona," after a racing yacht then belonging to H.R.H. These three peaks really seem to rival Mount St. Elias in height, and must approach 18,000 feet in height. None of them showed any sign of volcanic activity.

While we scanned the wide prospect, endeavouring to fix in our memory each detail of the wondrous scene, multitudinous thoughts and feelings crowded upon us. The labyrinth of dark lines, the pure white plains, the chaos of rock and ice, blended in our minds with familiar scenes of marvellous beauty in our own Alpine world.

But sheer physical weariness soon unfits the mind for contemplation of so much supernatural grandeur. We feel vaguely crushed by the immensity; a desolating sense of isolation comes to us from those infinite wastes of ice, and from the solemn, oppressive silence of nature. Once the first excitement [has] worn off, we are dazed by the radiance of the sunlight striking through the cold air; we suffer from distress caused by the altitude, and before long our only desire is to hasten down the peak as fast as we can.

By 1 o'clock P.M. we had gathered up our few possessions, arranged the different caravans, and begun the descent in the same order observed during the climb. We had spent an hour and a half on the summit.

Long glissades bore us quickly down the slopes we had so laboriously toiled up, and the few crevasses, being mostly filled with snow, were easily crossed. A little wind blowing in sudden gusts swept the face of the mountain, and assailed us with volleys of icy dust. As we drew near to the col the snow was in worse condition, and we had to plough through it knee-deep for long intervals. Nevertheless, we got on fast, slipping, falling, regaining our feet, plastered with snow from head to foot, but eager to reach camp, to escape from all that blinding, white glare, into the comforting shade of our tents. Between 4 and 5 o'clock P.M. we overtook on the col H.R.H.'s caravan, which had descended the great snow-slope in two hours and a half.

We had only a little broken sleep that night, and awoke early on the 1st of August in a very battered, aching, and stiffened condition. The same evening we camped again on the upper Newton plateau.

First Up Mt. Blackburn

— Dora Keen —

Mountaineering literature, like the sport itself, has traditionally been dominated by the male perspective. While that is becoming less true, the fact remains: relatively few women have, over the years, participated in Alaska expeditions. Even fewer have published stories about their Alaska climbs. A notable exception is Dora Keen (1871–1963).

Born and raised in Philadelphia, Keen graduated from Bryn Mawr College in 1896; a few years later, she began traveling the world. By her late thirties, Dora's adventurous spirit had led her into mountaineering, and before her fortieth birthday she'd climbed numerous peaks in the Canadian Rockies, the Andes, and the Alps, including 15,781-foot Mont Blanc and Ecuador's 20,561-foot Chimborazo. For the more demanding mountains, she routinely hired experienced alpine guides.

In 1911, Keen came to Alaska "merely as a tourist." But soon after her arrival she read about a high peak "worthy of the hardiest mountaineer." Inspired by the report, Keen decided to attempt 16,523-foot Mount Blackburn, highest of the Wrangell Mountains and fourth highest in the state. To put her ambition in perspective, only one of Alaska's great mountains had so far been

climbed: 18,008-foot Mount St. Elias. Organized on the fly, her 1911 expedi-
tion—which included four local prospectors, a dog team, and 750 pounds of
gear—was turned back at 8,700 feet by stormy weather and dwindling sup-
plies. (Keen's account of the attempt later appeared in Scribner's Magazine.)
Undeterred, Keen returned the following spring for a second attempt. And
with immeasurable help from several McCarthy residents—most notably
George Handy and Bill Lang—she reached the mountain's top on May 19,
1912, after thirty-three days on Blackburn.

Remarkably, the team's southerly approach has never been repeated.
Aided by air access, later climbers have ascended Blackburn from its more
remote, but safer, northern side. Keen's accomplishment was reported in a vari-
ety of magazines, and she addressed The American Alpine Club at its 1912
winter meeting.

In 1916 Keen would marry George Handy, the only man to accompany
her to the top of Blackburn. Fifty years after her historic Blackburn ascent,
Keen visited Alaska one last time, at the age of ninety-one. In tribute to her, the
U.S. Board of Geographic Names in 1965 officially named a portion of Alaska's
Chugach Mountains the Dora Keen Range.

Dora Keen's account, "First Up Mt. Blackburn," is taken from
the November 1913 edition of The World's Work.

"I HAVEN'T LOST ANYTHING at the top of Mt. Blackburn," remarked John
Bloomquist, a big Finn. We were sitting in his cabin, 1,500 feet above sea
level, at the foot of the great Kennicott Glacier. At the head of it rose Mt.
Blackburn. It was thirty-five miles away, but its glistening summit was
plainly visible from above the Copper River Railway which passed the
door. I had just arrived from the port of Cordova, 192 miles away, to
make a second attempt to climb this great mass of snow and ice, and
Bloomquist was assuring me that, for him at least, it "ain't going to be
no pleasure trip."

No one had ever tried Mt. Blackburn until my expedition of the previous year. Indeed, Mt. St. Elias, 18,100 feet, was the one difficult Alaskan
peak that had been successfully ascended and that by the fifth expedition
to try it. Mt. Blackburn was only 16,140 feet high, only as high as the base
of the great peaks of the Himalayas, where one may camp on rocks or

moraine ice, and find willows at 13,000 or 15,000 feet. It was just a little higher than Mt. Blanc, and about as steep as the Italian side of the monarch of the Alps. Had it been in the same latitude I could have climbed it, as I had Mt. Blanc, in two days, but the previous August four men and I, with three dogs, had spent thirteen days in the attempt and in the end had been obliged to give it up because our supplies had been calculated for a twelve-day ascent only.

My kindly, courageous, and efficient leader of the year before and the rest were scattered and unable to go, all but Mr. John E. Barrett, who had driven the dog team. He was to lead this year and to engage the other men, so he and I were the only ones, of our party of eight, who had ever been near the mountain before. On March 25, 1912, I had wired to him in Alaska that if conditions were favorable I should arrive at Kennicott, the starting point, at the end of the Copper River Railway, and four miles above the end of Kennicott Glacier, on April 16th. He had merely replied, "Favorable. Come as quickly as possible." All preparations I had to work out alone, at once, and far away, and the previous expedition was the only one on which I had ever been. That I was only five feet tall would matter very little. Success would depend rather upon judgment, endurance, courage, and organization.

Thus was every condition reversed this time. It was winter instead of summer, I knew in advance the seriousness of the undertaking and this time there was no one to help me to organize the expedition, so the task of hasty organization was almost as difficult as the ascent of the mountain.

I was going again because I had need of courage and inspiration and because on the high mountains I find them as no where else.

Success and safety would depend upon haste, and yet I could not reach Cordova before April 16th. Bad news greeted me. The season was a month early. One slide had already interrupted travel on the railroad for a week. The ice in the Copper River was breaking up. It might carry away the railroad bridge at Chitina any day. "It usually went out about the 22nd," I was told. I crossed it on the 19th. With some mistrust of my own judgment, I had brought a German from Cordova, Mr. G. W. Handy, to be one of my expedition. He had been recommended as a good man and a good climber and had prospected near another side of Mt. Blackburn. I might rate him with the least, he said, and he would try to be the best man. The other six men were Axel Waldstrom, Bob Isaacson, "Bill" Lang, C. W. Kolb, John Bloomquist, and Mr. Barrett, all prospectors and all living within view of Mt. Blackburn at the foot of Kennicott Glacier, up which lay the "easiest" way to our mountain.

At 5 o'clock in the morning on the 22nd of April we were off. Our 2,000 pounds of outfit had been hauled up the 200-foot wall of Kennicott Glacier by a pulley and stood lashed to the eight sleds and trailers to which the dogs were harnessed. It was only 18°, yet in an hour, just as the going became smooth, the snow began to soften. Spring had come. As we made camp on an "island" in the glacier that afternoon, for the sake of having timber, we were all exhausted and to come four miles had taken eleven hours of hard labor. The very next morning the best pulling dog of our nine escaped and went home. Still, they all agreed that Doodles was "an ornery dog and crooked anyhow." Altogether, the prospects were anything but encouraging. Here at 2,500 feet, as we knew, would be our only camp fire and our only game, the tame little ptarmigan.

To make speed we tried relaying the loads. One day we would put half ahead and the next day move camp still farther ahead with the other half, bringing up the first half at night. Still, by the third day it was clear that we had come too late to have an easy or quick approach to our glacier-surrounded mountain.

With temperatures around 18°, every morning about 1 o'clock in unheated tents the men would draw on their frozen shoe-packs—I slept on mine to prevent their freezing—cook and eat breakfast and pack up while it was still dark and cold, in order to be ready to travel as soon as we could see, at 3:30 o'clock. When it was cloudy we could not tell a hole from a hill nor even see the leader's snow-shoe trail ten feet away. Mr. Barrett kept ahead with his "crevice puncher." Roping was unnecessary. Every day snow-shoes had to be put on as soon as the sun shone, but even so by about 10 o'clock the cutting through of sled runners and dogs' feet would oblige us to stop for the day. All we could do then was to eat, sleep, wait for the night to give a crust and for the dawn to show the way.

At night the thermometer would drop to 12°, zero, or even 6° below, but by day it showed 59° or 70°, and in the sun even 96°. By day the glare made sleep difficult and we had hardly got to sleep after supper before we must get up again. On the third day, at only 3,300 feet, we had to resort to the oil stoves and they consumed as much time as oil.

Thus slowly in six days we raised nearly a ton of outfit 3,500 feet in thirty-one miles. Travel and spirits improved with elevation and the last day we made fifteen miles in seven and a half hours. Yet it was the 26th of

April when we reached the foot of Mt. Blackburn. For the last twenty-four miles there had been no sign of life. Snow, only snow and ice were to be seen. We had started on ice and snow at 2,000 feet and after five days of toil up a glacier we were only at 5,500 feet and had only snow to camp on.

We had reached the main sources of Kennicott Glacier. In a horse-shoe curve above us rose a majestic amphitheatre of lofty snow peaks, jagged ridges, and precipitous walls. Between the ridges tumbled the mighty ice falls of seven great glaciers. We seemed like atoms before these impregnable fortresses as we prepared to pit our human littleness against the pitiless forces of Nature. The snowy dome of Mt. Blackburn lay nearly 11,000 feet above us.

We had noted the summer before that the flow of the avalanches from these steep glaciers at times extended three miles, so a mound in the centre, out of the lines of flow and far from all walls, seemed the safest place for our base camp. Here dogs and sleds must be left with one man, Kolb, because of the crevasses and ice falls above.

All the long way from Kennicott we had been studying the best route up the mountain, and only from afar could angles and distances be correctly judged, for as we approached the true lines became flattened and distorted by foreshortening; but not until we came close could we judge of surfaces. Once at the foot of the mountain, we were all agreed that, although Barrett Glacier was the steepest of all, it offered probably the only route by which there was any hope of ascending this side of Mt. Blackburn at this time. I had named it for Mr. Barrett the year before. Then I had called him back at only 8,700 feet on account of the avalanches. So far we could surely go again, but above that point for the next 3,500 feet the ice was so steep and broken that only an exploring party could determine whether there was any route that would be safe from avalanches—for even on the high mountains the slides had begun.

Already at 11 o'clock the next morning our route and our success seemed determined, for, starting at daybreak with fairly good snow, four men and I had reached 8,700 feet and were back before the slides had begun. There, in a snow dug-out to which supplies were now relayed, the three best climbers, Barrett, Handy, and Waldstrom, would sleep the next night, after exploring the 3,500 feet above.

Again neither snow-shoes nor creepers were required as another dawn found all of us leaving the base with more packs to start up the mountain. A half hour brought us to the first steep slope, and after an hour's steady snow ascent it was no longer possible to avoid the crevasses. From here up progress was slow as we threaded our way through a maze of crevasses to camp in their midst. Two days of sun had made a difference in them. They had widened considerably. Bridges none too strong or wide before now made but a flimsy crossing over depths to which we could see no bottom. In approved Alpine fashion the men ahead and behind would hold the rope taut for each one's safety as he crossed, but they had never been roped before, and as much because of their daring as their inexperience I had constantly to remind them to keep as far apart as the rope would permit. Profiting by our experience of the year before, we had brought up two eight-foot "gee-poles"—steering poles from the sleds—to bridge the worst places. When their ends seemed to find no solid support, we would lighten our weight by throwing our loads over first. Bloomquist's eyes fairly bulged as once with his pack on his back he crawled over on all fours the better to distribute his weight.

Even the miseries of a heavy pack were repaid by the sights about us, and once established on another mound at "Crevice Camp"—there could be no other name for it—there was nothing to mar the exhilaration of the scene. As the sun had grown hot, immediately on all sides the ice cliffs had begun to break off and the powdery snow to slide from the walls of rock between which we were rising. We were safe from all slides and could enjoy their beauty to the full. In the Alps one keeps to the rocks and avoids glacier travel whenever he can, but at the same altitudes in Alaska all the rocks have a perpetual crest of ice hundreds of feet in thickness. When the thawing begins fragments fall; hence in Alaska the rocks are places to keep away from. If glaciers and snow ridges offer no safe route, the mountain cannot be climbed. There are no intermissions on dry rocks to the snow and ice work of which Alaskan mountaineering consists.

The slides were a subject of constant study; we could calculate how to avoid them and had time to observe their movements before venturing in their path, and the men assured me that "you could most generally always side-step them in time after you heard the first crack overhead." They had dodged them before now while hunting and prospecting.

"We've found a route up," said Mr. Barrett, as we set up our tents with our three explorers at Crevice Camp; but the gulch up which he pointed was so steep, so studded with bulging ice masses which must sweep us away if they broke off, and so near some rocks whence the ice was always breaking, that I hesitated.

"It's all right if we go early," he assured me. "But I tell you," and his face grew serious, "we'll have to go light and rush it; for that gulch is going to slide sometime, and if we keep a-traveling up and down it till we get all the stuff up, somebody's going to get killed. Just take food and what you have to have, and we men can sleep in the sun."

Again I hesitated. Suppose a storm came? That was just the reason he was urging me to "rush it," said my leader. They were unanimous, and they thought it the only way. "Anyway," they said, they would all "rather take a chance than to pack all that junk up and down again any further"— our shelter and fuel!

Thus were my carefully laid plans to be altered, almost daily, according to the conditions and the humor of the men—men, who think women whimsical.

Certainly our night among the crevasses emphasized the need for getting up and down the mountain as soon as possible; for fearful splits in the ice, apparently right under our tents, kept waking us, making us wonder whether we were about to be engulfed as we slept.

As the dawn showed the way amid the crevasses, we shouldered our packs, all but one man who was indisposed and remained in camp. It was the 30th of April. Fortune favored. The snow stayed firm and we rose rapidly merely with creepers and axes, no step-chopping, no roping, although for fully 3,000 feet the average angle of the slope was 60°. Twice the level showed 76°. Each took his own gait, the men's a top speed with rests, mine the slow but steady plodding of the Alps. My pack of 25 pounds exhausted me and, unasked, Isaacson and Lang generously added it to their already heavy loads. Generally I had 15 pounds, but on that slope camera, glasses, and instruments were all that I could well carry, although the men bore 50 pounds apiece. When there was ice underneath we went carefully. Crevasses were few and visible. The snow showed no tendency to slide. Our chief concern was due to the fearful ice masses which stood out to right and left, always one just overhead in our zigzag trail. Impressive as were their sizes and shapes, it was an anxious three hours and a half until we got above instead of below one after another that looked ready to fall on us. No icicles were breaking, no snowballs coming down, and yet we dared not relax our speed until at length we stood at the top of that perilous gulch. We had fixed 9 o'clock in the morning as the end of safe travel, and it was only eight. We had climbed about 3,500 feet in four hours and a half with all that was necessary to life for three days on our backs.

For the next hour we had but one thought—water—and no way to melt it except to hold tin cups full of snow patiently over candles. Just above and quite too near for safety, a sheer wall of ice 150 feet high seemed to block every path. From this source had already fallen those gigantic pieces that lay so dangerously near the head of our gulch. It would have taken only one of them to slide it. To camp here seemed unsafe, to find a way up apparently impossible. On every side loomed huge blocks, pillars, and towers, as large as houses.

The only way led right under and between lofty ice needles fantastic in shape. As we clambered carefully around the snow-hidden holes between the shattered remnants of those that now lay prostrate, stopping when we dared, through spaces a few feet wide we could look down a sheer 6,500 feet to our base camp, and on far across Kennicott Glacier up to the very summits of Mt. Regal and distant Mt. Natazhat. It seemed too marvelous to be true that mortal eye could look upon these enormous leaning towers of ice.

We dared not linger. Sharp angles and lines of cleavage told that some of these beautiful ice turrets close under the perpendicular sides of which we were passing had but lately broken from that wall and stood ready to fall on us. In Cordova Mr. Handy had had a small anchor made for throwing a rope over crevasses. By means of it a rope and then a man were quickly up the wall, at a point where the ice lay piled to within twenty feet of the top, without the delay of chopping steps, and soon all of us and our packs were safe.

We had reached 12,400 feet, and could now trace a route right up to the top. Indeed, the way seemed so clear that I estimated five to seven hours as all that would be needed to climb the 4,000 feet that remained, but it was impossible to proceed at once, for the snow had softened. It would be better to wait until daybreak.

Avalanches were pouring off the ridges below like loveliest bridal veil falls. We were too far up to hear or see any but the high ones. New mountains were in view, one far distant peak that seemed by its shape to be of volcanic origin, and by compass due east, 150 miles away, and per-haps 16,000 feet high. The panorama was one to linger over, but a chill breeze decided us to dig "igloos" or caves in the snow. The shovel flew and soon I "holed in" to mine, which reminded me of a sleeping-car berth—if only it had been as warm. "The smaller the warmer," they said, but it had the chill of the grave, and I had had to leave blanket and sleeping-suit at Crevice Camp. Whenever I sat up or moved or arranged my hair, elbows and hair got full of snow. A flag pole marked each cave, lest some one step through the roof. The thermometer went down to 12° and even with mits and sweater on in my fur sleeping-bag my feet were barely warm enough for me to sleep.

It was broad daylight when I awoke, to realize that I had not been called. Had the men then frozen to death? I wondered, as I hurried out to see. A snowstorm was raging. Stamping and tramping to keep warm, sitting on a snow-shoe, or huddled over two candles trying to melt water and to warm it for tea or bouillon, I found five silent, cold, weary men. Unless we descended at once the trail would be covered and the rations for the summit depleted; but to venture down that fearful gulch in a blinding storm seemed to me out of the question. Moreover, I hoped that the weather would clear in time for us to go to the top and back without the added labor and danger of climbing down and up that gulch anew. So we stayed, stayed three days, until the food was so nearly gone that there was no choice but to go down. Each day the storm had grown worse. Two feet of snow fell in 24 hours. By day I would lend my sleeping-bag to two men at a time, who would take turns lying on it for two hours at a time, but to cover them I had only the maps of the now invisible glaciers. I had already lent both my extra sweaters. A snow-shoe for a carpet kept our feet off the snow. I sat on my leather mits, kept my hands in my arm-pits, and stamped my feet like the rest. At least numbers and candles made their cave warmer than mine. The next morning they dug me out three times and finally dug a small burrow off their cave for me. Outside it was warmer, but wet. They told me stories of their life in the wilderness, and always their talk was of timber and water and game. By the second day to climb out required four steps instead of two and inside it was darker.

On the 3d of May we went out into a howling, freezing, driving snow storm to grope our way down the awful 3,500 feet that lay between us and more food.

"It don't look good to me," said my leader, as finally we found the top of the gulch. Without a word Mr. Handy took the lead, tested the snow, and started down. It was too cold to discuss the question. The slope was so steep and the snow so deep as to keep us wet to the waist half the time. Over crevasses and on down a now trailless path of danger, we seemed always to be just on the brink of some precipice or crevasse. We could not see fifty feet ahead, sometimes not twenty—and yet they did not call it a blizzard. For just such a storm had I brought long bamboo flag poles to mark the trail, but because they were troublesome in climbing, without asking me, the men had left them at Crevice Camp.

On went Mr. Handy, through all the hours never hesitating, except for the way when we could not see, never afraid, merely shouting back occasional warnings of crevasses or of steep ice underneath. For the latter Lang would anchor his ice axe and "snub us down," and the rope stood every test. It was as cool and brilliant a piece of leadership as I have ever seen. In four hours we were safely down that gulch to Crevice Camp.

We were back to the bedding, back to tents and a stove—but to wet bedding! The man at the camp had let the snow pile up on the tents and the bedding get against their wet walls. It was the last straw, wet bedding after three nights without any in a 16° snow cave!

The next morning it was still snowing. Mr. Barrett wanted to go for wood, the Finn and the two Swedes for good, and they left us, here at 8,700 feet, on the 4th of May.

"To wait for the haymaker"—as Lang called the sun—to dry the bedding was the only way, and that might mean rheumatism for life. Moreover, they thought that even when the storm ceased we should have to wait a week for that gulch either to slide or settle. Meantime the food would probably run short and the mountain grow too dangerous because of the rapidly advancing season. Thus they argued, and I would not ask any one to go where he thought it unsafe. I had brought three extra men for the relaying only because I thought them needed to save time and I did not see how we could well go on without them, but Mr. Handy said, "Don't turn back unless you want to. We will get up without them." I had brought food and fuel for five weeks.

On the 9th day of May a widely published Associated Press despatch told of three men and two dogs that had "staggered into Kennicott, telling a thrilling tale," sent back—so the newspapers said—for more food and fuel. So they reported us *Marooned near Top Mt. Blackburn, Facing Starvation.*

"Once more the Arctic silence closed about them," said the newspapers.

On Mt. Blanc people perish when overtaken by sudden storms, unless they can get to one of the refuge huts 4,000 feet apart. We had not even had tents, but we had dug caves in the snow, and had lived in them for three days with temperatures of 16° to 32° and no stove.

Amid the yawning crevasses of Barrett Glacier, Mr. Handy, Lang, and I were all that were now left of the eight that had set out two weeks before for the summit of Mt. Blackburn. We had all the worst part to climb over again. We were only at 8,700 feet and it was already the 5th of May, but we were snowbound, and "May and June are the months of slides" had been my warning before I started.

Mr. Barrett had wished to see how Kolb and the dogs were faring and had gone down to the base camp the day before with the three men that were homeward bound. Today he was to come up again, bringing his tiny wood stove and the wood from the hardtack boxes. Mr. Handy and Lang went down to meet him. With Kolb and the dogs to help, Mr. Barrett was bringing up a big load of supplies on a sled as far as the crevasses.

We seemed safe on our mound, safely away from all walls and far from all lines of breakage and flow. Suddenly a thundering roar made Lang step out. On the other side of the glacier, somewhere near our gulch, a great mass of ice had broken off and was falling. It had dropped 2,000 feet and came rolling onward like a great wave of surf and spray. It was flowing into the wide basin below us with a momentum which nothing could withstand. It was a mile away and on the side of the glacier where lay our trail to the base, and we were watching to see whether it would extend so far—when all of a sudden an icy, snow-laden gust told us to run for our lives to our dug-out and, before we could get in, Lang and I were covered. We had got only a smart sprinkling, but the cloud of "spray" remained about five minutes or more, and when it had settled, so far as we could miss any mass on so huge and broken a glacier, it seemed as if a great area of ice had broken not from our gulch but from the ice cliffs above the rocks beside it.

It was snowing again and 26° as we turned into our comfortable tents—the last time that we were to use them for seventeen days. The next morning the men were wet as they came from the crevasses with more packs; and the intervals without snow were too brief to dry anything. Over a hot dinner we held a council of war. We had all been thinking: what if a big slide were to come from our side of the glacier, from above us? It could not fail to sweep us away, tents and all. Mr. Barrett decided to go down to the base camp, even if he had to cross the crevasses alone; but the chief part of the supplies was up now, and at the base we should be one day farther from the summit, so the rest of us preferred to stay and to make ourselves slide-proof in a snow cave. By tunnelling into the steepest slope of our mound we would be safe, no matter how many slides went down over us, provided only that our roof were solid. Hence the cave must be small, just big enough for us to live in; and we three did live in it for nine days. It was about the size of a bathroom and half as high, 10 feet by 6, with 4 feet to stand in. Anything left out in the storm was lost in an hour, so everything had to be stowed away inside. In one end I managed to raise my tent just enough for me to crawl into at night and to keep my possessions dry.

The thermometer often went down to 21° inside, but we could not have heat lest we weaken our snow roof or run out of oil, so between meals we would crawl into our sleeping-bags. The hardest thing was to keep dry, for every time we went out we were in snow to our knees at the least and got wet all over, and the only way to dry anything was to sleep on it. Sometimes it would snow three feet in a day or a night. And yet, during the nine days in that snow cave we slept more, ate more, laughed more, even washed more than all the rest of the time put together, and I think the thing I minded most about the entire expedition was that there were days when there was not enough water for me to brush my teeth.

One day Mr. Handy said, "I think Barrett and Kolb will be wanting to turn back also; but I have spoken to Lang and he agrees that we two can get you to the top of the mountain alone, so don't you turn back, unless you want to."

On the 10th of May, the tenth day of the storm (which had abated a little), for the first time it seemed safe to descend far enough to meet Mr. Barrett and Kolb. Mr. Barrett was anxious lest his wife worry and he lose his position by too long absence. Both wished to go back; and with them would go the remaining dogs. Thus did we burn our bridges behind us; but Mr. Barrett was to return in two weeks to search for us if we had not then appeared. We turned and faced the wind to go back to our cave. The storm grew wild and we could barely follow our trail of two hours before.

For another three days the snow continued. We could do nothing but talk. Lang loved to repeat the German fairy stories of his childhood, *Snow White and Rose Red,* and the rest, interlarding his philosophy of life. He was as simple as a child, although he was an old hunter and trapper from Eastern Ontario. The wilds had no terrors for him. He "would just as lief be 1,500 miles away from the nearest man as not," and "could climb any mountain alone." He had neither received nor written a letter for fifteen years, but he "knew everyone in Alaska, pretty much," and he didn't want them to say, "Well, Bill, you couldn't make it, could you!" Alaska was getting too settled for him and he "guessed he'd be going to the Mackenzie River soon, where game was more plentiful-like."

Mr. Handy was the son of a German army officer. He was adventurous and daring by nature, but a disciplined soldier and always the first to subordinate his own interests to the good of the whole. He had been trained in a German technical school, had done his military service in Southwest Africa, and had mined in South America, Mexico, California, and Alaska. He had even been a cowboy in Texas. For money he cared nothing, but he had enlisted for the summit of Mt. Blackburn and he always said, "Don't worry. We shall get to the top."

On the 13th of May, there came a lull in the storm, and at last we could venture to the base camp for some necessaries. As we were upward bound, the skies cleared. The thirteen-day snowstorm was over. Although it was 9:30 o'clock at night the sunset was only beginning to fade as we got back to our cave at Crevice Camp, and five hours later it was sunrise again as for the second time we were preparing to start up the mountain. Midsummer was upon us! Still, during the last seven days of the storm uniform temperatures had prevented all slides, the snow seemed to pack quickly, and we thought it safe to try our gulch at once.

Twenty feet or more of new snow now necessitated a long zigzag approach to the gulch on snow-shoes instead of the former direct climb up across the basin at its foot. To sound and break the trail as they relayed two packs and to test the gulch was all that could be done that day. They could go faster without me, and their parting words were, "If we don't come back, do you think you can get home alone?" and my reply, "I'll try." In half an hour I saw them disappear. Was it forever, or were they behind that hill? They had seemed to be making straight for the place where, just as they started, a great pinnacle of ice had fallen from 2,000 feet above. At last I saw them again, far above, and this time in the path of the slides from that cliff next to our gulch. "Well," Lang had said, "if we're killed we'll get our names in the papers, anyhow."

They thought the gulch safe, but the perpetual daylight of the Northern summer had come. Henceforth daytime travel would be unsafe and the nights might prove too short and warm for the freezing which alone prevented slides and gave a crust. At 10 that night, 11, midnight, still there was no crust. Although I sank to my hips as I put on my snow-shoes, we could wait no longer.

At dawn on the 15th of May, for the second time we lost sight of Crevice Camp, once again to strain every nerve to get up that gulch before the slides should begin. Once more we had left tents and stove behind, but this time I had insisted that the men take their bedding. So there were five loads for two men, there was no relay party, and the deep new snow would be certain to double the time; and the hours of safe travel had dwindled to the brief period of a dusk and dawn that could hardly be told apart. Indeed, all the conditions were changed, and the ascent would now be twice as hard as before the storm. The difficulties were as great or greater than the previous August when we had given up this route as too dangerous, but I knew my men and I trusted their judgment and ability.

The night was clear and I could drink in the beauty of it all while the men rested from their heavy packs. Lang would roll his pack off, exclaiming, "There, you've been lying on me long enough! It's my turn to lie on you awhile."

At 2 o'clock in the morning we were under the treacherous rock-cliffs and amid huge snowballs, tell-tales of slides. Lang pointed to the overhanging upper lip of a big crevasse beside us now drifted half full of snow, saying, "There, that's the kind of a place to get in if a slide comes." Hardly had he spoken when there was a loud report overhead as of an explosion, and we looked up to see ice cliffs descending upon us. "Come here!" cried Lang from behind, and as we were roped we had to, although the quickest way to safety lay ahead. As I turned, the tails of my snow-shoes caught and I upset. Two of us had yet to cross a narrow slanting ledge of ice overhanging a crevasse, but somehow we reached shelter just in time to be half way under as the slide came on. As we crouched, "Dig in your ice pick!" were the last words I heard. A moment and it had passed, and for a second time we had only two inches of snow all over us, for an intervening gulley had received most of the slide. The route the men had chosen *was* a safe one.

Once at the foot of the gulch, despite the softness of the snow the angle necessitated creepers. The sun was already hot as at 3:15 o'clock we began the ascent of that 3,000-foot nightmare gulch. To climb the first 150 feet I had to take hold of the rope, for it was 76° and all ice underneath, but Mr. Handy had not even chopped steps as he had taken the rope up to anchor it. The steeper the slope the better he liked it. He did not call the zigzag method climbing. He was never afraid, yet he never led us into danger. Until 9 o'clock we would be safe even here, and by that hour surely we hoped to be in our cave above the wall. A deep groove like a toboggan slide told where something had come down, and I was glad when the last pack and the last man were above instead of beside it.

Hauling seemed the quickest and easiest way for two men to get five packs up so steep a gulch. To a "sleigh" or "buggy," as he called it, made from two snow-shoes, Lang would tie two packs at a time, and around an anchored ice axe Mr. Handy would "line them" up eighty feet at a time. I helped to haul or broke trail ahead. I had to choose the steepest places in order that the sled might slide; yet, work as we would, by 5 o'clock in the morning it would no longer slide either up or down. Trail breaking had become such deep, steep work that I was pressing first one knee and then the other ahead and still rising only three inches at a time. By 7 o'clock the snow was so soft and the slope so steep that bits of snow, "snowballs," were rolling down on us—warning of slides to follow. We were exhausting ourselves and still we were making no progress. It was time to be out of such a place, and yet we could not hope to get up the remaining 1,200 feet to our cave before the slides should begin. We were only two-thirds of the way up the gulch, and I could not see even a safe place to camp. Indeed, to look up was appalling, for to right and left beetling ice cliffs loomed threateningly overhead. It was the only time when I felt that we were really in grave danger and saw no way out of it; but Lang had more experience than I. "Why," he said, "we can camp 'most anywhere as far as that goes," and he pointed to the "shelter" of one ice mound after another as a good camp site! Under an eyelid of ice, as it were, deep in the recesses of a snow-filled ice cave, we spread our bedding and awaited the night. A great crack right across our roof warned us away from its edge. A fringe of icicles, like eyelashes, dripped merrily—so long as the sun was on them—giving us water.

We were safe from anything that might come, and yet I could not sleep for the thunder of the many slides on every side. None came near us until midday, when twice the rolling of falling ice made me sit up with a start just as a great mass went sweeping by. They were the most awe-inspiring sight that I have ever seen, so wonderful, so thrilling to watch, that I wished I did not need sleep. They passed so close that it was as if the American Falls at Niagara were suddenly overwhelming us. It was the most exciting day of the entire ascent. Still nothing came over us, and at 3:30 in the afternoon I got up. The higher we rose the fewer the slides— but on the descent the opposite would be true. I looked down and there at the foot of our gulch, 2,000 feet below, lay the fragments of a great slide spread out like a fan. It had gone down since we had come up just there a few hours before. It was the third big slide we had escaped, and again it was judgment more than good fortune that had saved us. We had been there at an hour that was safe.

We had reached 11,000 feet, and still there was no crust as again we started upward at 10 o'clock in the evening, none until the cold breeze of dawn found us on a glazed slope where a crust left no foothold. Just as we seemed to have reached the top of the gulch, bad crevasses caused delay. It grew late and we looked upward anxiously. Weary from lack of food we had to stop to eat in none too safe a place. At the top, steps had to be chopped and when at length we were up, utterly weary from the disheartening struggle in knee-deep snow, the most we could do was to crawl into a shaded shelter as far as possible from the great ice wall above. For lack of a relay party and because of the advance in the season, it had taken thirteen hours to get merely food, bedding, and essential outfit up 1,000 feet.

In the seventeen days since we had dug our first cave above this wall all had changed. New blocks had parted from it. The great 60-foot ice needles under which we had once hurried had fallen. Landmarks were gone and just to find the way up 200 feet again to our "igloo" and to dig it out took all that night. Only by the bare tip of a bamboo pole did we discover it. It had become a burrow and to descend into it required twelve steps. We had been four days regaining the 3,500 feet which we had before climbed in as many hours. For the second time we had reached 12,400 feet. Between 10,000 and 12,500 feet what appeared to be a volcanic ash discolored the snow.

At 9:30 o'clock in the evening it seemed as if we should really reach the summit that night. The slope was easier, slides were improbable so high up, and although snow-shoes were still required, moccasins had replaced rubber shoe-packs lest our feet freeze. We had only 4,000 feet to go, and to avoid further relaying the men decided to leave their bedding.

At midnight the wind pierced us as we exchanged snow-shoes for creepers, only to need the snow-shoes again when they were far behind.

62 ▲ A<small>LASKA</small> A<small>SCENTS</small>

For an hour we were wallowing to our knees. Then a thin crust made us take to all fours, and still we broke through. For the breakfast halt we sought shelter but found none, until Lang dug a third cave. The distance had been considerable and although it was 3 o'clock in the morning we had reached only 14,000 feet. An ocean of billowy clouds covered Kennicott Glacier. The earth lay hidden from view and only the mountain tops appeared as the tints of the dawn added the last touch to the most superb view of my life. As we watched, the peaks took fire and in a moment over the snowy spires of Mt. Reynolds the sun crept forth.

Although at 3:30 o'clock the thermometer showed only 6°, before we could start again trail breaking had become so arduous that it seemed best to wait for the shadows. With makeshift coverings and moving as the sun moved we slept a little. At 5 o'clock in the evening Lang started up the last 2,000 feet. He was ploughing to his knees and the slope had become steep enough for him to zigzag.

At 15,000 feet our packs made us begin to feel the altitude a little. Because of the moccasins my creepers refused to stay firm, and to rebind them was a long, cold process. We were not getting up very fast, but it was no place for a slip. At 9 o'clock at night we saw Lang depositing my bedding above, at the only level spot. Presently we also would be there with the shovel to dig a last cave, the fourth—for a brief rest. The next moment he was running down, pausing as he passed only long enough to say that he felt a little sick and, since he "had no bet on getting to the top," he thought he would go down to his bedding and wait. After twenty-seven days of misery he had turned down within 500 feet of the top. Of the seven men in our party that had started, one alone remained.

It was zero at midnight. Even at sunrise it was only 3°. To thaw a tin of salmon over two candles took an hour. The final slope was steep and slippery, and even so high there were holes. We were a full hour climbing it, and when at length we thought the summit attained, we found that it was a half mile plateau on which a half hour's wandering and use of the level were necessary in order to determine the highest point. Indeed, at first a twin summit at least two miles away to the northwest appeared the higher one. A long snow saddle connected them. Finally, however, at the northeast edge of the southeast summit we seemed to be standing on the top of Mt. Blackburn, all that were left of us, two of eight. It was 8:30 o'clock in the morning and the 19th of May. Even a temperature of 6° and an icy gale from which there was no shelter failed to mar the satisfaction of achievement in the accomplishment of a difficult task. It had taken four weeks.

There was nothing to impair a view upon which our eyes were the first that had ever looked and the panorama seemed limited only by the haze of distance as we gazed a full 200 miles on every side. Probably nowhere except in Alaska, not even in the Himalayas, could mortal man attain to the centre of so vast and imposing a stretch of unbroken snow over great glaciers and high snow peaks. Literally hundreds of them rose above the line of perpetual snow. The limited snow areas of the Alps, the Canadian Rocky Mountains, even the high Andes, faded into insignificance in my memory. We were in the very midst of the Wrangell Mountains, of which Mt. Blackburn was [the highest.] All were snow peaks, and at least six of them rose above 12,000 feet, more than 9,000 feet above the snow line. Each could be plainly distinguished and identified, Mt. Sanford, the [second highest,] Mt. Drum, Mt. Jarvis, and Mt. Wrangell, from the volcanic cone of which a faint column of white smoke was rising lazily. Although many miles away, no doubt this was the source of the fragments of burnt-out granite with which our plateau was strewn.

Between us and Mt. Jarvis to the north lay the immense unbroken snow field of the Nabesna Glacier. It was seemingly three times as extensive as the great Kennicott Glacier up which it had taken us five days to come. From Mt. Blackburn's summit two precipitous glaciers descended to it, contradicting my prediction of an easy northeast slope. On the west side, if anywhere, would lie the better route. We had hoped to explore all sides of our peak, but its area, the wind, the fatigue of climbing up again whenever we went down, and the long descent we had yet to make prevented.

With aching hands and in wind-hardened snow—for lack of any rock at all—we planted and guyed the bamboo flag-pole which we had dragged up, burying beneath it a brief record of the first ascent of this great 16,140-foot [the official height is now 16,523 feet] sub-arctic peak.

After four hours and a half, relief from the cold wind became imperative and we turned downward to rejoin Lang below.

With crevasses opening all but under us as we waited for snow bridges to harden, three days of anxious work brought us to the base, and two days more to Kennicott on the 24th of May.

Because of the latitude, to climb up and down 11,000 feet of snow and ice had required 26 days. After 33 days entirely on snow and ice, of which 22 nights had been spent without tents and 10 days without fuel, we were back—back to wood and water, to green grass and spring flowers, to civilization and friends.

Alaskan mountaineering is so new that the whole undertaking had been an experiment. Latitude and location are as important as altitude in determining the difficulty of a mountain ascent, and chiefly because of its latitude the problems of Alaskan mountaineering are new and wholly different from those of other regions. It is like Arctic exploration. Elsewhere difficulties of approach may be as great, the time required as long, and altitudes higher, but nowhere else is the time on snow and ice so long. Nowhere else does one have to climb 14,000 feet above the snow line, as on Mt. Blackburn, or even 17,000 feet, as on Mt. McKinley, which is only 20,300 feet high. Nowhere but in Alaska is the mountaineer obliged to be entirely on snow and ice and to choose between safety at the price of almost unendurable cold, or soft snow and avalanches, according as he goes early or late in the only season at which an ascent can be attempted. Not even in the Himalayas are the glaciers so extensive.

On Mt. Blackburn and Mt. McKinley, the discoverer of the North Pole has said, the problem of Alaskan mountaineering has been solved. The Parker–Browne expeditions and mine have proved that the secret of success lies in going early and in using dogs. Our 1911 expedition had been the first to use dogs on a mountain and the one here recounted was the first to succeed without Swiss guides, the first to live in snow caves, the first to make a prolonged night ascent, the first to succeed on an avalanche-swept southeast side, and the only Alaskan ascent in which a woman has taken part—to the credit of the men be it said. We succeeded because one man cared to succeed.

Ice-Cliff and Earthquake:
Mount Fairweather

– Paddy Sherman –

Often hidden by coastal clouds and battered by North Pacific storms, Mount Fairweather, when visible, is considered to be among Alaska's most spectacular sights, "an uncommonly beautiful peak," as mountaineer Allen Carpé reported in 1931. Fairweather got its name in 1778, when English captain James Cook sighted "a very high peaked mountain" after a prolonged siege of coastal storms. Eventually, an entire group of peaks within the St. Elias Mountains would be named the Fairweather Range.

Fifteen miles from the North Pacific in what is now Glacier Bay National Park, 15,320-foot Fairweather is one of the world's highest coastal mountains. Its great height—and, in clear weather, its visibility from great distances—made Fairweather a natural choice of surveyors, who used it as a boundary mountain to mark the Alaska-Canada border. Fairweather's height and rugged beauty have also made it a natural target of climbers. Beyond the Alaska Range giants and perhaps St. Elias, it is arguably the state's greatest mountaineering "prize."

One measure of Fairweather's status is its inclusion in Steve Roper and Allen Steck's Fifty Classic Climbs of North America. *Another is its climbing history. The first attempt on its summit was made in 1926, years before Alaskan giants such as Foraker or Hunter would attract mountaineers. William Ladd, Allen Carpé, and Andy Taylor—the latter two considered among the best climbers of their day—reached 9,200 feet before retreating. Four years later, Bradford Washburn led a group of Harvard classmates up the west ridge, but reached only 6,700 feet. Then, in 1931, Ladd, Carpé, and Taylor returned with well-known mountaineer and scholar Terris Moore. The foursome ascended what Steck and Roper call "the most demanding and technical route done [to that time] in North America."*

More than a quarter century passed before the next attempt. In 1958, a group of Canadians ascended the mountain as part of British Columbia's centennial celebration. The team's leader: climber and journalist Paddy Sherman. Born in Newport, Monmouthshire, in 1928, Sherman moved to Vancouver, B.C., in 1952 and spent much of the next thirty-seven years climbing and working as a newspaper journalist. He retired as president of Southam Newspapers—Canada's largest chain—in 1989, but even in his mid-sixties he remains an active climber, skier, and writer. Most of Sherman's mountaineering efforts have been within British Columbia's Coast Mountains, but he's also ascended Denali and Ecuador's 19,347-foot Cotopaxi and 20,561-foot Chimborazo.

Paddy Sherman's account, "Ice-Cliff and Earthquake: Mount Fairweather," is taken from his book Cloud Walkers, *published in 1965 by St. Martin's Press in New York.*

NINE HUNDRED MILES NORTH-WEST of Vancouver, on a shoreline thrashed by the turbulent North Pacific Ocean, stands one of the tallest coastal mountains in the world. It is a glittering peak, which for almost two hundred years has been a guide to explorers gingerly probing the mysteries of the wild, ice-chiselled coast of Alaska.

A map published after exploration of the coast in 1786 by the French Captain La Pérouse shows the mountain as "Mont Beautems." Today it is known as Mount Fairweather, and from its summit at 15,300 feet rivers of ice plunge right into the ocean.

Everest has a snow and ice zone of around 13,000 feet. Mount Logan, the Yukon giant that rises to almost 20,000 feet, stands 14,000 feet above the general level of the terrain around it. Fairweather's glacial armour soars more than 15,000 feet right out of the sea.

Dr. W. S. Ladd, an early Alaskan mountaineer who tried to climb it in 1926 and 1931, was enthralled by its splendour. He wrote: "Its pyramidal central summit, and broad shoulders approached only by the steepest of great snow and ice arêtes, give delight in a symmetrical grace and beauty that I know of [in] no other great massif. From an altitude of 3,000 feet, its fluted walls rise almost too steeply for the mountaineer on every side. The snow and ice hang as if glued upon them. Upon every line of approach that the eye follows in an effort to plan a route to the summit, there is some obstacle demanding the best art of the mountaineer."

It would have taken the best art of the magician to persuade the early explorers to try to climb it, though several of La Pérouse's men set foot on one of the glaciers. For them, battling the gales and currents brewed in the hell's-kitchen of the wild Pacific weather, mere survival was enough. They were content to marvel—in the rare moments when nature would allow them. Calling this ocean the "Pacific" was one of the great misnomers of all time. Surely whoever first named Fairweather had his tongue in his cheek, going along with the irony of Balboa's blunder when he named the Pacific almost 3,000 miles to the south.

One tempest after another whines in from the vast, cold ocean throughout the winter. Bad weather is generated in low-pressure areas, and the pressure around Fairweather is so low, according to Allen Carpé, one of the earliest climbers in the region, that average pressures on its peak are about ten per cent lower than would be expected. They are as low as would be found on inland mountains of almost 17,000 feet.

The pressure may be low, but precipitation is high. For week after week, with rarely a break, snow falls steadily for most of the winter, piling up enormous drifts that make the landscape arctic. All along this brooding coast, the resulting glaciers rumble and fan out to the sea. The pocks and veins of age and decay now mar their once-white faces.

High on the slopes of the peaks the ice is still young and active, worrying and grinding at the age-old rock of the earth's hard crust. Here at the tattered fringe of ocean, many glaciers are stagnant. Steaming and sweating in the summer sun, they look like the worn-out limbs of a mountain monster that has outlived its day and withered on its suicidal rush to the sea.

Towering over the surrounding peaks, Fairweather was a striking challenge to the mountaineering pioneer. In 1926 Dr. Ladd made the first attempt to climb it. With him were two of the best climbers then active in North America—Andy Taylor and Allen Carpé—fresh from their great ascent of Mount Logan.

They reached a height of 9,000 feet, after an exciting time ferrying supplies ashore at Cape Fairweather through the rolling ocean surf. In 1930, Dr. Bradford Washburn took up the attack. He was to compile perhaps the greatest record in Alaskan climbing history, but that year he reached only 6,700 feet amid the jumbled pinnacles of ice. He did not have another chance, because Ladd, Taylor, and Carpé came back in 1931, with Dr. Terris Moore, later president of the University of Alaska.

Their expedition took two months, and the weather was so bad at the start that it took them ten days to make the trip by boat from Juneau to Lituya Bay that normally took twenty hours.

Moore and Carpé reached the summit after climbing through the night of June 7, and found that Dr. Ladd was right about the steepness of the snow-slopes. They measured great faces at an angle of fifty-five degrees throughout their length. In many places they steepened to sixty degrees. After it was all over, Carpé confessed to his friend Henry Hall that Fairweather was technically the toughest peak he had climbed in his outstanding Alaskan career. And when an account of the climb appeared in that year's *Alpine Journal* in London, the editor, E. L. Strutt, wrote in an introduction: "The ascent of Mt. Fairweather is, we understand, the hardest yet accomplished among the 'Arctic' mountains of North America."

Fairweather had fascinated me since just after I moved to Canada in 1952, but early efforts to attempt it shattered on the twin reefs of time and money. Then an oddity of geography and the centenary of British Columbia's birth suddenly made it feasible.

A glance at the map will show what I mean about the geography. Northern British Columbia's access to the sea is cut off for hundreds of miles by the Alaska Panhandle, a long strip of United States coastline. At the north end, the boundary of British Columbia reaches far out into the Panhandle. The boundary surveyors chose Fairweather as one of the boundary points, so that the British Columbia–Alaska border runs right over the top.

This made it far and away the highest point in British Columbia— and a peak so far unclimbed by Canadians. In 1957, L. J. Wallace, chairman of the committee preparing the centennial celebrations for 1958, thought it would be a good idea if a mountainous province could start the program with a mountaineering feat, much as the ascent of Everest opened the reign of Queen Elizabeth. On behalf of the Alpine Club of Canada, I suggested an ascent of Mount Fairweather, and this was immediately approved.

It is a fundamental principle of mountaineering that the difficulty and steepness of a mountain decrease in direct ratio to the distance of the challengers from the peak. Otherwise, of course, there would be few attempts on major mountains. Who, in his right mind, would cold-bloodedly plan to scale a difficult mountain if he could actually see the difficulties as he planned? When he actually sees the difficulties, of course, it is too late: he is committed!

In our minds we climbed Fairweather a dozen times the year before we even saw it. Optimistic routes were planned on aerial photographs, camp-sites were picked from the inaccurate map with a blithe disregard for the fact that the previous party had trouble finding even one place big enough for a tent. Ian Kay, our one-man technical planning committee, more or less "delivered" the mountain to us gift-wrapped, when he completed a masterpiece of planning on the assault schedule.

It came in the form of a series of tables, which would tell at a glance how long two, three, or four, or eight men should take to reach the summit, how much food they would have to carry, and whether or not they should leave the tents standing on Day 3 when they left Camp Two. We were sure it covered every possible combination of circumstances on the mountain. But I was perversely glad to find that by a flagrant breach of organizational etiquette we finally attempted the summit by an "unplanned plan," in the best tradition of individualistic mountaineers.

There were several reasons why we suggested Mount Fairweather to the centennial planners. First, of course, it was time Canadians tried to reach the highest point of British Columbia. Second, it was a first-class climb, and regular progress bulletins by radio from base camp would, we thought, make a worth-while addition to the many other projects being reported, and focus attention on the least-known part of the province. Third, it would give the Alpine Club and the British Columbia Mountaineering Club experience in planning and making a major expedition which could help to raise the standards of both clubs in the years ahead.

Therefore, we set up many committees to look after various aspects of the expedition, and Roy Mason and I spent a hectic winter coordinating their work. The Royal Canadian Air Force came into the picture, and we earnestly discussed details of where our goods should be parachuted and how they should be packaged, and a hundred other details. Here again, nature knocked holes in our plans, and our elaborate, well-conceived system of alternative drop-sites had to be abandoned at the last minute.

The Canadian Broadcasting Corporation decided shortly before we left to send with us, at their own expense, a television producer and a cameraman. We had to start getting them into shape, so I undertook to hike with them, before work each day, up 2,300 feet of the steep ski-lift track on Grouse Mountain, a few miles from Vancouver. Michael Rothery and Kelly Duncan were the two who finally came, and they proved willing and firm friends of the whole party.

But the cameraman who showed up for the first early-morning training session was a bit of a problem. We had met briefly on several assignments, and he knew that I was a reporter. He had no idea that I was a climber too—in fact, by this time I had been named the leader of the expedition.

He was waiting when I arrived at the foot of the ski-lift, and said, "Oh, are you going too?" I confessed that I was thinking of doing so. Then he confided, "I don't know what all the fuss is about. They tell me this is just a promotion stunt. They say this mountain is so easy that our television cameras could be waiting on top when the party reaches there, and make a good movie. But the climbers don't want their glory stolen, and have insisted that we won't be able to go above 5,000 feet. They will take a camera on to the top."

I didn't ask him who "they" were, knowing that only one man still lived who had stood on Fairweather's top—Dr. Terris Moore, who was far away in the United States. So, very meanly, I murmured, "Well, that sounds interesting."

This encouraged him, having dug his own trap, to blunder headlong in. "This training program," he went on, "is just a waste of time. I used to be a national champion in cycling. I don't need any training."

Up to this moment, I had been about to explain the situation to him as we stood around waiting for the late-comer. Instead I suggested we hike up without waiting for Michael. My confidant shot away up the slope at a great rate, and in the first hundred feet rapidly opened up a gap between us. I plodded along, and by the time we had climbed 300 feet, I was a yard behind him, listening to his furious panting. Sweat poured from him, and I asked if he wanted to rest. He replied, "Okay, *pant* if you *pant pant* need *pant* the rest *pant pant* . . . " So while his heart gradually stopped its pounding, I told him the score and gave him a few pointers on how to make uphill travel a little easier.

He performed very well for a beginner, but on the way down he said he had had an ulcer some time before and was worried that he might have trouble if he were away for a month in remote Alaska.

When I reached home, I telephoned the expedition doctor, Denis Moore, and asked his opinion. "Well," said Denis, "tell him I think a month away from civilization will probably do his ulcer a world of good. If anything does go wrong, we'll be able to fix him up all right. It won't be quite the same as being in hospital, but we'll manage."

With visions of a flashing scalpel in a billowing tent on a glacier, I told him. Next day a different cameraman went into training.

Our climbing training had been under way for some months, with fourteen climbers getting into excellent condition for the final selection. I found some of the training was rather risky when we were not on the mountains.

Each night through the winter I ran a couple of miles in the dark on the streets near my home. One night as I pounded down the road, a police car came roaring up and I was asked a barrage of questions. They had set a trap, it seemed, for a peeping Tom who was busy in the neighbour-hood—and sprinting Sherman just answered the description nicely! Eventually I persuaded them I was crazy but harmless, and too tired anyway, so they let me go.

Another night, as I ran as hard as I could along the final stretch, another car pulled in beside me. The door was flung open and a voice shouted, "I don't know where you're going, Buster, but wherever it is I'll drive you, if you're in that much of a hurry."

We practised crevasse rescue techniques on the glaciers of Mount Baker, in Washington State, and completed the program by hauling fifty-pound packs to the top of the 10,800-foot mountain. We camped one night at the 9,000-foot level, and then set up our expedition tents for another night on the summit, giving our basic equipment a thorough work-out. This gave us, for a day, the delightful sensation of starting our climbing downhill, then making high-standard ice-climbs back up to the tent. Even the weather co-operated. For the climbing it was perfect. For the summit camp and the descent it turned into a howling blizzard that made route-finding difficult even with the green bamboo canes we had put up as markers the day before.

The eight climbers were chosen by a personnel committee headed by the veteran climber Eric Brooks. They were:

Paul Binkert, an astonishingly fit and able man of fifty who had amassed tremendous experience in Europe, the Andes, and Canada.

David Blair, born in British Columbia, with experience of many difficult climbs on British Columbia mountains.

Fips Broda, from Austria, an instructor in mountain warfare in the last war, with a fine record in the Alps, the Caucasus, and the Canadian Coast Range. I always considered him the climbing leader.

Joseph Hutton, a Scot, with wide experience in Europe and Canada.

Dr. Denis Moore, another recent arrival from Scotland, who had been climbing difficult mountains for years.

Walter Romanes, a quiet, incredibly strong New Zealander who had climbed in many parts of the world, and was at twenty-seven the youngest member of the party. A few weeks after the expedition finished, he was able, being a carefree bachelor, to dash back to New Zealand and join an expedition to the Antarctic. Later he went to the Himalayas with Hillary.

Russell Yard, a strong, heavily bearded climber who was the second Canadian-born member of the party, thoroughly at home in the tall, tough mountains of the province.

I came from England in 1952 after climbing in Britain and the Pyrenees, and was soon fascinated by Coast Range exploration.

Two more names were yet to be added to our roster. The centennial authorities wanted to issue reports on our progress, which raised a difficult problem. In the Himalayas, runners can often do the job. Here there were no trade paths or regular routes, just a wilderness of mountains and glaciers bordered by the ocean. A radio was the only answer—but we needed a powerful radio transmitter at the spot to be sure of sending our messages 1,000 miles to Vancouver.

The British Columbia Amateur Radio Association solved the problem by offering to put a complete station at Lituya Bay, twenty-four miles from our peak, and right at the base of operations. Two experienced "hams," George Kitson, a detective, and Ken McMillan, agreed to man the station for the whole month.

The climbing party carried a portable transmitter right into base camp, and the nightly chattering back and forth became essential listening for the many "hams" on the Alaska Panhandle network. They went to considerable trouble to make arrangements for us, and, once the climbing was on, obtained special weather forecasts for us every day.

The climbers kept their equipment down to a minimum and this was fortunate—for when the radio operators arrived at Vancouver Airport, they had a small mountain of sets and spares and generators. By the time it was all aboard and we took off at 8 AM on June 16, 1958, there was just no room for us to sit. We settled down among the crates, and flew until after 8 PM trying to get into Lituya Bay, which is about a hundred miles north and west of Juneau.

As we headed from Juneau towards the ocean coast, a solid wall of cloud built up ahead and forced us back. We tried again the following morning, despite thick cloud and rain. The pilots, Flight Lieutenants Don Hill and Ed Cameron, managed to creep down to within two hundred feet of the sea through a hole in the clouds, and we were astonished to spot a small aeroplane on the beach, only a few yards from the Pacific rollers.

Where it had stopped, a tent was set up—our first indication of the way Alaskan glacier and bush pilots seem willing and able to land almost anywhere. We also spotted Lituya Bay near by; so Don Hill offered to put the big Canso amphibian down on the beach near the other aircraft. The shade of green that spread over my face must have put him off, and instead we headed for the bay.

This had been gloomy and dispiriting work, with the crew doing wonders even to find the place, which is the only harbour for more than one hundred miles along this inhospitable coast.

Now, as we swung low over the surrounding trees, patches of cloud were hanging down almost to the water. Through the gloom we suddenly saw a dozen fishing-boats dotting the likeliest landing-place—and here and there the glint of icebergs from glaciers at the head of the bay.

This was the second try, and, like the first, it failed. Visibility was too poor to land in the circumstances, and gas was getting low; so back we went once more to Juneau. Morale was getting a little low, too, as we climbed slowly through the layers of cloud. Then, at 6,000 feet, we were on top of the weather for an instant. For perhaps ten seconds we had a view of Fairweather floating an impossible distance above us. A few obscure little brain cells did the rest, and in a moment everybody was enthusiastic once more.

Just before 3 PM we landed at Lituya and work got rapidly under way. Everything was most efficiently set up. The television boys were waiting for us on the beach, flown in earlier by bush pilot Ken Loken, to whom flying blindfold seemed to be second nature. A rubber boat was inflated, an outboard motor attached, and away went the first load. So did the motor. It swamped on landing and for the next couple of hours we rowed.

Only five minutes' walk from the sandy beach just inside the spit guarding the entrance to Lituya Bay was a small lake surrounded by tall timber. It was sheltered from the wind, had plenty of fresh water, and was ideal for stringing aerials for the radios.

It was raining when we left the radio camp the next morning, and we all carried big packs, but nobody cared. At last we were really on the way to our mountain. So far we had been passengers, but now everything depended on us.

The route took us a dozen miles along the ocean shore to Cape Fairweather, then a similar distance up Fairweather Glacier to a point right under the southern cliffs of the mountain. We expected the walk to be hard, trudging along twelve miles of shifting sand, but the day turned out to be one of delightful surprises.

First, we found a trail good enough for a park. It had been built by prospectors many years before, and we found many signs of their activity. A decayed cabin here, a broken sluice there where they had panned for gold, even the wreckage of an old steam-engine that had almost rusted away. The bears that abounded here had also made full use of the trail, and their big feet had worn deep, regular holes in the track.

In mid-afternoon we reached a camp of modern-style prospectors. Mark and Walter Gilkey, both in their sixties, had a very comfortable camp, every item of which had been flown in by the small plane we had seen the day before. They had found good showings of titanium, more precious than gold in this day of jet planes and satellites, and were enthusiastically planning to develop their claims.

Our walk from here made us feel ashamed when we reflected on our arm-chair visions of the tough travel in Alaska. We strolled through won-

derful fields of lupine on a narrow fringe of land between the ocean and
the forest. For literally miles we trod on beds of wild strawberries, with
the occasional ripe one promising vitamin orgies on our way back from
the peak.

Half an hour short of camp, the Canso roared at pebble-whipping
height along the beach looking for us. The pilot radioed that he had
dropped all our supplies—but at neither of the places we had selected in
advance. The lower site was hidden in cloud, he said, and the upper one
was an impossible maze of crevasses. So he picked the only reasonable
place he could see, and dropped a marked map to guide us. Then a waggle
of the wings and he was gone. We were on our own for a month.

That night we camped on the beach, sheltering under plastic sheets
to keep out the spray from the sea. It was a most unlikely approach to a
big mountain. As we turned in after 11 PM, the sun was still shining
brightly, the surf was pounding with a resonant roar, and porpoises
leaped about in the waves. Just before we turned in, the little white plane
sped by, and we waved. The pilot must have been dumbfounded to see us
there with our roaring fire, and probably thought we were shipwrecked
sailors. He banked and flew in low for a closer look. Finally we managed
to convince him that we did not need rescuing just yet.

On June 19, we quickly reached a big river flowing from the foot of
Fairweather Glacier, and there had our first ground-level view of the
mountain. It was magnificent—and rather frightening. As Dr. Ladd had
said, every side looked almost too steep for the mountaineer to climb. We
lost sight of it almost immediately, ploughing our way through thick bush.
In the three hours to lunch-time we covered only two miles.

On the way we first saw that peculiar Alaskan phenomenon, a stagnant glacier out of which a veritable jungle was growing. The ice, here
about a hundred feet thick, and right at sea-level, had accumulated
enough gravel and silt to support luxuriant stands of slide alder. We were
quite fascinated and intrigued—until we tried to make our way through
it. Alder, with its snaking, springy branches, is hard enough to penetrate at
the best of times. Now the footing was completely unreliable, as the slightest pressure from the boot sent the soil sliding off the ice.

Soon, however, we had worked our sweating way through this and
were out on open moraine. This was easier going, but it, too, had its problems, consisting as it did of millions of slabs of rock poised on the dead ice.
It was a huge moraine, dwarfing anything in Europe. We threaded our

way through vast piles of rock that looked like exaggerated slag heaps from Welsh mining villages. Some of the effects were striking. On all sides were weird caves and grottoes with water cascading in. Large chuckling streams of melt-water just vanished in mid-gurgle.

As we went, we built rock cairns, for we could see from the great size of the moraine that we would have trouble finding our way back across it in a fog. Camp this night was in a slate-lined hollow in the ice half a mile from the active white ice of the glacier, about seven miles from the air-drop. We were still sleeping out, as the tents were in the air-drop, but we built small sheltering walls of rock, and made our beds on flat rock slabs.

Within half an hour next day, we were on the main Fairweather Glacier, ready at last to cope with something more interesting than bushwhacking. It looked as if we would have plenty to cope with. From here, the sweep of the glacier soared up in two vast steps to the 5,000-foot level where we hoped to put our main base camp. The first ice-fall appeared easy enough, and we managed to pass it on the right after several false starts.

Then, as we stood wearily, high on a side-hill late that evening, we spotted the air-drop parachutes lying on the snow on the far side of yet another glacier. They were in a flat and seemingly stable spot right on our line of approach, and we blessed the good sense of the airmen who had dropped them. We reached them at 9:45 PM, after almost fifteen hours of travel.

The Royal Canadian Air Force had picked the only feasible spot in the circumstances—at the edge of a small glacier coming in from the south. All the thirteen parachutes were within an area of 300 yards, a fine piece of precision dropping by Para-rescue expert Jake Dyck, considering the problems. Only one 'chute could be dropped at a time as the Canso lumbered by, and each time it had to circle a mountain, climb over a high pass, and then descend to the drop-zone. Again it would bank steeply and circle the mountain—all the time dodging layers of clouds.

It was the best site available, but, even at that, what a horrible spot it turned out to be. Within half an hour, six members of the party sank part-way into masked crevasses, which made recovering the parachuted parcels containing the tents a nerve-wracking business. We probed the snow until we found a safe area big enough to hold the tents, and marked it out with bamboo sticks. Nobody could leave this tiny camp-site alone or unroped. Five minutes after the last tent was up, rain began to fall—the first since we had left Lituya Bay three days before.

Here we were at 3,500 feet. The next day, Walter, Fips, and I set out to find a route beyond the second ice-fall to the 5,000-foot level, whence the steep south-south-east ridge sprang more than 10,000 vertical feet to the summit.

The ice-fall was a bewildering maze of decaying ice-towers, quite impossible to negotiate in safety. Time and again we saw blocks break off and collapse in a shower of splinters. Everything here was on a titanic scale, and it was hard to realize that often these pieces of tilted ice were bigger than apartment buildings.

On the south side of the glacier, however, we could make our way slowly along the mountain wall that hemmed the glacier in. This, too, was mostly glacier, steep and soft, but manageable. As we crossed one of the snow-bridges, the upper reaches of the mountain cleared enough to show us the final part of the route to the summit. But the key was still beyond our reach. Cloud blocked out the view of the way from the glacier onto the steep ridge. All we could see was an assortment of cliffs and crumbling ice-falls that seemed to hold no promise of success.

By the time we had reached the centre of the glacier that passed beneath the ridge, we had abandoned any hope of setting up our base camp here. None of us had ever seen such a dangerous place before. Weather reports we had received earlier from Alaska indicated that the amount of snow-fall in the area the previous winter was probably the lightest on record. The glacier confirmed this. Where one could reasonably expect a thick blanket of snow at this time of year, crevasses puckered their lips on every side. The weather was abnormally warm, and the strength that frost gives to the snow was conspicuously lacking. Crevasse edges would constantly crumble beneath us as the vast glacier defied most of the laws with which well-behaved ice is expected to conform.

It was eerie, walking just beneath the clouds and listening to the constant battlefront roar of avalanches that we could never see. When we rejoined the others, we learned that several of them had again dropped into crevasses while bringing in the rest of the bundles. So there was no difficulty deciding that camp had to be moved, and quickly. Seven hundred feet above, on a mound of rocks offering safety from the snow-slopes of the mountain side above, was a good potential site.

Sunday, the traditional day of rest, was an excellent illustration of why North Americans cannot be hired as back-packers, as can mountain people of some countries. They just would not stand for the work involved—and you could hardly blame them.

We had to move our whole camp up 700 feet on the steep, loose mountain side, and each man had to make three round trips. The first time, I carried four ration boxes, containing food for four men for four days, and weighing a total of forty pounds. On my second trip I carried over sixty pounds; on the final one I was afraid to weigh the pack. I could barely move. Yet most of the others carried more, particularly Denis, who yields little to the bears in the matter of strength.

The rock pile at 4,300 feet might have looked inviting to the marmots who whistled all around us, but it took the eye of faith to see comfort in it. Fips, however, is an architect and designer to whom anything but order is anathema. Quickly we all set to work levelling platforms for the tents. When we finished, Fips had us building patios at the entrances, shelter walls, and finally smooth, neat paths from the tents to the cooking area.

From the "kitchen," which consisted of two tea chests containing a two-burner stove and the pressure cookers, the view was almost overwhelming. To the west, the glacier streaming in rhythmic steps down to the silver-scaled ocean; at our feet, the chaotic beauty of the ice-fall, with sparkling turquoise pools in the hollows; and everywhere the flash of greens and blues from the glistening ice.

And to the north-east, Fairweather loomed, two vertical miles of ice and snow. Already, it seemed, our presence was causing it some discontent. Throughout the day it growled at us, occasionally roaring defiance as ice-cliffs on its face danced angrily and fell. The arm-chair traveller through far-off lands may smugly smile when he reads of natives who fear the mountain gods. But in places like this it is easy to credit the superstitious fear that attributes supernatural power to the garrulous rantings of an ice-clad peak.

Now we were established in safety and comfort, and it was time to get on with the climbing. The consistently warm weather worried us, for each day of it made glacier travel more dangerous. Later, we found that the surface did not refreeze even in the couple of hours of twilight that passed for night in these northern latitudes. So we decided that the next day we would all go up to the foot of the so-called Carpé Ridge and try to find a way onto it.

Fips, Paul, Joe, and Walter would put an overnight camp (Camp One) on the glacier, and try to establish a more permanent Camp Two at

9,000 feet or higher. Then they would make the first try for the summit.

The need for speed became evident as we moved out of base camp on Monday, June 23—Fips's birthday. In the few days since our first visit to the upper glacier, the surface had become much worse. Four of us dropped through rotten bridges in the five hours we took to reach the foot of the ridge. Fips's party stopped about four hundred yards out from the edge of the glacier and set up camp on a small and spectacular spot. It was an ice-block about eight feet wide and twenty feet long, with deep crevasses on all sides—the sort of place where one needed to keep one's eyes down and watch where one was stepping. But the temptation to look up was almost irresistible. All around us now were beautiful, unclimbed peaks.

And right in front of us, big, steep cliffs and bigger mountains of crumbling ice guarded the way to upper slopes that looked easier. There seemed no easy way, but we were looking at the route end-on, and there is no way of finding out the degree of difficulty on a climb without rubbing your nose against the problem. As my party set off back to base that evening, Fips and Paul went off one way, and Joe and Walter another, hunting anxiously for the key to the first big battlement door.

That night, the weather cleared, and at base camp the temperature dropped to a few degrees below freezing. What a difference it made to crossing the glacier! We reached Camp One with a load of supplies in a mere hour and a half, compared with five hours the day before. Everybody was still there when we arrived, and our hearts sank. Had they been turned back? Fortunately, one reason they were so late was that they had prospected until midnight before finding a way up. Another reason: one of the pairs had forgotten its stove.

We wished them well, and watched as they climbed a fairly safe fan of old snow and then vanished like ants amid the gullies in the rock cliffs. We pushed on up the main glacier, looking for routes up peaks we hoped to climb when and if Fairweather was in the bag.

Very soon we were a mile or more east along Fairweather Glacier in perfect weather. It seemed the sort of place that should be reserved for (morally) good mountaineers in the next world.

Mount Lituya (11,750 feet) was built of meringue-like masses of snow and ice piled dizzily one atop the other, promising almost a surfeit of snow-craft. To its west, Mount Sabine (named after Fips's daughter) lowered a fluted fin of ice right to our feet. As we watched, one avalanche from this peak fell a clear 3,000 feet through space before its debris billowed like smoke from the glacier. There is an exquisitely graceful air to a free-falling avalanche—but it is sobering to find at close range that the "tiny flakes" floating down through the air can be blocks of ice as big as houses.

To the north, Mount Quincy Adams, at 13,650 feet, was one of the highest unclimbed peaks left in North America. It obviously would not succumb to anything less than a first-class party. East of it was one of the most beautiful peaks we had ever seen.

Its classical summit, small in area, was supported by ridges of rock that were scornfully steep. Two others, about 11,000 feet, would be outstanding in almost any mountain range in the world. Small snow-fields clung to them at angles we all swore were impossible.

Every turn of the head, every slightly changed angle, every shadow from a fast-flitting cloud, served only to heighten the feeling that this was a special place in the mountains. It seemed almost too beautiful to desecrate with our unshaven presence, and was in itself adequate reason, if reason you need, why people climb mountains. Our constant stream of superlatives seemed thin and threadbare in the face of such grandeur.

We used adjectives of a different sort that night. As we reached base camp, clouds were filtering down the mountain sides to meet others boiling in from the sea. The next morning, we were sitting in the middle of a cloudy rain, listening to the cheery "ham" giving our weather forecast: cloud right up to 14,000 feet, rain and snow, and no sign of any improvement.

For a while our camp cleared, showing us a lot of new snow on the rocks above 6,000 feet. There was little chance that Fips and his companions would be climbing today—but the arrangement was for them to come down the next day and let us take our turn.

On Thursday, June 26, we moved up as planned, though nobody really expected the others to be coming down. Then, as we neared Camp One, the veil of cloud shivered and split, and we could see four tiny dots on an ice-field 5,000 feet above our heads. They were a day late, and had obviously made a late start that morning. By 9:30 they should have been several thousand feet higher than the 10,000-foot level they had reached.

Soon the clouds closed in again, and we approached the foot of the ridge. From some of the earlier accounts of the climb, we had assumed that Carpé and Moore had climbed this ridge, a little to the west of the route we took. In fact, neither of them had set foot on the ridge. Fuller research showed me they had in fact climbed a steep snow-face half a mile east of our route. Our routes joined just above the 9,000-foot level.

However, the fact that an ice-mountain has been climbed before means very little. Changes in the ice in a single season can make last year's easy walk a hair-raising climb, and vice versa. In more than a quarter of a century, major changes had probably occurred.

Now we kicked slowly up the inactive east edge of the ice-fall, to the west of the ridge. Once again, the nose-rubbing test proved the slopes not as steep as they seemed, though they were more than steep enough with our forty-five-pound packs. Almost 1,000 feet of this went slowly by; then suddenly we were on top of the cliffs. Ahead was an ice-fall, so we put on crampons, the iron spikes that make it possible to ascend steep ice without step-cutting. At 3 PM we came out of the clouds at 7,700 feet, and could see where the others had wandered onto a snow-face beneath some cliffs and pinnacles of rotten ice.

Now a stream of debris poured down towards their steps; so we kept clear and headed up a steep rock ridge. It, too, was rotten, and occasionally we had to remove our packs and haul them up after us on a rope.

How slow, how tedious it now became, and how desperately we equivocated to find excuses for stopping. Look at the view—take another photograph—tighten the crampons in case they came loose—what about the bootlaces? Any excuse would do, and nobody needed any coaxing to stop. The 600 feet up to 8,900 feet took us one and a half hours, but this was almost sprinting compared with the dispirited trudge that took us up the final 450 feet in the same time.

It was more or less chance that Dave spotted Camp Two, for nothing that even remotely resembled a camp-site had been visible on the continuously steep slope. And "Camp Two" was more a brave title than a place in which to relax.

It was just a spot where the plunging slopes paused for breath before hurtling headlong down again. A 500-foot slope of very steep ice came right to the edge of a cliff, where a few bare rocks showed through. Then the cliff dropped about 3,000 feet to a rutted glacier below. A big boulder protruded through the ice like a worn-down tooth at the rock line, almost as if its angry snarl was holding back the countless tons of ice.

In front of it was a ledge perhaps fifteen feet long, sloping down, and nowhere wide enough for the tents. Fips and his crew had humped dozens of small rocks to build up the ledge, but even then the tents could not be fully erected because the rock and ice got in the way.

However, the rock, by partly shielding both tents, gave an illusion of safety from avalanches that might swish down from the steep wide slopes above. When we arrived at 5:40 PM, water was running out from under the foot of the ice-slope, which was very convenient for cooking. But the minute the sun moved around and left the spot in shadow, it froze. The narrow space along the edge of the cliff turned into a skating-rink.

For some reason, we were all reluctant to move out of the tents that evening, though the insides were a shambles, with pools of water and sodden equipment after a storm that dumped sixteen inches of snow on Fips's party in twenty-four hours. Our staying inside was doubtless based on the same magic principle that gives a child complete immunity from robbers or charging elephants by simply pulling a flimsy sheet over his head.

As we ate, cooking in a small area between the facing tent-sleeves, we wondered how eight of us would manage to preserve the social amenities while sleeping in two tents designed to hold two men each. As the evening wore on, however, we turned into our down sleeping-bags, easily rationalizing our selfishness with the thought that the boys had started so late they could not possibly get back until morning.

After a few hours of half-sleep, we were up before 3 AM preparing breakfast. Suddenly there was a splattering against the canvas, and I wondered for a moment if a slide had started above us. Pieces of ice began hitting the side of the tents in a torrent, and then we could hear faint voices. Several hundred feet above, the four climbers were chipping steps in the ice on the last lap down to camp.

It was almost 3:30 AM when they reached the tents, after more than nineteen hours of difficult climbing. All were tired, but bubbling with enthusiasm at their success. Said Fips: "What a mountain! It has everything. You think you are never going to get there. We first estimated we would reach the top at 4 PM, then we changed it to 5. When we finally got there, it was almost 10 PM. Just wait till you reach the wall of green ice near the top—Oh boy!"

Paul, with his lifetime of climbing experience, said simply, "It is a fantastic mountain. The best climb I ever made." Walter alone was a little quiet. His feet had been frozen, and he thought he had frost-bite. It turned out later that one big toe actually was frost-bitten, but the doctor snipped a little flesh off and there were no ill effects.

For a long time the mountain fairly rang with our excited chatter. Much of the rum bottle's contents gurgled into the coffee cups of Fips, Paul, Walter, and Joe; then we stepped out to leave them room to sleep. At long last, it was our turn.

When I was rock-climbing in the English Lake District, there was a constant grumble from rock-artists who had to walk for half an hour before they could express themselves on their favourite crags. These purists bitterly protested that energy not spent on serious, steep, and technical work was an utter waste.

From that point of view, even the purest of English mountaineers could not have complained about our Camp Two. We climbed out of bed, put on the rope, sidled six feet along the ice-covered ledge, and then stepped unsteadily up onto a wall of ice and snow. The 500-foot slope was one of the steepest of the whole climb, and finding it at the start of the day was rather too much of a good thing.

The time: 4:25 AM. Our total of rest: very little. But our enthusiasm, for some obscure reason on which the psychologists need to do more research, was high. I have never had much use for the idea of slogging up a peak behind professional guides who were cutting all the steps, but this was the nearest I ever came to sympathizing with climbers who employ them. The steps that Fips's party had nicked down the slope were most welcome. It had frozen hard during the night, and the snow that covered the glacier slope was so firm that our crampons, with their store-sharp points, made hardly a mark.

It was exhilarating, and it is only in retrospect, as I see again our figures almost bouncing up the steep snow at that unearthly hour, that I realize Wilfred Noyes was right. After years of climbing in the Alps and the Himalayas, and just as many years studying his motives with an introspective poet's eye, he confirmed what my unimaginative friends had been telling me for years—that the urge to climb remains a flaw in the otherwise reasonable personality. His phrasing was more polite than theirs, however.

Our spirits were high as we pushed on, roped in pairs. There is a rhythm of motion, a harmony of step and action, that comes only at times when high training is joined with enthusiasm—times such as this.

Usually we moved together, but on steeper sections one would stop and pay out the rope around the shaft of his deep-pressed axe. There were crevasses everywhere, with morning-wide jaws, but the mountain was somnolent now, in a vast deep-freeze that stilled for a while the crumbling, sliding, melting of decay.

By 5 AM we had reached 10,200 feet, according to the small pocket aneroid I carried. By 7:30 we were almost 12,000 feet above the sea. At a time when human beings begin to think of breakfast, we decided to have breakfast too. But no breakfast nook in a modern, boxlike palace of gracious living ever had a view like this.

Three lonely fangs of rock pushed through the ice that had now almost completely enfolded our mountain. One was flat enough to hold the two small stoves, and, as breakfast drinks bubbled merrily away, we chewed on cheese and nuts and chocolate and watched the sun act as back-lighting to a gem-encrusted world of peaks.

The sun was clear, with no clouds to bar its rays, but the light that flickered from a myriad facets of the glaciers had no more warmth than the Northern Lights.

We went on refreshed, and the character of the climbing slowly changed. So far, it had been over wide and open slopes that made up the steep faces of the mountain. Now at last it began to turn to the slender, knife-edged ridge of snow that brings a tingle to the toes with every step. We arrived in the middle of a ridge, as our open slope faded into a long ridge gliding up from below.

Soon we were creeping up slowly, moving only one at a time with the speculative eye ever on the drop of a thousand feet to the left and even more to the right. It steepened, and, as I twisted in the axe and brought Denis up to lead on through, the sickle-edged curve of snow led my reluctant eye in a flash to the glacier 7,000 feet below. But the foot of new snow was well frozen to the ice, and our belays were safe.

A second similar arête of snow took us well up the mountain, and now the ridge had faded once again into the massive mountain face that gave it birth. The wind here had whipped the snow away and left a glistening sheet of bottle-green ice. It was just too steep in places for comfortable cramponing, and we chipped out steps that landed us on a luncheon platform at 13,500 feet. The time was now 11:30 AM, and as our stoves roared away in a hole in the wind-swept ice, we could see signs not only of travelling hopefully, but perhaps of finally arriving.

While we had been climbing with our faces turned in to the steep slopes, some cosmic jester had been sprinkling the rest of the world with diminishing-powder. The peaks and towers that had loomed sky-high for so long had finally dwindled.

For the first time in years I idly recalled—and promptly believed—what the geography master had said: that the world would be smoother than a billiard ball if scaled down to the same diameter.

This pleasant, idle cogitation made it no easier to climb slowly on. That 800 feet ahead of us now was no billiard table, but a sloping wall of rough green ice that wearily seemed to stay the same size no matter how far along it we trod, mechanically avoiding the blue-lined crevasse pockets.

It took forty-five minutes, each one longer than the last, to reach the top of the slope and find ourselves on top of the South-East Shoulder at 14,000 feet. The going was flattish now for over half a mile, and then headed up in a series of steps to The Nose, the thought of which had been niggling at our minds for hours.

Everybody still felt fine, with no sign of mountain sickness, but it was obvious that we had come up too far too fast and not allowed enough time to adjust to the thinness of the air. Nobody felt any real discomfort, but when we pushed the throttle down nothing happened. Our brave flow of movement had shrunk to a trickle. Each in turn stopped and sat, rummaging through his day-pack. We had brought only essentials with us, of course, but now, when the ounces counted, the "essentials" turned out to be a flock of unconsidered trifles.

Packs and spare clothing began to litter the snow, limp reminders of our arm-chair bravado, 1,000 miles away and 14,000 feet nearer the sea. I bitterly cursed the misguided enthusiasm that had led me to carry about nine pounds of movie camera and film to the summit, in case Walter's shots of the day before did not turn out. Naturally, not a scrap of the film I shot was ever used.

The 400 feet of ascent to the bottom of the ice-nose took us one and a quarter hours, and as we reached it we could easily see why Walter and Fips, both craftsmen in ice-climbing, had chortled with glee when they spoke of it. They were chortling in retrospect, thinking of how the nasty Nose would knock the steam out of us.

Carved from clear green ice, it curved superciliously for about 150 feet before merging with a brow of cold grey cloud that suddenly appeared from nowhere. Grim as it looked, The Nose was the only line to take. On the right, ice-cliffs dropped sheer away with little prospect of climbing. On the left, steep ice thinly smeared with snow dropped to some ice-coated rocks and then bounded out of sight.

The wind was howling now, to remind us that we were getting close to 15,000 feet, where even a summer's day is arctic. Clouds whipped coldly past us as Denis hammered in a long ice piton and Dave led up yesterday's small steps, now jammed full of wind-blown snow. Slowly onward, each step an effort, and I tried the last steep move that would get us over the difficulty. Hand- and foot-holds nicked on a near-vertical wall of ice led around a fog-shrouded corner into a steep and shallow gully that faded upwards out of sight.

My courage then was on a par with my strength. At the awkward move from wall to gully I hesitated and was lost. Back I crept, ready to stop right there and leave the greater things to greater people. Once again Dave went ahead and vanished around the minatory corner. A few scrapes, some very quiet moments that seemed eternal, and the rope swung around to dangle vertically down the wall of ice beneath which we cowered. He was up. So, in a few more minutes, were we.

It takes but seconds to tell, though the doing took more than two hours. Now the aneroid said we were at 15,000 feet, with only 300 feet to go if its indications were accurate.

They took us an hour of plodding, and when we reached the top the infernal little machine read 15,600 feet. The route wound in and out of the most impressive scenery. Turrets and battlements of ice, formed into fantastic shapes by the never-ending gales, stood guard around the big summit plateau, but fortunately we were able to weave our way easily among them. It was no effort for all of us to weave by now—in fact it would have been almost impossible for us to tread a straight line. Again, nobody felt unwell, but there was just no energy to call on. A single step often needed two or three gasping breaths.

We reached the top at 5:25 PM, and as Russ's beard quickly vanished under a coating of ice, we realized we were not going to see much of this high point of British Columbia that we had come 1,000 miles to reach.

The cloud flashed by in horizontal streamers, cutting visibility to about fifty feet. Not a rock was to be seen in the wilderness of snow and ice, and there was no way to build the traditional cairn anywhere near. I buried a rock piton in the snow, and after ten minutes of formal photography, mainly of British Columbia's centennial flag, we were on our way down.

The great moment we had dreamed about for more than a year turned out to be, like so many other "great moments," memorable only in prospect and retrospect.

For some of the descent, things were easier, as the pull of gravity was on our side. But soon we were tensed and working harder than we had on the way up. The beautiful snow arêtes, the essence of classical climbing, had crumbled in the day of steady sun. Now they were as stable and steady as porridge smeared on tilted glass. Each move was stilted, made individually, and "safeguarded" by a belay that was mainly psychological.

Slopes we rhythmically strode up in the morning took two or three times as long to descend, as the snow peeled limply off the underlying ice.

It was midnight when we reached the top of the last, steep slope above the tents. The strain of coming down, even more than the labour of climbing up, had wearied us. A maze of crevasses that we had crossed that morning on a bridge of faith and frost now tripped us up at every step. Denis and I were roped together, the biggest and smallest in the party. Half a dozen times he broke into concealed crevasses. As I held him on a tight rope, he would half-swim out and flounder right into another. I was so tired that little flashes of light kept popping behind my eyes, and no tent in the world ever held so much promise of comfort and rest—and rest—and rest . . .

Getting to it, however, was still quite a problem. The sun had long gone off the slopes, and they should have been freezing, by all the rules, for we were almost 10,000 feet above sea-level. They stayed like mush, and though we were over the viper's nest of crevasses, we still sank knee-deep at every step. Under this soft snow was ice into which the shaft of the axe could not be forced to make an anchor.

The slope steepened, and we caught up with Russ and Dave, who felt they could go no farther in safety—even though they were now only 350 feet from the tents, and in full sight of them.

I shared the feelings, and decided it would be wise to go back uphill to a comparatively safe spot and give the snow a chance to harden, making movement safer.

Then one of those odd things happened, of the type that occurs only under conditions of great stress and fatigue, and, probably, a slight lack of oxygen. The late Frank Smythe has written of the time when, as second man on a rope of two, he turned to offer some food to the third man he felt had been with them all day. Others have talked to non-existent companions, and one wrote at great length about the old man of the mountains he quite matter-of-factly sensed on a peak.

No stranger appeared on my rope, but when quiet, competent Denis calmly said he would like to see what he could do, he began to grow before my very eyes. His voice deepened and boomed in my ears, and within seconds he was no longer just Denis but a huge, commanding figure. I had no difficulty accepting the evidence of my eyes that here was a giant rivalling those in fairy tales, and once I had accepted it I thought no more about it. A giant had come along to help us out of a tough spot, and what could be more natural?

I let him down 120 feet until the rope ran out, and then he stamped and cut a hole through the snow to the ice. The ice itself was rotten, and in no shape to hold a piton if any real strain came on it. But Denis hammered one home; then, after we climbed down to join him, he joined both ropes together and fixed one end to the piton. The other he dropped right onto the tents. As calmly as if we were taking a Sunday stroll through the park, we all walked down, using the rope as a "safety" handrail.

We made only a quick drink when we reached the tent just after 1 AM, almost twenty-one hours after we had left it, and fell quickly asleep. We left the piton and ropes where they were, as we were too tired to attempt to retrieve them.

About 9:30 AM, the warmth of the sun on the tent woke us up. A few minutes later there was a gentle, slithering sound, followed by a metallic clang. The piton had fallen out of the ice, and our "safety line" slid gently down onto our sheltering rock.

The less said about the stumbling descent to base camp on Saturday, June 28, the better for our battered egos. Feeling very tired, and carrying heavy packs, including the gear Fips's party had left for us, we spent ten hours descending 4,000 feet. It was after midday when we left Camp Two, though we realized that the lateness would complicate our problem by softening the snow.

Proof of this presented itself the moment we stepped onto the main Fairweather Glacier at 10:30 PM. A big snow-bridge we had used to cross one crevasse on the way up had collapsed. We followed the faint tracks of the first party, but they soon ran into another collapsed bridge. So we climbed down into the crevasse, fortunately a small one, and up the other side. The food cache was in a most precarious position. The block of ice on which it stood was melting rapidly, and canting a little. All the pitons holding down the plastic tarpaulin had melted out of the ice.

There was a rousing welcome when we reached base camp at 12:30 AM. A bonfire was burning brightly, though it did not last long, as the fuel consisted mainly of cardboard boxes. A couple of the flares we carried for emergencies chased away the arctic twilight. As tall tales of our difficult peak followed the rum bottle around the circle, we spent two hours building the atmosphere of dangers shared and problems solved that makes most expedition members friends for life.

Next day we loafed, finding comfort on our rock pile and quietly studying our surroundings. The ocean was neatly packed in silver-white layers of long-ribbed clouds that delighted the eye. But Ken and George, at radio camp, were beneath them, and complained that it had not stopped raining for days down at the beach. Due south, a range of peaks little over 6,000 feet high stood stark of ridge and pregnant with ice. For hours we looked north at Fairweather and marvelled at how deceptive a mountain could be.

In the interests of accuracy for the taxpayers who were paying the bills, Fips's party scrambled up the rocks and snow above camp so that Mike and Kelly could shoot some photographs of them "nearing the summit." These were to fill in the blanks that Walter had left in the artistic whole, though he actually did take many shots on the summit and the approach to it. Fortunately, as these sequences were supposed to have been taken by Walter, he did not have to appear in them. He was able to stay in camp while Denis snipped off some of his frost-bitten flesh.

Our camp was certainly remote, but the peace normally associated with such remoteness was rarely evident. The scorching sun was speeding the tempo of disintegration, and always there was the thunder of avalanches. Many of them roared on for minutes at a time, and one was the biggest we had ever seen. Hundreds of thousands of tons of rock billowed down a mountain on the north side of the glacier, and bubbled like a chaotic flow of lava far out onto the ice.

While we were watching this primeval battle of attrition that had changed little in thousands of years, we were in constant touch with modernity. As Kelly lounged in breech-clout and sun-glasses, reading *The Theory of the Leisure Class*, Mike was on the radio, arranging to be picked up by Ken Loken, and for a hotel room in Juneau and a supply of fresh fruit!

The pilot was due to arrive on July 1, but even the best of radios cannot prevent human forgetfulness, and it was July 2 when he arrived. We rushed down the cliffs to our old camp-site and saw his little ski-plane a mile or so away, in the middle of the glacier running in from the south.

The crevasses were bad, and it took us some time to reach him. When we got there, we found he had dumped several cans of gasoline there as a mountain base, and was going to fly the boys out one at a time. It was awe-inspiring to watch him take off, bumping and swaying over the undulating surface of the glacier before staggering into the air.

He landed them, on skis, on a sandy beach about a mile from the radio camp. Then he flew back to Juneau, changed to a bigger plane on floats, and flew them and their equipment back to civilization.

It was odd, listening to him chat between flights, to realize just how true is the trite, tired old phrase about one man's meat being another man's poison. He nodded towards Fairweather with a big grin and asked how we ever acquired the nerve to climb such a mountain. He wouldn't even think of it, he said—far too dangerous.

Yet this assessment came from a man who made his living flying far-from-new single-engined aircraft in what is undeniably some of the most dangerous flying country in the world. In thousands of square miles there is nobody to help him if his motor fails. The weather is notorious for its rapid, lethal changes, and much of the time he flies completely alone. We shuddered at the thought. I shudder even more now that I have acquired my own pilot's licence. Eventually we each agreed that the other was a fool to tackle such dangers without some degree of alarm.

This time, however, the odds were on the pilot's side. The weather stayed perfect for flying, but all around us the snow and ice peaks began to peel and disintegrate in the unusually prolonged heat. Some of us attempted Mount Lituya, an unclimbed monster of 11,750 feet. I called that one off on a razor-edge of ice just 200 feet below the summit. The rotten ice had a consistency of little more than granulated water, and I called to Paul as he hacked out ice-spray, "Let's call it a day. This is no place for the fathers of sixteen children to be." To get down we had to "swim" over rotten crevasse bridges, and avalanches were born of their own volition in front of our eyes.

All this had been great sport, but as we rested on July 4 we all agreed things had become far too dangerous to permit any more big climbs. The mountains echoed with avalanches, and we saw one that seemed to sweep over the site of our Camp Two, perched like an eagle's nest way up on Fairweather. As we returned to base camp, bridges collapsed on all sides and one climber muttered, "Let's get back to the beach. It's far healthier eating up strawberries than pushing up daisies."

We radioed to the Royal Canadian Air Force, asking them to pick us up on Thursday, July 10, instead of July 12 as planned. On Monday, July 7, we headed out to Lituya Bay.

Lituya Bay is about seven miles long and T-shaped. The short north and south arms of the T are fjords made by long glaciers that come right into the water. Great peaks rise from its head, and lesser peaks clad in forest and flowers flank both sides. The entrance is very narrow and may be used only at certain stages of the tide because currents boil through it at up to fourteen knots.

La Pérouse came here in 1786 on his voyage around the world. With infinite seamanship he pushed his sailing ships into the bay. He was overpowered by it and considered that the arms at the head probably led to the fabled inland sea of North America. In this he was rapidly disappointed, but he wrote in his diaries: "Its scenery has no parallel, and I doubt whether the lofty mountains and deep valleys of the Alps and Pyrenees afford so tremendous yet so picturesque a spectacle, well deserving the attention of the curious, were it not placed at the extremity of the earth."

He declared its harbour was equal to the finest in all France, and suggested that on the island in the centre French traders could establish a profitable trading-post. He suggested, too, that the Indian women of the local village—which no longer exists—were the most disgusting in the whole world.

The island in the bay is now called Cenotaph Island, a name bestowed by La Pérouse himself after a tragedy marred the splendour of his stay. Twenty-one of his men drowned when two of his boats overturned while they were testing the state of the tide near the entrance.

There was no thought in our minds of this tragedy as we came back to the peaceful bay that Wednesday. In a lily-dappled lake we had our first bath for weeks, ate bread that tasted wonderful despite the green mould on it, and listened to Ken's and George's tales of curious bears and monster fish. The plane was not due until 7 AM next day, so we had time to

wander around the beaches picking spiny sea-urchin shells and other souvenirs for civilized planters a thousand miles away.

At 6 PM, before we had even had supper, I heard the sound of Canso
engines. The plane skimmed low and landed, and Ed Cameron urged us
to get out as soon as we could. He was worried that there might be sea-fog
the next morning, and he wanted to be safely in Juneau with us overnight.
We cursed him roundly, but he would not even stop for a bite to eat. We
whisked up trees to dismantle aerials, piled equipment helter-skelter into
boxes, and hurriedly loaded the aircraft. I opened a can of stew with my
knife and grumpily munched it cold on the beach as the rubber boat came
in for the last load. At 9 PM we took off, just as several fishing-boats came
through the turbulent entrance, seeking shelter for the night.

Two hours and seventeen minutes later, an earthquake and a mountainous tidal wave all but destroyed Lituya Bay. The quake was one of the
most powerful in recent times, with a magnitude of eight on the Richter
Scale. It was more powerful than the one that killed 10,000 people at
Agadir, and similar to the one of Good Friday, 1964, that laid waste
Alaska's cities. But the wave that followed was the biggest yet recorded
anywhere in the world.

The cause of it all is well known to geologists—the Fairweather fault
that runs right along the T-shaped head of Lituya Bay and under the glaciers on either side. Geologists who were flown to the scene measured a
horizontal movement of the ground extending for twenty-one and one-
half feet, and a vertical upheaval of three and one-half feet.

Eighty miles to the north, in Yakutat Bay, Mr. and Mrs. Robert
Tibbles, who worked at the airport, and Mrs. J. W. Walton, a cannery
owner, were having a picnic on Khantaak Island. Just as they were ready
to leave, an enormous portion of the island suddenly reared into the air
and then plunged under the sea. All three were drowned.

In Lituya Bay, a gigantic section of the mountain side at the head of
the T was shaken off by the quake. Estimated to weigh 90 million tons, it
dropped into the inlet and sent a jet of water spouting 1,700 vertical feet
up the hill side on the north side of the inlet. A triangular section of forest
a mile wide at the base was stripped to bedrock. When geologists
inspected the apex 1,700 feet above sea-level they found whole trees
hurled even higher up the slopes into still-standing timber. This, according
to the United States Geological Survey, was eight times as high as any similar wave on record.

This awful wave raced across the inlet and then bounced from one shore to the other, compounding havoc and destruction as it went. The farther it went, the lower it became, and the trim-line of timber, some of which had the bark stripped clean, sank gradually towards the entrance. But part way down the inlet, the wave surged over Cenotaph Island, which is several hundred feet high at the centre.

Three fishing-boats were at anchor inside Lituya Bay when the earthquake struck. Bill and Vivian Swanson were aboard the *Badger*, which was just inside La Chaussee Spit in Anchorage Bay just off our camp. Near them was the *Sunmore*, with Orville Wagner and his wife, Mickey, aboard. The 38-foot *Edrie*, carrying Howard Ulrich and his seven-year-old son Sonny, was anchored a mile away, near the southern shore of the inlet.

Mr. Ulrich wrote later in the magazine *Alaska Sportsman* that he saw the mountains shake and dance, throw clouds of snow and rocks into the air, and unleash great avalanches.

"I saw a gigantic wall of water, 1,800 feet high, erupt against the west mountain. I saw it lash against the island, which rises 320 feet above sea-level, and cut a fifty-foot swath through the trees of its centre. I saw it backlash against the southern shore, sweeping away the timber to a height of more than 500 feet.

"Finally I saw a fifty-foot wave come out of this churning turmoil and move along the southern shore directly towards me."

Mr. Ulrich tried to pull in the anchor chain, but it would not budge. His account continued: "As the *Edrie* began her almost perpendicular ascent to the crest of the wave, the chain snapped and a short end whipped back and wrapped itself around the pilothouse.

"As we were swept along by the wave, over what had recently been dry land and a timber-covered shore, I was sure that the end of the world had come for Sonny and me and our boat. There seemed to be no hope for survival.

"I wanted my wife, back in the fishing village of Pelican, to know where and how her husband and her first-born had been lost, and I grabbed the radiophone and yelled into it: 'Mayday, mayday. This is the *Edrie* in Lituya Bay. All hell has broken loose here. I think we've had it. Goodbye.' "

Astonishingly, the *Edrie* survived. As the waves subsided, Mr. Ulrich escaped by what seemed to him an almost suicidal run through the narrows.

The Wagners, aboard the *Sunmore,* were killed. They saw the wave coming and tried to race it through the narrow entrance. It caught them, flicked them into the air, and hurled the boat over the spit and into the ocean.

The Swansons, quite incomprehensibly, survived the nightmare. The wave picked up their boat as if it were a matchstick, raised it fifty feet into the air, and bore it rapidly towards the spit. At this point, the spit is about 200 yards wide, covered with huge boulders and trees.

The *Badger* flew right over the trees and boulders. Then she was dumped stern first into the Pacific. The Swansons had time to launch a dinghy before she sank, and were rescued hours later.

The only detail that remains to be told is what happened to our camp, which we had been so reluctant to leave. The Gilkey brothers, who knew we were due to stay the night there, flew down early in the morning to see if there was any sign of life.

The camp had vanished, the trees, the lake—all wiped from the earth in one instant of that night when the mountain fell. It was the sort of shattering climax which, had it torn some other range asunder, would have convinced the natives for ever that their gods were angry because the peak was climbed.

The Devils Thumb

– JON KRAKAUER –

Jon Krakauer traces his relationship with mountaineering to 1962, when his parents, as a birthday gift, gave their eight-year-old son an ice axe and then took him up an Oregon volcano. Though something of an emotional disaster (as Krakauer recounts in "The Devils [sic] Thumb"), the aborted ascent sparked a growing desire. By the age of eighteen, Krakauer says, "climbing was the only thing I cared about."

His obsession deepened in 1974, on a month-long expedition to Alaska's Arrigetch Peaks. Not only did that trip intensify his longing for mountains, it launched a writing career. Krakauer's Arrigetch account in The American Alpine Journal *was his first published story. With the urging of friend and mentor David Roberts, Krakauer continued to write, and by the age of twenty-nine, the former carpenter and climbing bum had traded his tool belt for a word processor. Now, some two decades after his AAJ piece, the Seattle-based freelancer writes about subjects that range from adventure travel to popular culture, commercial fishing, and architecture.*

For Krakauer, mountaineering isn't the all-consuming passion it was for him in the 1970s—in fact, he quit the sport for a while in the early 1980s—but he still climbs. Over the years he's ascended hundreds of mountains: in South America, Iceland, the Alps, Canada, and the Pacific Northwest. Alaska remains a favorite destination. Here he's put up several new routes, including one on Devils Thumb, the 9,077-foot granite spire in Southeast Alaska's Coast Range that proved to be his quintessential obsession: it occupied his thoughts for fifteen years.

A mountain with Yosemite-like walls, Devils Thumb had been first attempted in 1946, by a team that included two of the world's most talented mountaineers, Fritz Wiessner and Fred Beckey. Their attempt failed and Wiessner was injured, but Beckey returned later that summer with two part-ners to complete what Krakauer calls "the most technical ascent ever done [at that time] in Alaska." Over the next thirty years, three other teams reached the mountain's summit. But none scaled the Thumb's great north face, which rises 6,000 feet from bottom to top. So in 1977, Krakauer left a carpentry job in Colorado to seek out the mountain, and the granitic wall, that he felt sure would transform his life.

"The Devils Thumb" first appeared in Krakauer's collection Eiger Dreams: Ventures Among Men and Mountains, *published in 1990 by Lyons & Burford.*

BY THE TIME I REACHED THE interstate I was having trouble keeping my eyes open. I'd been okay on the twisting two-lane blacktop between Fort Collins and Laramie, but when the Pontiac eased onto the smooth, unswerving pavement of I-80, the soporific hiss of the tires began to gnaw at my wakefulness like ants in a dead tree.

That afternoon, after nine hours of humping 2x10s and pounding recalcitrant nails, I'd told my boss I was quitting: "No, not in a couple of weeks, Steve; right now was more like what I had in mind." It took me three more hours to clear my tools and other belongings out of the rust-stained construction trailer that had served as my home in Boulder. I loaded everything into the car, drove up Pearl Street to Tom's Tavern, and downed a ceremonial beer. Then I was gone.

At 1 AM, thirty miles east of Rawlins, the strain of the day caught up to me. The euphoria that had flowed so freely in the wake of my quick escape gave way to overpowering fatigue; suddenly I felt tired to the bone. The highway stretched straight and empty to the horizon and beyond. Outside the car the night air was cold, and the stark Wyoming plains glowed in the moonlight like Rousseau's painting of the sleeping gypsy. I wanted very badly just then to be that gypsy, conked out on my back beneath the stars. I shut my eyes—just for a second, but it was a second of bliss. It seemed to revive me, if only briefly. The Pontiac, a sturdy behemoth from the Eisenhower years, floated down the road on its long-gone shocks like a raft on an ocean swell. The lights of an oil rig twinkled reassuringly in the distance. I closed my eyes a second time, and kept them closed a few moments longer. The sensation was sweeter than sex.

A few minutes later I let my eyelids fall again. I'm not sure how long I nodded off this time—it might have been for five seconds, it might have been for thirty—but when I awoke it was to the rude sensation of the Pontiac bucking violently along the dirt shoulder at seventy miles per hour. By all rights, the car should have sailed off into the rabbitbrush and rolled. The rear wheels fishtailed wildly six or seven times, but I eventually managed to guide the unruly machine back onto the pavement without so much as blowing a tire, and let it coast gradually to a stop. I loosened my death grip on the wheel, took several deep breaths to quiet the pounding in my chest, then slipped the shifter back into drive and continued down the highway.

Pulling over to sleep would have been the sensible thing to do, but I was on my way to Alaska to change my life, and patience was a concept well beyond my twenty-three-year-old ken.

Sixteen months earlier I'd graduated from college with little distinction and even less in the way of marketable skills. In the interim an off-again, on-again four-year relationship—the first serious romance of my life—had come to a messy, long-overdue end; nearly a year later, my love life was still zip. To support myself I worked on a house-framing crew, grunting under crippling loads of plywood, counting the minutes until the next coffee break, scratching in vain at the sawdust stuck *in perpetuum* to the sweat on the back of my neck. Somehow, blighting the Colorado landscape with condominiums and tract houses for three-fifty an hour wasn't the sort of career I'd dreamed of as a boy.

Late one evening I was mulling all this over on a barstool at Tom's, picking unhappily at my existential scabs, when an idea came to me, a scheme for righting what was wrong in my life. It was wonderfully uncomplicated, and the more I thought about it, the better the plan sounded. By the bottom of the pitcher its merits seemed unassailable. The plan consisted, in its entirety, of climbing a mountain in Alaska called the Devils Thumb.

The Devils Thumb is a prong of exfoliated diorite that presents an imposing profile from any point of the compass, but especially so from the north: its great north wall, which had never been climbed, rises sheer and clean for six thousand vertical feet from the glacier at its base. Twice the height of Yosemite's El Capitan, the north face of the Thumb is one of the biggest granitic walls on the continent; it may well be one of the biggest in the world. I would go to Alaska, ski across the Stikine Icecap to the Devils Thumb, and make the first ascent of its notorious nordwand. It seemed, midway through the second pitcher, like a particularly good idea to do all of this solo.

Writing these words more than a dozen years later, it's no longer entirely clear just *how* I thought soloing the Devils Thumb would transform my life. It had something to do with the fact that climbing was the first and only thing I'd ever been good at. My reasoning, such as it was, was fueled by the scattershot passions of youth, and a literary diet overly rich in the works of Nietzsche, Kerouac, and John Menlove Edwards—the latter a deeply troubled writer/psychiatrist who, before putting an end to his life with a cyanide capsule in 1958, had been one of the preeminent British rock climbers of the day.

Dr. Edwards regarded climbing as a "psycho-neurotic tendency" rather than sport; he climbed not for fun but to find refuge from the inner torment that characterized his existence. I remember, that spring of 1977, being especially taken by a passage from an Edwards short story titled "Letter From a Man":

> So, as you would imagine, I grew up exuberant in body but with a nervy, craving mind. It was wanting something more, something tangible. It sought for reality intensely, always, if it were not there . . . .
> But you see at once what I do. I climb.

To one enamored of this sort of prose, the Thumb beckoned like a beacon. My belief in the plan became unshakable. I was dimly aware that I might be getting in over my head, but if I could somehow get to the top of the Devils Thumb, I was convinced, everything that followed would turn out all right. And thus did I push the accelerator a little closer to the floor and, buoyed by the jolt of adrenalin that followed the Pontiac's brush with destruction, speed west into the night.

You can't actually get very close to the Devils Thumb by car. The peak stands in the Boundary Ranges on the Alaska–British Columbia border, not far from the fishing village of Petersburg, a place accessible only by boat or plane. There is regular jet service to Petersburg, but the sum of my liquid assets amounted to the Pontiac and two hundred dollars in cash, not even enough for one-way airfare, so I took the car as far as Gig Harbor, Washington, then hitched a ride on a northbound seine boat that was short on crew. Five days out, when the *Ocean Queen* pulled into Petersburg to take on fuel and water, I jumped ship, shouldered my backpack, and walked down the dock in a steady Alaskan rain.

Back in Boulder, without exception, every person with whom I'd shared my plans about the Thumb had been blunt and to the point: I'd been smoking too much pot, they said; it was a monumentally bad idea; I was grossly overestimating my abilities as a climber; I'd never be able to hack a month completely by myself; I would fall into a crevasse and die.

The residents of Petersburg reacted differently. Being Alaskans, they were accustomed to people with screwball ideas; a sizeable percentage of the state's population, after all, was sitting on half-baked schemes to mine uranium in the Brooks Range, or sell icebergs to the Japanese, or market mail-order moose droppings. Most of the Alaskans I met, if they reacted at all, simply asked how much money there was in climbing a mountain like the Devils Thumb.

In any case, one of the appealing things about climbing the Thumb—and one of the appealing things about the sport of mountain climbing in general—was that it didn't matter a rat's ass what anyone else thought. Getting the scheme off the ground didn't hinge on winning the approval of some personnel director, admissions committee, licensing board, or panel of stern-faced judges; if I felt like taking a shot at some unclimbed alpine wall, all I had to do was get myself to the foot of the mountain and start swinging my ice axes.

Petersburg sits on an island, the Devils Thumb rises from the mainland. To get myself to the foot of the Thumb it was first necessary to cross twenty-five miles of salt water. For most of a day I walked the docks,

trying without success to hire a boat to ferry me across Frederick Sound.
Then I bumped into Bart and Benjamin.

Bart and Benjamin were ponytailed constituents of a Woodstock
Nation tree-planting collective called the Hodads. We struck up a conversation. I mentioned that I, too, had once worked as a tree planter. The
Hodads allowed that they had chartered a floatplane to fly them to their
camp on the mainland the next morning. "It's your lucky day, kid," Bart
told me. "For twenty bucks you can ride over with us. Get you to your
fuckin' mountain in style." On May 3, a day and a half after arriving in
Petersburg, I stepped off the Hodads' Cessna, waded onto the tidal flats at
the head of Thomas Bay, and began the long trudge inland.

The Devils Thumb pokes up out of the Stikine Icecap, an immense,
labyrinthine network of glaciers that hugs the crest of the Alaskan panhandle like an octopus, with myriad tentacles that snake down, down to
the sea from the craggy uplands along the Canadian frontier. In putting
ashore at Thomas Bay I was gambling that one of these frozen arms, the
Baird Glacier, would lead me safely to the bottom of the Thumb, thirty
miles distant.

An hour of gravel beach led to the tortured blue tongue of the Baird.
A logger in Petersburg had suggested I keep an eye out for grizzlies along
this stretch of shore. "Them bears over there is just waking up this time of
year," he smiled. "Tend to be kinda cantankerous after not eatin' all winter. But you keep your gun handy, you shouldn't have no problem."
Problem was, I didn't have a gun. As it turned out, my only encounter
with hostile wildlife involved a flock of gulls who dive-bombed my head
with Hitchcockian fury. Between the avian assault and my ursine anxiety, it was with no small amount of relief that I turned my back to the
beach, donned crampons, and scrambled up onto the glacier's broad, lifeless snout.

After three or four miles I came to the snowline, where I exchanged
crampons for skis. Putting the boards on my feet cut fifteen pounds from
the awful load on my back and made the going much faster besides. But
now that the ice was covered with snow, many of the glacier's crevasses
were hidden, making solitary travel extremely dangerous.

In Seattle, anticipating this hazard, I'd stopped at a hardware store
and purchased a pair of stout aluminum curtain rods, each ten feet long.
Upon reaching the snowline, I lashed the rods together at right angles,

then strapped the arrangement to the hip belt on my backpack so the poles extended horizontally over the snow. Staggering slowly up the glacier with my overloaded backpack, bearing the queer tin cross, I felt like some kind of strange *penitente*. Were I to break through the veneer of snow over a hidden crevasse, though, the curtain rods would—I hoped mightily—span the slot and keep me from dropping into the chilly bowels of the Baird.

The first climbers to venture onto the Stikine Icecap were Bestor Robinson and Fritz Wiessner, the legendary German–American alpinist, who spent a stormy month in the Boundary Ranges in 1937 but failed to reach any major summits. Wiessner returned in 1946 with Donald Brown and Fred Beckey to attempt the Devils Thumb, the nastiest looking peak in the Stikine. On that trip Fritz mangled a knee during a fall on the hike in and limped home in disgust, but Beckey went back that same summer with Bob Craig and Cliff Schmidtke. On August 25, after several aborted tries and some exceedingly hairy climbing on the peak's east ridge, Beckey and company sat on the Thumb's wafer-thin summit tower in a tired, giddy daze. It was far and away the most technical ascent ever done in Alaska, an important milestone in the history of American mountaineering.

In the ensuing decades three other teams also made it to the top of the Thumb, but all steered clear of the big north face. Reading accounts of these expeditions, I had wondered why none of them had approached the peak by what appeared, from the map at least, to be the easiest and most logical route, the Baird. I wondered a little less after coming across an article by Beckey in which the distinguished mountaineer cautioned, "Long, steep icefalls block the route from the Baird Glacier to the icecap near Devils Thumb," but after studying aerial photographs I decided that Beckey was mistaken, that the icefalls weren't so big or so bad. The Baird, I was certain, really was the best way to reach the mountain.

For two days I slogged steadily up the glacier without incident, congratulating myself for discovering such a clever path to the Thumb. On the third day, I arrived beneath the Stikine Icecap proper, where the long arm of the Baird joins the main body of ice. Here, the glacier spills abruptly over the edge of a high plateau, dropping seaward through the gap between two peaks in a phantasmagoria of shattered ice. Seeing the icefall in the flesh left a different impression than the photos had. As I stared at the tumult from a mile away, for the first time since leaving

Colorado the thought crossed my mind that maybe this Devils Thumb trip wasn't the best idea I'd ever had.

The icefall was a maze of crevasses and teetering seracs. From afar it brought to mind a bad train wreck, as if scores of ghostly white boxcars had derailed at the lip of the icecap and tumbled down the slope willy-nilly. The closer I got, the more unpleasant it looked. My ten-foot curtain rods seemed a poor defense against crevasses that were forty feet across and two hundred fifty feet deep. Before I could finish figuring out a course through the icefall, the wind came up and snow began to slant hard out of the clouds, stinging my face and reducing visibility to almost nothing.

In my impetuosity, I decided to carry on anyway. For the better part of the day I groped blindly through the labyrinth in the whiteout, retracing my steps from one dead end to another. Time after time I'd think I'd found a way out, only to wind up in a deep blue cul de sac, or stranded atop a detached pillar of ice. My efforts were lent a sense of urgency by the noises emanating underfoot. A madrigal of creaks and sharp reports—the sort of protests a large fir limb makes when it's slowly bent to the breaking point—served as a reminder that it is the nature of glaciers to move, the habit of seracs to topple.

As much as I feared being flattened by a wall of collapsing ice, I was even more afraid of falling into a crevasse, a fear that intensified when I put a foot through a snow bridge over a slot so deep I couldn't see the bottom of it. A little later I broke through another bridge to my waist; the poles kept me out of the hundred-foot hole, but after I extricated myself I was bent double with dry heaves thinking about what it would be like to be lying in a pile at the bottom of the crevasse, waiting for death to come, with nobody even aware of how or where I'd met my end.

Night had nearly fallen by the time I emerged from the top of the serac slope onto the empty, wind-scoured expanse of the high glacial plateau. In shock and chilled to the core, I skied far enough past the icefall to put its rumblings out of earshot, pitched the tent, crawled into my sleeping bag, and shivered myself to a fitful sleep.

Although my plan to climb the Devils Thumb wasn't fully hatched until the spring of 1977, the mountain had been lurking in the recesses of my mind for about fifteen years—since April 12, 1962, to be exact. The occasion was my eighth birthday. When it came time to open birthday presents, my parents announced that they were offering me a choice of gifts: according to my wishes, they would either escort me to the new Seattle World's Fair to ride the Monorail and see the Space Needle, or give me an introductory taste of mountain climbing by taking me up the third highest peak in Oregon, a long-dormant volcano called the South Sister that, on clear days, was visible from my bedroom window. It was a tough call. I thought the matter over at length, then settled on the climb.

To prepare me for the rigors of the ascent, my father handed over a copy of *Mountaineering: The Freedom of the Hills,* the leading how-to manual of the day, a thick tome that weighed only slightly less than a bowling ball. Thenceforth I spent most of my waking hours poring over its pages, memorizing the intricacies of pitoncraft and bolt placement, the shoulder stand and the tension traverse. None of which, as it happened, was of any use on my inaugural ascent, for the South Sister turned out to be a decidedly less than extreme climb that demanded nothing more in the way of technical skill than energetic walking, and was in fact ascended by hundreds of farmers, house pets, and small children every summer.

Which is not to suggest that my parents and I conquered the mighty volcano: From the pages and pages of perilous situations depicted in *Mountaineering: The Freedom of the Hills,* I had concluded that climbing was a life-and-death matter, always. Halfway up the South Sister I suddenly remembered this. In the middle of a twenty-degree snow slope that would be impossible to fall from if you tried, I decided that I was in mortal jeopardy and burst into tears, bringing the ascent to a halt.

Perversely, after the South Sister debacle my interest in climbing only intensified. I resumed my obsessive studies of *Mountaineering.* There was something about the scariness of the activities portrayed in those pages that just wouldn't leave me alone. In addition to the scores of line drawings— most of them cartoons of a little man in a jaunty Tyrolean cap—employed to illustrate arcana like the boot-axe belay and the Bilgeri rescue, the book contained sixteen black-and-white plates of notable peaks in the Pacific Northwest and Alaska. All the photographs were striking, but the one on page 147 was much, much more than that: it made my skin crawl. An aerial photo by glaciologist Maynard Miller, it showed a singularly sinister tower of ice-plastered black rock. There wasn't a place on the entire mountain that looked safe or secure; I couldn't imagine anyone climbing it. At the bottom of the page the mountain was identified as the Devils Thumb.

From the first time I saw it, the picture—a portrait of the Thumb's north wall—held an almost pornographic fascination for me. On hundreds—no, make that thousands—of occasions over the decade and a half that followed I took my copy of *Mountaineering* down from the shelf, opened it to page 147, and quietly stared. How would it feel, I wondered over and over, to be on that thumbnail-thin summit ridge, worrying over the storm clouds building on the horizon, hunched against the wind and dunning cold, contemplating the horrible drop on either side? How could anyone keep it together? Would I, if I found myself high on the north wall, clinging to that frozen rock, even attempt to keep it together? Or would I simply decide to surrender to the inevitable straight away, and jump?

I had planned on spending between three weeks and a month on the Stikine Icecap. Not relishing the prospect of carrying a four-week load of food, heavy winter camping gear, and a small mountain of climbing hard-ware all the way up the Baird on my back, before leaving Petersburg I paid a bush pilot a hundred and fifty dollars—the last of my cash—to have six cardboard cartons of supplies dropped from an airplane when I reached the foot of the Thumb. I showed the pilot exactly where, on his map, I intended to be, and told him to give me three days to get there; he promised to fly over and make the drop as soon thereafter as the weather permitted.

On May 6 I set up a base camp on the Icecap just northeast of the Thumb and waited for the airdrop. For the next four days it snowed, nixing any chance for a flight. Too terrified of crevasses to wander far from camp, I occasionally went out for a short ski to kill time, but mostly I lay silently in the tent—the ceiling was too low to sit upright—with my thoughts, fighting a rising chorus of doubts.

As the days passed, I grew increasingly anxious. I had no radio, nor any other means of communicating with the outside world. It had been many years since anyone had visited this part of the Stikine Icecap, and many more would likely pass before anyone did so again. I was nearly out of stove fuel, and down to a single chunk of cheese, my last pack-age of ramen noodles, and half a box of Cocoa Puffs. This, I figured, could sustain me for three or four more days if need be, but then what would I do? It would only take two days to ski back down the Baird to Thomas Bay, but then a week or more might easily pass before a fisher-man happened by who could give me a lift back to Petersburg (the Hodads with whom I'd ridden over were camped fifteen miles down the impassable, headland-studded coast, and could be reached only by boat or plane).

When I went to bed on the evening of May 10 it was still snowing and blowing hard. I was going back and forth on whether to head for the coast in the morning or stick it out on the icecap, gambling that the pilot would show before I starved or died of thirst, when, just for a moment, I heard a faint whine, like a mosquito. I tore open the tent door. Most of the clouds had lifted, but there was no airplane in sight. The whine returned, louder this time. Then I saw it: a tiny red-and-white speck, high in the western sky, droning my way.

A few minutes later the plane passed directly overhead. The pilot, however, was unaccustomed to glacier flying and he'd badly misjudged the scale of the terrain. Worried about winding up too low and getting nailed by unexpected turbulence, he flew a good thousand feet above me—believing all the while he was just off the deck—and never saw my tent in the flat evening light. My waving and screaming were to no avail; from that altitude I was indistinguishable from a pile of rocks. For the next hour he circled the icecap, scanning its barren contours without success. But the pilot, to his credit, appreciated the gravity of my predicament and didn't give up. Frantic, I tied my sleeping bag to the end of one of the crevasse poles and waved it for all I was worth. When the plane banked sharply and began to fly straight at me, I felt tears of joy well in my eyes.

The pilot buzzed my tent three times in quick succession, dropping two boxes on each pass, then the airplane disappeared over a ridge and I was alone. As silence again settled over the glacier I felt abandoned, vulnerable, lost. I realized that I was sobbing. Embarrassed, I halted the blubbering by screaming obscenities until I grew hoarse.

I awoke early on May 11 to clear skies and the relatively warm temperature of twenty degrees Fahrenheit. Startled by the good weather, mentally unprepared to commence the actual climb, I hurriedly packed up a rucksack nonetheless, and began skiing toward the base of the Thumb. Two previous Alaskan expeditions had taught me that, ready or not, you simply can't afford to waste a day of perfect weather if you expect to get up anything.

A small hanging glacier extends out from the lip of the icecap, leading up and across the north face of the Thumb like a catwalk. My plan was to follow this catwalk to a prominent rock prow in the center of the wall, and thereby execute an end run around the ugly, avalanche-swept lower half of the face.

The catwalk turned out to be a series of fifty-degree ice fields blanketed with knee-deep powder snow and riddled with crevasses. The depth of the snow made the going slow and exhausting; by the time I front-pointed up the overhanging wall of the uppermost *bergschrund*, some three or four hours after leaving camp, I was whipped. And I hadn't even gotten to the "real" climbing yet. That would begin immediately above, where the hanging glacier gave way to vertical rock.

The rock, exhibiting a dearth of holds and coated with six inches of crumbly rime, did not look promising, but just left of the main prow was an inside corner—what climbers call an open book—glazed with frozen melt water. This ribbon of ice led straight up for two or three hundred feet, and if the ice proved substantial enough to support the picks of my ice axes, the line might go. I hacked out a small platform in the snow slope, the last flat ground I expected to feel underfoot for some time, and stopped to eat a candy bar and collect my thoughts. Fifteen minutes later I shouldered my pack and inched over to the bottom of the corner. Gingerly, I swung my right axe into the two-inch-thick ice. It was solid, plastic—a little thinner than I would have liked but otherwise perfect. I was on my way.

The climbing was steep and spectacular, so exposed it made my head spin. Beneath my boot soles, the wall fell away for three thousand feet to the dirty, avalanche-scarred cirque of the Witches Cauldron Glacier. Above, the prow soared with authority toward the summit ridge, a vertical half-mile above. Each time I planted one of my ice axes, that distance shrank by another twenty inches.

The higher I climbed, the more comfortable I became. All that held me to the mountainside, all that held me to the world, were six thin spikes of chrome-molybdenum stuck half an inch into a smear of frozen water, yet I began to feel invincible, weightless, like those lizards that live on the ceilings of cheap Mexican hotels. Early on a difficult climb, especially a difficult solo climb, you're hyperaware of the abyss pulling at your back. You constantly feel its call, its immense hunger. To resist takes a tremendous conscious effort; you don't dare let your guard down for an instant. The siren song of the void puts you on edge; it makes your movements tentative, clumsy, herky-jerky. But as the climb goes on, you grow accustomed to the exposure, you get used to rubbing shoulders with doom, you come to believe in the reliability of your hands and feet and head. You learn to trust your self-control.

By and by, your attention becomes so intensely focused that you no longer notice the raw knuckles, the cramping thighs, the strain of maintaining nonstop concentration. A trance-like state settles over your efforts; the climb becomes a clear-eyed dream. Hours slide by like minutes. The accrued guilt and clutter of day-to-day existence—the lapses of conscience, the unpaid bills, the bungled opportunities, the dust under the couch, the festering familial sores, the inescapable prison of your genes—all of it is temporarily forgotten, crowded from your thoughts by an overpowering clarity of purpose, and by the seriousness of the task at hand.

At such moments, something like happiness actually stirs in your chest, but it isn't the sort of emotion you want to lean on very hard. In solo climbing, the whole enterprise is held together with little more than chutzpa, not the most reliable adhesive. Late in the day on the north face of the Thumb, I felt the glue disintegrate with a single swing of an ice axe.

I'd gained nearly seven hundred feet of altitude since stepping off the hanging glacier, all of it on crampon front-points and the picks of my axes. The ribbon of frozen melt water had ended three hundred feet up, and was followed by a crumbly armor of frost feathers. Though just barely substantial enough to support body weight, the rime was plastered over the rock to a thickness of two or three feet, so I kept plugging upward. The wall, however, had been growing imperceptibly steeper, and as it did so the frost feathers became thinner. I'd fallen into a slow, hypnotic rhythm—swing, swing; kick, kick; swing, swing; kick, kick—when my left ice axe slammed into a slab of diorite a few inches beneath the rime.

I tried left, then right, but kept striking rock. The frost feathers holding me up, it became apparent, were maybe five inches thick and had the structural integrity of stale cornbread. Below was thirty-seven hundred feet of air, and I was balanced atop a house of cards. Waves of panic rose in my throat. My eyesight blurred, I began to hyperventilate, my calves started to vibrate. I shuffled a few feet farther to the right, hoping to find thicker ice, but managed only to bend an ice axe on the rock.

Awkwardly, stiff with fear, I started working my way back down. The rime gradually thickened, and after descending about eighty feet I got back on reasonably solid ground. I stopped for a long time to let my nerves settle, then leaned back from my tools and stared up at the face

above, searching for a hint of solid ice, for some variation in the underlying rock strata, for anything that would allow passage over the frosted
slabs. I looked until my neck ached, but nothing appeared. The climb was
over. The only place to go was down.

Heavy snow and incessant winds kept me inside the tent for most of
the next three days. The hours passed slowly. In the attempt to hurry them
along I chain-smoked for as long as my supply of cigarettes held out, and
read. I'd made a number of bad decisions on the trip, there was no getting around it, and one of them concerned the reading matter I'd chosen to
pack along: three back issues of *The Village Voice*, and Joan Didion's latest
novel, *A Book of Common Prayer*. The *Voice* was amusing enough—there on
the icecap, the subject matter took on an edge, a certain sense of the
absurd, from which the paper (through no fault of its own) benefited
greatly—but in that tent, under those circumstances, Didion's necrotic
take on the world hit a little too close to home.

Near the end of *Common Prayer*, one of Didion's characters says to
another, "You don't get any real points for staying here, Charlotte."
Charlotte replies, "I can't seem to tell what you do get real points for, so I
guess I'll stick around here for awhile."

When I ran out of things to read, I was reduced to studying the rip-
stop pattern woven into the tent ceiling. This I did for hours on end, flat
on my back, while engaging in an extended and very heated self-debate:
should I leave for the coast as soon as the weather broke, or stay put long
enough to make another attempt on the mountain? In truth, my little
escapade on the north face had left me badly shaken, and I didn't want to
go up on the Thumb again at all. On the other hand, the thought of returning to Boulder in defeat—of parking the Pontiac behind the trailer, buck-
ling on my tool belt, and going back to the same brain-dead drill I'd so
triumphantly walked away from just a month before—that wasn't very
appealing, either. Most of all, I couldn't stomach the thought of having to
endure the smug expressions of condolence from all the chumps and nim-
rods who were certain I'd fail right from the get-go.

By the third afternoon of the storm I couldn't stand it any longer: the
lumps of frozen snow poking me in the back, the clammy nylon walls
brushing against my face, the incredible smell drifting up from the depths
of my sleeping bag. I pawed through the mess at my feet until I located a
small green stuff sack, in which there was a metal film can containing the

makings of what I'd hoped would be a sort of victory cigar. I'd intended to save it for my return from the summit, but what the hey, it wasn't looking like I'd be visiting the top any time soon. I poured most of the can's contents onto a leaf of cigarette paper, rolled it into a crooked, sorry-looking joint, and promptly smoked it down to the roach.

The reefer, of course, only made the tent seem even more cramped, more suffocating, more impossible to bear. It also made me terribly hungry. I decided a little oatmeal would put things right. Making it, however, was a long, ridiculously involved process: a potful of snow had to be gathered outside in the tempest, the stove assembled and lit, the oatmeal and sugar located, the remnants of yesterday's dinner scraped from my bowl. I'd gotten the stove going and was melting the snow when I smelled something burning. A thorough check of the stove and its environs revealed nothing. Mystified, I was ready to chalk it up to my chemically enhanced imagination when I heard something crackle directly behind me.

I whirled around in time to see a bag of garbage, into which I'd tossed the match I'd used to light the stove, flare up into a conflagration. Beating on the fire with my hands, I had it out in a few seconds, but not before a large section of the tent's inner wall vaporized before my eyes. The tent's built-in rainfly escaped the flames, so the shelter was still more or less weatherproof; now, however, it was approximately thirty degrees cooler inside. My left palm began to sting. Examining it, I noticed the pink welt of a burn. What troubled me most, though, was that the tent wasn't even mine—I'd borrowed the shelter from my father. An expensive Early Winters OmnipoTent, it had been brand new before my trip—the hang-tags were still attached—and had been loaned reluctantly. For several minutes I sat dumbstruck, staring at the wreckage of the shelter's once-graceful form amid the acrid scent of singed hair and melted nylon. You had to hand it to me, I thought: I had a real knack for living up to the old man's worst expectations.

The fire sent me into a funk that no drug known to man could have alleviated. By the time I'd finished cooking the oatmeal my mind was made up: the moment the storm was over, I was breaking camp and booking for Thomas Bay.

Twenty-four hours later, I was huddled inside a bivouac sack under the lip of the *bergschrund* on the Thumb's north face. The weather was as bad as I'd seen it. It was snowing hard, probably an inch every hour. Spindrift avalanches hissed down from the wall above and washed over me like surf, completely burying the sack every twenty minutes.

The day had begun well enough. When I emerged from the tent, clouds still clung to the ridge tops but the wind was down and the icecap was speckled with sunbreaks. A patch of sunlight, almost blinding in its brilliance, slid lazily over the camp. I put down a foam sleeping mat and sprawled on the glacier in my long johns. Wallowing in the radiant heat, I felt the gratitude of a prisoner whose sentence has just been commuted.

As I lay there, a narrow chimney that curved up the east half of the Thumb's north face, well to the left of the route I'd tried before the storm, caught my eye. I twisted a telephoto lens onto my camera. Through it I could make out a smear of shiny grey ice—solid, trustworthy, hard-frozen ice—plastered to the back of the cleft. The alignment of the chimney made it impossible to discern if the ice continued in an unbroken line from top to bottom. If it did, the chimney might well provide passage over the rime-covered slabs that had foiled my first attempt. Lying there in the sun, I began to think about how much I'd hate myself a month hence if I threw in the towel after a single try, if I scrapped the whole expedition on account of a little bad weather. Within the hour I had assembled my gear and was skiing toward the base of the wall.

The ice in the chimney did in fact prove to be continuous, but it was very, very thin—just a gossamer film of verglas. Additionally, the cleft was a natural funnel for any debris that happened to slough off the wall; as I scratched my way up the chimney I was hosed by a continuous stream of powder snow, ice chips, and small stones. One hundred twenty feet up the groove the last remnants of my composure flaked away like old plaster, and I turned around.

Instead of descending all the way to base camp, I decided to spend the night in the 'schrund beneath the chimney, on the off chance that my head would be more together the next morning. The fair skies that had ushered in the day, however, turned out to be but a momentary lull in a five-day gale.

By midafternoon the storm was back in all its glory, and my bivouac site became a less than pleasant place to hang around. The ledge on which I crouched was continually swept by small spindrift avalanches. Five times my bivvy sack—a thin nylon envelope, shaped exactly like a Baggies brand sandwich bag, only bigger—was buried up to the level of the breathing slit. After digging myself out the fifth time, I decided I'd had enough. I threw all my gear in my pack and made a break for base camp.

The descent was terrifying. Between the clouds, the ground blizzard, and the flat, fading light, I couldn't tell snow from sky, nor whether a slope went up or down. I worried, with ample reason, that I might step blindly off the top of a serac and end up at the bottom of the Witches Cauldron, a half-mile below. When I finally arrived on the frozen plain of the icecap, I found that my tracks had long since drifted over. I didn't have a clue how to locate the tent on the featureless glacial plateau. I skied in circles for an hour or so, hoping I'd get lucky and stumble across camp, until I put a foot into a small crevasse and realized I was acting like an idiot—that I should hunker down right where I was and wait out the storm.

I dug a shallow hole, wrapped myself in the bivvy bag, and sat on my pack in the swirling snow. Drifts piled up around me. My feet became numb. A damp chill crept down my chest from the base of my neck, where spindrift had gotten inside my parka and soaked my shirt. If only I had a cigarette, I thought, a single cigarette, I could summon the strength of character to put a good face on this fucked-up situation, on the whole fucked-up trip. "If we had some ham, we could have ham and eggs, if we had some eggs." I remembered my friend Nate uttering that line in a similar storm, two years before, high on another Alaskan peak, the Moose's Tooth. It had struck me as hilarious at the time; I'd actually laughed out loud. Recalling the line now, it no longer seemed funny. I pulled the bivvy sack tighter around my shoulders. The wind ripped at my back. Beyond shame, I cradled my head in my arms and embarked on an orgy of self-pity.

I knew that people sometimes died climbing mountains. But at the age of twenty-three personal mortality—the idea of my own death—was still largely outside my conceptual grasp; it was as abstract a notion as non-Euclidean geometry or marriage. When I decamped from Boulder in April, 1977, my head swimming with visions of glory and redemption on the Devils Thumb, it didn't occur to me that I might be bound by the same cause-effect relationships that governed the actions of others. I'd never heard of hubris. Because I wanted to climb the mountain so badly, because I had thought about the Thumb so intensely for so long, it seemed beyond the realm of possibility that some minor obstacle like the weather or crevasses or rime-covered rock might ultimately thwart my will.

At sunset the wind died and the ceiling lifted one hundred fifty feet off the glacier, enabling me to locate base camp. I made it back to the tent intact, but it was no longer possible to ignore the fact that the Thumb had made hash of my plans. I was forced to acknowledge that volition alone, however powerful, was not going to get me up the north wall. I saw, finally, that nothing was.

There still existed an opportunity for salvaging the expedition, however. A week earlier I'd skied over to the southeast side of the mountain to take a look at the route Fred Beckey had pioneered in 1946—the route by which I'd intended to descend the peak after climbing the north wall. During that reconnaissance I'd noticed an obvious unclimbed line to the left of the Beckey route—a patchy network of ice angling across the southeast face—that struck me as a relatively easy way to achieve the summit. At the time, I'd considered this route unworthy of my attentions. Now, on the rebound from my calamitous entanglement with the nordwand, I was prepared to lower my sights.

On the afternoon of May 15, when the blizzard finally petered out, I returned to the southeast face and climbed to the top of a slender ridge that abutted the upper peak like a flying buttress on a Gothic cathedral. I decided to spend the night there, on the airy, knife-edged ridge crest, sixteen hundred feet below the summit.

The evening sky was cold and cloudless. I could see all the way to tidewater and beyond. At dusk I watched, transfixed, as the house lights of Petersburg blinked on in the west. The closest thing I'd had to human contact since the airdrop, the distant lights set off a flood of emotion that caught me completely off guard. I imagined people watching the Red Sox on the tube, eating fried chicken in brightly lit kitchens, drinking beer, making love. When I lay down to sleep I was overcome by a soul-wrenching loneliness. I'd never felt so alone, ever.

That night I had troubled dreams, of cops and vampires and a gangland-style execution. I heard someone whisper, "He's in there. As soon as he comes out, waste him." I sat bolt upright and opened my eyes. The sun was about to rise. The entire sky was scarlet. It was still clear, but wisps of high cirrus were streaming in from the southwest, and a dark line was visible just above the horizon. I pulled on my boots and hurriedly strapped on my crampons. Five minutes after waking up, I was front-pointing away from the bivouac.

I carried no rope, no tent or bivouac gear, no hardware save my ice axes. My plan was to go ultralight and ultrafast, to hit the summit and make it back down before the weather turned. Pushing myself, continually out of breath, I scurried up and to the left across small snowfields linked by narrow runnels of verglas and short rock bands. The climbing was almost fun—the rock was covered with large, in-cut holds, and the ice, though thin, never got steep enough to feel extreme—but I was anxious about the bands of clouds racing in from the Pacific, covering the sky.

In what seemed like no time (I didn't have a watch on the trip) I was on the distinctive final ice field. By now the sky was completely overcast. It looked easier to keep angling to the left, but quicker to go straight for the top. Paranoid about being caught by a storm high on the peak without any kind of shelter, I opted for the direct route. The ice steepened, then steepened some more, and as it did so it grew thin. I swung my left ice axe and struck rock. I aimed for another spot, and once again it glanced off unyielding diorite with a dull, sickening clank. And again, and again: it was a reprise of my first attempt on the north face. Looking between my legs, I stole a glance at the glacier, more than two thousand feet below. My stomach churned. I felt my poise slipping away like smoke in the wind.

Forty-five feet above, the wall eased back onto the sloping summit shoulder. Forty-five more feet, half the distance between third base and home plate, and the mountain would be mine. I clung stiffly to my axes, unmoving, paralyzed with fear and indecision. I looked down at the dizzying drop to the glacier again, then up, then scraped away the film of ice above my head. I hooked the pick of my left axe on a nickel-thin lip of rock, and weighted it. It held. I pulled my right axe from the ice, reached up, and twisted the pick into a crooked half-inch crack until it jammed. Barely breathing now, I moved my feet up, scrabbling my crampon points across the verglas. Reaching as high as I could with my left arm, I swung the axe gently at the shiny, opaque surface, not knowing what I'd hit beneath it. The pick went in with a heartening *THUNK!* A few minutes later I was standing on a broad, rounded ledge. The summit proper, a series of slender fins sprouting a grotesque meringue of atmospheric ice, stood twenty feet directly above.

The insubstantial frost feathers ensured that those last twenty feet remained hard, scary, onerous. But then, suddenly, there was no place higher to go. It wasn't possible; I couldn't believe it. I felt my cracked lips stretch into a huge, painful grin. I was on top of the Devils Thumb.

Fittingly, the summit was a surreal, malevolent place, an improbably slender fan of rock and rime no wider than a filing cabinet. It did not encourage loitering. As I straddled the highest point, the north face fell away beneath my left boot for six thousand feet; beneath my right boot the south face dropped off for twenty-five hundred. I took some pictures to prove I'd been there, and spent a few minutes trying to straighten a bent pick. Then I stood up, carefully turned around, and headed for home.

Five days later I was camped in the rain beside the sea, marveling at the sight of moss, willows, mosquitoes. Two days after that, a small skiff motored into Thomas Bay and pulled up on the beach not far from my tent. The man driving the boat introduced himself as Jim Freeman, a timber faller from Petersburg. It was his day off, he said, and he'd made the trip to show his family the glacier, and to look for bears. He asked me if I'd "been huntin', or what?"

"No," I replied sheepishly. "Actually, I just climbed the Devils Thumb. I've been over here twenty days."

Freeman kept fiddling with a cleat on the boat, and didn't say anything for a while. Then he looked at me real hard and spat, "You wouldn't be givin' me double talk now, wouldja, friend?" Taken aback, I stammered out a denial. Freeman, it was obvious, didn't believe me for a minute. Nor did he seem wild about my snarled shoulder-length hair or the way I smelled. When I asked if he could give me a lift back to town, however, he offered a grudging, "I don't see why not."

The water was choppy, and the ride across Frederick Sound took two hours. The more we talked, the more Freeman warmed up. He still didn't believe I'd climbed the Thumb, but by the time he steered the skiff into Wrangell Narrows he pretended to. When we got off the boat, he insisted on buying me a cheeseburger. That night he even let me sleep in a derelict step-van parked in his backyard.

I lay down in the rear of the old truck for a while but couldn't sleep, so I got up and walked to a bar called Kito's Kave. The euphoria, the overwhelming sense of relief, that had initially accompanied my return to Petersburg faded, and an unexpected melancholy took its place. The people I chatted with in Kito's didn't seem to doubt that I'd been to the top of the Thumb; they just didn't much care. As the night wore on the place emptied except for me and an Indian at a back table. I drank alone, putting quarters in the jukebox, playing the same five songs over and over, until the barmaid yelled angrily, "Hey! Give it a fucking rest, kid! If I hear 'Fifty Ways to Lose Your Lover' one more time, *I'm* gonna be the one who loses it." I mumbled an apology, quickly headed for the door, and lurched back to Freeman's step-van. There, surrounded by the sweet scent of old motor oil, I lay down on the floorboards next to a gutted transmission and passed out.

It is easy, when you are young, to believe that what you desire is no less than what you deserve, to assume that if you want something badly enough it is your God-given right to have it. Less than a month after sitting on the summit of the Thumb I was back in Boulder, nailing up siding on the Spruce Street Townhouses, the same condos I'd been framing when I left for Alaska. I got a raise, to four dollars an hour, and at the end of the summer moved out of the job-site trailer to a studio apartment on West Pearl, but little else in my life seemed to change. Somehow, it didn't add up to the glorious transformation I'd imagined in April.

Climbing the Devils Thumb, however, had nudged me a little further away from the obdurate innocence of childhood. It taught me something about what mountains can and can't do, about the limits of dreams. I didn't recognize that at the time, of course, but I'm grateful for it now.

▲ Part II ▲

THE CHUGACH RANGE

The Ascent of Mt. St. Agnes
[Mount Marcus Baker]

– BRADFORD WASHBURN –

No one is more intimately connected with Alaska's mountaineering history than New Englander Bradford Washburn. Born in Cambridge, Massachusetts, in 1910, Washburn served as director of the Boston Museum of Science for forty-one years (he is now honorary director), and has earned fame worldwide as a scientist, photographer, author, lecturer, cartographer, explorer, and mountaineer. Much of his most celebrated work has occurred in Alaska.

Mount Fairweather, in Southeast Alaska, was the first peak to lure Washburn north. Though he and his Harvard teammates proved unsuccessful in reaching the summit, the expedition marked the start of a long relationship that continues to this day: over the past sixty-six years, Washburn has visited Alaska more than fifty times, and almost a third have been climbing expeditions. Over the years, he's become most closely associated with Mount McKinley—a name he prefers over Denali, because it is the officially recognized one. Indeed, in some quarters he's known as "Mr. McKinley." Since his first photographic and aerial flights over the peak in 1936, he's devoted much of his life to its study and exploration. In all, he's spent more than 200 days on McKinley's slopes, visited it in every month except February, and climbed the mountain three times, once (in 1947) with wife Barbara, the first woman to reach McKinley's summit. In 1951, he established what has become the mountain's standard route, via the West Buttress, and ten years later he completed his highly acclaimed Mount McKinley map. Besides all that, his photographic record of the mountain is unmatched.

Because Washburn's McKinley connection is so strong, it's overshadowed his other mountaineering accomplishments. Between 1930 and 1955, he participated in first ascents of ten major Alaska peaks. The following story chronicles, in characteristic Washburn detail, the first ascent of the Chugach Range's Mount Marcus Baker in 1938.

Measured in absolute numbers, the Chugach is not especially grand; Marcus Baker, its tallest peak, is only 13,176 feet high. But measured from base to summit, the Chugach is Alaska's second-highest coastal range, behind only the St. Elias Mountains. When first ascended, the mountain was called Mount St. Agnes. Says Washburn: "Colonel James W. Bagley of the U.S. Geological Survey named Mount St. Agnes after his wife—knowing full well that it wouldn't be formally approved by the U.S. Board of Geographic Names because she was very much alive (I knew them both very well). Finally the USGS discovered this trick and renamed it after one of their stars!"

"The Ascent of Mt. St. Agnes," by Bradford Washburn, originally appeared in 1939 in The American Alpine Journal.

TOWERING IN A BROAD ARC about the deep fjords of Prince William Sound stand the Chugach Mountains, magnificent western ramparts of the St. Elias Range. Although three of its peaks rise to heights of greater than 12,000 ft., and more than a dozen of its summits are greater than 10,000 ft. high, this range is still one of the least known among all the mountain ranges of North America. Its glaciers tumbling to tide water only a few hundred yards from a well-travelled steamship line, the eastern snow-slopes virtually dropping into the streets of Valdez, and scarcely one of its great peaks more than 100 miles from Seward, Anchorage or Cordova, it is hard to imagine why until this last summer not a single peak in the range had ever been reached.

The approaches to Mt. St. Agnes (13,250 ft.) and Mt. Witherspoon (12,100 ft.) from the head of College Fjord, which has often been visited

by expeditions for the study of its beautiful glaciers, are particularly forbidding. The rock of the Chugach Mountains is dominantly schistose or
volcanic and terribly rotten. The huge glaciers which drain the S. flank of
the range are exceedingly steep and rough, with the sole exception of the
great Columbia Glacier. Access to the N. side of the range is difficult
because of inadequate means of transportation. The Matanuska Valley, the
valley of the Knik River, and those of the Nelchina and Tazlina Rivers,
which drain this side of the range, are as yet uninhabited. The shortest of
the glaciers, leading from the heart of the range to the head of these various valleys, is nearly 30 miles in length, and, in each case, to approach the
glacier's end, a walk of at least 30 miles is necessary through country
which has not been extensively travelled since the days of the Gold Rush.
Horses are not available anywhere on the N. side of the range as they are
for approach to climbs in the Mt. McKinley and the Wrangell areas, and
the gravel-bars in the heads of the rivers are for the most part far too
rough to be used for an airplane landing.

Aside from the mere inaccessibility of the one side of the Chugach
Mountains which seems to be most easily climbable, the greatest deter-
rent to the exploration of the Chugach Range has been the unbelievably
terrible weather which sweeps the slopes of these mountains almost every
day of the entire year. Alaskan weather, at best, is notoriously bad; in the
mountains fringing Prince William Sound it is awful beyond the most
remote limit of the imagination.

During the winter and spring of 1938, a small expedition was
planned at the Harvard Institute of Geography to attempt the ascent of
Mt. St. Agnes, the highest peak in the Chugachs, and to make a series of
aerial photographic flights, which would fill in the great blank on this part
of the Alaskan map.

Early in June, 1937, on a flight between Seward and Valdez, I had an
excellent opportunity to study the Seward face of Mt. St. Agnes, which
seemed particularly steep and rugged. Although there appeared to be two
routes on this side of the mountain which might prove possible for climbing under excellent snow conditions, we decided, however, it would be
worth while to make a further reconnaissance flight on the N. side of the
range before blundering on to one of these very steep and exposed S.
ridges. Russell Dow and pilot Bob Reeve of Valdez succeeded in making a
flight along the N. edge of the range early in February, 1938, as soon as
the sun had risen high enough to make photography on this side of the

mountains possible. These pictures were sent to Cambridge by air-mail where they were developed, and we discovered an ideal route to the summit of St. Agnes by way of a great ridge which dropped N. from the peak to the head of Matanuska Glacier. This glacier, only the snout of which appears on the U.S.G.S. map, melts into the Matanuska River, near the mouth of which the Federal Relief Colony has been established some 40 miles down the valley near the shores of Cook Inlet.

Without the possibility of obtaining any pack-horses on this side of the range, the long rough approach up the Matanuska Valley was not a cheering prospect, in view of the weather which we must almost certainly face. On the new aerial pictures showing the Matanuska Glacier, there appeared to be a beautifully smooth, high plateau about 8 miles below its head. Reeve was certain, after examining the head of the glacier on this February flight, that he would be able to land both our party and supplies somewhere on this plateau. In order to do this, he agreed to use his ski-equipped plane, taking off from the Valdez mud-flats as we had done on the Mt. Lucania trip the year before.

The advance guard of our small party, consisting of Peter Gabriel, Norman Bright and Norman Dyhrenfurth, arrived with all of our supplies in Valdez on April 30th. I planned to reach Alaska in the middle of May and we hoped by that time Reeve and the other three men would have been able to move our entire outfit to a base camp on the glacier and start the reconnaissance of the lower part of the mountain. The Chugach weather, however, now got to work. The flight from Valdez to the glacier, including time taken to unload the plane, was only a matter of about two hours. When I arrived in Valdez on the afternoon of May 16th, I learned that the first clear two-hour period had been early that morning. My three companions were still in Valdez and only one of our four loads had been flown to the glacier. Ten more days of bitter storms followed, and at last, very early on the morning of May 27th, Reeve, Gabriel and I made a flight to the glacier and a temporary camp was set up beside our landing place. The weather on this trip was far from good and Reeve was forced to fly almost 50 miles out of his way in order to get back to Valdez, as the passages over which we had flown but two hours before were completely clogged with clouds on his return.

Fog and rain again enveloped Valdez for several days, and although our weather on the N. side of the mountains was moderately good, there was no hope whatever of bringing in the last two loads from the coast.

Gabriel and I were comfortably established on the glacier with ample food for several weeks, and in constant communication with Valdez and Anchorage by means of our small portable radio telephone. Situated as we were on exactly the opposite side of this range from Valdez, it was impossible to tell what sort of weather to expect in either place, no matter how clear it might be in the other. The radio proved a marvelous boon to the efficient freighting in of the last two loads, as well as in getting the party safely out to civilization at the close of the trip.

Two lovely mornings on May 31st and June 1st brought the remainder of our party in from Valdez and united us all safely on the glacier. Gabriel and I had reconnoitered 4 miles about the base camp the day after our arrival and had marked the trail clearly with willow-wands as far as we felt it safe for two people to travel alone. On June 2nd we started sledging supplies ahead up the valley to a camp at 5950 ft., 2 miles above our base. The reason for the exceedingly short distances between all our camps on St. Agnes was the weather. It snowed heavily almost every night, and during the day when it was not actually snowing or blowing a hurricane, the lower glacier was usually blanketed in dense fog. In order to keep the trail broken out, we made our camps close together and relayed twice each day instead of once.

Camp 2 was established on the night of June 4th, and on the 5th and 6th, we had the most terrific storm of the entire trip. Two of our heavy bamboo tent-poles were smashed to pieces and the new trail, both above and below camp, was completely buried. Thick fog settled down over the glacier for the next three days, but we managed during short clear streaks to mark a good trail to the top of the low icefall, slightly more than 2 miles above camp. Heavy rain on the 9th and 10th reduced the fresh fall of snow to a sea of slush, and when we finally managed to drag the last of our three light loads into Camp 3, we were utterly disgusted with the weather. During the 14 days that Gabriel and I had been on the glacier, we had only once been able to glimpse the summit ridge of St. Agnes, and then only for a few moments.

The morning of June 11th dawned cloudless after a night of dense fog and light snow. We made an early start and sledged a load to a point about a mile from the base of the northerly ridge of St. Agnes, and then bogged down on the glacier in a mass of slush. We made another trip late that night after a crust had formed, finding our way to the cache only by means of the willow-wands. More fog and still more snow hampered the next three relays, which finally established us at a fourth camp on a fine level patch of snow, 7500 ft. high, at the very base of St. Agnes. Although essentially a rock ridge, this northerly buttress of St. Agnes is so exposed to the force of the easterly storms that its entire length is capped with a beautiful arête of snow. By following the crest of this buttress to a height of about 10,000 ft., we hoped to attain the main summit ridge of St. Agnes at a pass about 11,000 ft. high. This route had the disadvantage of forcing us to climb over the tops of two distinct peaks, each one followed by a descent of more than 500 ft. before reaching the actual summit cone of the mountain.

Unfortunately the easier and more direct routes of approach which lay at the very head of the Matanuska Glacier were far too badly swept by avalanches for consideration. We had at first hoped to relay our final camp up the N. ridge to 10,000 ft. without any intermediate depot. In fact, if it had not been for the uncertainty of the weather and the length of this climb, involving two descents, we should certainly have tackled the summit directly from Camp 4 without any further advance at all.

A short clear-off on the night of June 13th gave us a chance for reconnaissance up the ridge to 10,000 ft., where we located a level though very exposed campsite. The clouds and blowing snow above this point hid all the upper part of the mountain in such a wild swirl that we were forced to return without having a chance to study the final approach to the 11,000-ft. pass. We beat our way back to camp down the narrow ridge in a gathering gale, and during the next three days we were scarcely able to leave the tents on account of a hurricane of wind and drifting snow.

In one short lull late on the night of the 14th, we managed to sneak one load to a sheltering rock outcrop on the ridge at about 8600 ft., but above that the wind was blowing so hard we could not work it up any harder. On the night of the 15th, we had a short break. The wind and snow suddenly died down at sunset after a constant blizzard all day. By working all night, we managed to break trail through oceans of powdered snow on the crest of the ridge, and by dawn had made two relays to the 8600-ft. shelf. We abandoned two sleeping-bags at the base of the ridge and only took with us the absolute necessities for ten days' existence on the mountain. We slept for a short time early in the morning of the 17th and then worked all through that day, pushing three relays through to our final camp at 10,000 ft. The freak good weather ended abruptly just before noon, and camp was finally set up just before supper in a frigid wind and driving snow. The last trip from the lower cache had been made entirely along willow-wands in dense fog and snow. That night we wondered why we had ever tried to climb Mt. St. Agnes!

The wind again rose to hurricane force. We had erected camp under such wretched conditions, had not been able to dig it in deep enough and just leveled out a space large enough for the tent and built a small wall to windward. It blew so hard about midnight that we had to pull down the tent poles for fear the whole camp would be demolished, and spent the remainder of the night half smothered underneath the flapping cloth, sitting up in bed every hour or so to throw off the drifting snow and keep it from burying us. The hurricane continued until the middle of the next afternoon, when we turned to in shifts, dug out camp and built a new and higher wall.

A lull late in the afternoon put Bright and myself on the trail, while Gabriel and Dyhrenfurth fortified camp for the coming night. In two hours of fog-groping through a maze of cracks, guided mainly by one of our aerial photographs, we found an excellent way to reach our 11,000-ft. col and willow-wanded trail through to the bottom of a smooth slope immediately below it. The new wall stood us in good stead that night, but we had little sleep. The wind and driving snow roared by ceaselessly at 80 or 90 miles an hour, having started up just before Bright and I got in from our afternoon's reconnaissance. At 6 o'clock on the morning of the 19th, the wind suddenly died and the clouds lifted, although the weather was still far from promising. We decided to make a quick start and work our way as far up the mountain as we possibly could. Our food supplies were limited; we had to count on flying out to Valdez no later than the end of the month, if we were still to have smooth snow for the airplane to take off.

The trip on foot down the Matanuska Valley would have been a long and difficult walk, and both Gabriel and I had to be in Valdez no later than July 1st—he to meet the Harvard ski party, and I to meet Terris and Katrina Moore for the Sanford climb. We had planned to spend two whole months on St. Agnes, but storms had forced us to waste all of May waiting in Valdez; bad weather had again caused us day after day of delay in reaching this final camp. We were certain that St. Agnes could be climbed. The problem now arose as to whether even two months were sufficient allowance in order to have a single clear day.

Shouldering two days of iron rations, our survey camera, the light movie cameras and some extra film, we set out at 9 o'clock on the morning of June 19th in hopes of at least finding out exactly what was in store for us on the upper ridge of the mountain. The new snow was abominable. We had to use snowshoes wherever it was possible to wear them. At 11 o'clock we made our pass and thence followed the ridge in warm sunlight to the bottom of Pk. 12,250 ft., which we had always hoped we might traverse on its right (W.) flank. This, however, proved absolutely impossible, as a 5000-ft. cliff of rock and ice tumbled abruptly from its very summit to the very head of the Knik Glacier, which stretched below us towards Anchorage. Peering towards the S. across this cliff and past Pk. 12,250 ft. we had the first glimpse of the actual summit of St. Agnes since we had landed at its base more than three weeks before. Still 3 miles ahead, it looked as if it were but a stone's throw away. With the added incentive of the summit in sight, we decided to press on over the top of the 12,250-ft. peak and mark a trail as far as we possibly could. The opposite side of this smaller peak is exceedingly steep and quite icy. By dropping down 800 ft., we attained a notch on the other side of which 2 miles of plateau-like snow fields brought us to an altitude of 12,500 ft., near the summit of our second intermediate mountain. We managed to avoid going over the actual top of Pk. 12,750 ft., a mile N. of St. Agnes, by slipping past it on a shoulder about 12,600 ft. high and thence wallowing down 400 ft. through waist-deep powder snow into the final pass, 12,200 ft.

We reached this pass at 3 PM without a single rest, even to eat, since leaving camp at 9 o'clock in the morning. The weather, though still calm, was very unsettled. The blue sky had disappeared shortly after we had descended the S. side of Pk. 12,250 ft. Heavy clouds were now rolling in towards us from the coast. A light southerly wind was picking up and patches of fog were rapidly forming all along the valley of the Knik Glacier to our right. As we sat shoulder deep in the loose snow with the summit rising 1000 ft. above us, now but a scant three-quarters of a mile away, we realized that this was our last chance. Another big southeaster would be sure to blockade us in camp until the end of our food. We had to strike now or give up the mountain. The clouds were rapidly closing in about the summit cone, so we carefully headed our trail across our broad pass toward the spot where the final pyramid seemed most easily climbable. Then the clouds completely hid the peak from view and we continued ahead holding a straight course by lining each new willow-wand up with the preceding ones, which we knew were heading us exactly where we wanted to go. This literally surveyed us through the fog to the bottom of a clear route up the summit cone. Once out of the pass, with its fathomless powder snow, the footing changed to hard ice. We put on our crampons once more and made fine headway. The wind and snow increased gently and the fog was impenetrable. At 4:40 PM, however, we hit the unmistakable final ridge. The last ten minutes we followed the crest of the ridge into a chilly southerly breeze, laden with hoarfrost and occasional snowflakes. At 4:50 PM the ridge abruptly ended; steep slopes dropped sharply about us on all sides through the fog, and we stood at last on the summit of St. Agnes.

The ascent of Mt. St. Agnes was a curious mixture of failure and success. Happy as we were at making a goal which we had virtually given up, we realized that one of the prime objectives of the trip—the photographic survey of the Chugach Range from the summit—could not possibly be accomplished. Nevertheless, we felt ourselves extremely lucky even to have made the climb, as we were certain beyond all doubt that this was the first day in more than six weeks that we could possibly have succeeded.

Our stay on top was short, partly on account of the cold, partly because of the late hour and the long struggle with its two uphill grades that still lay between us and camp. Our old trail entirely gone and nothing but twigs sticking through the drifting snow left to guide us, we finally reached camp at 9:50 that night, after a long, exhausting day—a combination of joy and bitter disappointment.

The storm hit that night with redoubled fury. The wind and snow were so bad on the following morning that we decided not to tackle the descent of the ridge until the usual evening lull. This arrived on schedule late in the afternoon, but it ended much sooner than usual and we descended the last half of the ridge in a veritable tornado of wind and blowing snow, arriving at Camp 4 late in the evening. The next night saw us safely back in Camp 2. Our old landing-field near Camp 1 had been completely wiped out by heavy rains. We were forced to spend the whole of the next day snowshoeing a safe solid runway 2000 ft. long and 80 ft. wide near Camp 2. The radio again rallied to our aid. The night of June 22nd was icy cold and magnificently clear, the only truly clear night on the entire expedition. We picked up Valdez on our first call at 6 o'clock in the evening. Reeve, fully warned by wireless of the shape and position of the new field, dropped from the skies early the next morning and spirited us safely out to Valdez in two quick flights.

Technically speaking the ascent of Mt. St. Agnes was not difficult. Two short stretches on the ridge below our final camp, as well as the descent on the S. side of Pk. 12,250 ft., were exceedingly steep and icy but presented no first-order difficulties. Similar in most respects to a good many other Alaskan mountains, the main problem on St. Agnes was that of reaching its base. The climb proper was accomplished from Valdez to Valdez in twenty-seven days, a time which would have been more than doubled had we not succeeded in making both our approach and retreat by air.

Repeated use of airplanes for stocking our base on the Yukon Expedition in 1935 and on Mt. Lucania a year ago furnished convincing proof that these flights cannot be carried out efficiently and safely without the use of reliable radio equipment at both ends. Our success on St. Agnes despite the desperate efforts of a hard-working climbing party was due in great part to the flawless operation of our radio and the expert piloting of Reeve, both of which contributed to make an isolated and strongly fortified mountain one which could easily be attacked.

▲ PART III ▲

DENALI

AND

THE

ALASKA

RANGE

The Sourdough Expedition, 1910
[Denali]

– BILL SHERWONIT –

Choosing the most significant mountaineering accomplishment in Alaska's climbing history is an imposing, if not impossible, task.

As Valdez physician and climber Andy Embick once commented, "There are just so many categories to consider. Are you talking about big-wall climbs? First ascents? Solo ascents? Winter climbs? Comparing those different kinds of climbs is like comparing apples and oranges. It just can't be done."

Perhaps. But, believing it would be fun—and educational—to try, in 1989 I conducted an informal telephone poll of approximately twenty veteran Alaska mountaineers, to see if those most devoted to climbing and exploring Alaska's high places could reach some consensus. I asked participants to name the mountaineering feat(s) they considered to be the most significant or noteworthy, with no limit on the number and types of choices.

The variety of responses was enormous. More than thirty expeditions received mention. Some, such as the first winter ascent of Denali by Art Davidson, Ray Genet, and Dave Johnston in 1967, are highly acclaimed, well-publicized mountaineering masterpieces. Others, such as John Waterman's five-month solo of Mount Hunter in 1978, have received little public attention but are considered classics within the mountaineering community.

From the many opinions offered, one expedition stood out from all the rest: the Sourdough Expedition of 1910.

More than any other group of climbers, past or present, the Sourdoughs seem to symbolize the pioneering spirit and adventurous nature of what is often called the Alaskan mystique. Over the past eighty-six years, their ascent has become the stuff of legend. This group of four gold miners challenged North America's highest peak with the most rudimentary gear and with no technical climbing experience, simply to disprove explorer Frederick Cook's claim that he reached the mountain's summit in 1906 and to demonstrate that Alaskans could outdo the exploits—whether real or imagined—of any "Easterners."

That they succeeded in a brazen style uniquely their own delights Todd Miner, who calls their ascent a "climbing masterpiece." "To me, one of the most appealing aspects of the expedition is that it was a bunch of locals doing it," said Miner, an Anchorage mountaineer who also coordinates the University of Alaska Anchorage's Alaska Wilderness Studies Program. "It's a classic case of Alaskans showing Outsiders how it's done."

"The Sourdough Expedition, 1910" is adapted from To the Top of Denali: Climbing Adventures on North America's Highest Peak, *published in 1990 by Alaska Northwest Books in Seattle.*

THE SOURDOUGH EXPEDITION REACHED its literal high point on April 3, 1910, when Billy Taylor and Pete Anderson reached the top of Denali's 19,470-foot North Peak, widely recognized as a more difficult ascent than the higher—and ultimately more prestigious—20,320-foot South Peak. The Sourdoughs' reason for choosing the North Peak seemed quite logical at the time; the miners hoped that the fourteen-foot spruce pole, complete with six-by-twelve-foot American flag they'd lugged up Denali, would be seen from Kantishna and serve as visible proof of their conquest.

Taylor and Anderson made their summit push from 11,000 feet. Hauling their flagpole, they climbed more than 8,000 vertical feet and then descended to camp in eighteen hours' time—an outstanding feat by any mountaineering standard. (By comparison, most present-day Denali expeditions climb no more than 3,000 to 4,000 vertical feet on summit day, which typically lasts ten to fifteen hours.) Yet the Sourdoughs' final incredible ascent is merely one chapter in an altogether remarkable story that for many years was steeped in controversy and, as Alaska historian Terrence Cole has noted, "is still shrouded in mystery."

As seems to be the case with so many legendary Alaskan adventures, the Sourdough Expedition began with some barroom braggadocio. Or so the story goes. The expedition's leader and instigator was Tom Lloyd, a Welshman and former Utah sheriff who came to Alaska during the Klondike gold rush, eventually settling in the Kantishna Hills north of Denali.

In the fall of 1909, Lloyd and several other patrons of a Fairbanks bar joined in a discussion that focused on Frederick Cook's claim that he'd reached Denali's summit in 1906. As the *Fairbanks Daily Times* noted in 1909, "Ever since Dr. Cook described his ascent of Mount McKinley, Alaskans have been suspicious of the accuracy of this explorer."

According to Lloyd's official account of the Sourdough Expedition, which appeared in *The New York Times Sunday Magazine* on June 5, 1910, "[Bar owner] Bill McPhee and me were talking one day of the possibility of getting to the summit of Mount McKinley and I said I thought if anyone could make the climb there were several pioneers of my acquaintance who could. Bill said he didn't believe that any living man could make the ascent."

McPhee argued that the fifty-year-old Lloyd was too old and overweight for such an undertaking, to which the miner responded that "for two cents" he'd show it could be done. To call Lloyd's bluff, McPhee offered to pay $500 to anyone who would climb McKinley and "prove whether that fellow Cook made the climb or not."

After two other businessmen agreed to put up $500 each, Lloyd accepted the challenge. The proposed expedition was big news in Fairbanks, and before long it made local headlines. Later, Lloyd admitted, "Of course, after the papers got hold of the story we hated the idea of ever coming back here defeated."

A seven-man party left Fairbanks in December 1909, accompanied by four horses, a mule, and a dog team. Their send-off included an editorial in the *Fairbanks Daily Times*, which promised, "Our boys will succeed . . . and they'll show up Dr. Cook and the other 'Outside' doctors and expeditions."

Original team members included Tom Lloyd, Billy Taylor, Pete Anderson, Charles McGonagall, C. E. Davidson, Bob Horne, and a person identified as W. Lloyd. But the latter three men quit before the actual climbing began, following a dispute—some accounts report a fist-fight—between Tom Lloyd and Davidson, a talented surveyor/photographer whose role with the expedition, according to Cole, was "to map the route and keep track of elevations." Thus the expedition was left with four members, all miners from the Kantishna District: Taylor was Lloyd's mining partner; McGonagall and Anderson each had worked several years for the two property owners.

The Sourdoughs spent most of February establishing a series of camps in the lowlands and foothills on Denali's north side. By the end of the month, they'd set up their mountain base of operations, the "Willows Camp," near the mouth of Cache Creek at an elevation of about 2,900 feet.

On March 1, the team began "prospecting for the big climb," Lloyd wrote in his expedition diary. "Anderson and McGonagall examined the [Muldrow] glacier today. We call it the 'Wall Street Glacier,' being enclosed by exceedingly high walls on each side." Three days later, they set up their first glacier camp. Lloyd, who'd lost the barometer loaned him by Davidson, estimated the camp's elevation at 9,000 to 10,000 feet, but it was probably much lower. Team members then descended and spent the next several days cutting firewood and hauling it up the glacier, along with a wood-burning stove.

Traversing the Muldrow proved to be quite intimidating. As Lloyd explained in his diary:

> For the first four or five miles there are no crevasses in sight, as they have been blown full of snow, but the next eight miles are terrible for crevasses. You can look down in them for distances stretching from 100 feet to Hades or China. Look down one of them and you never will forget it. . . . Most of them appear to be bottomless. These are not good things to look at.

Despite the danger of a crevasse fall, the climbers traveled unroped, a practice most contemporary Denali mountaineers would consider fool-hardy. There's no way to know whether the Sourdoughs' decision was made in ignorance or disdain for such protection. Years later, when asked why the team chose not to use climbing ropes, Taylor simply answered, "Didn't need them." Such an attitude seems to reflect the Sourdoughs' style. With the notable exception of their fourteen-foot flagpole, they chose to travel light.

The team had "less 'junk' with them than an Eastern excursion party would take along for a one-day's outing in the hills," wrote W. F. Thompson, editor of the *Fairbanks Daily News-Miner*, who prepared Lloyd's story for publication in *The New York Times*. The Sourdoughs' climbing gear consisted of only the bare essentials: snowshoes; homemade crampons, which they called creepers; and crude ice axes, which Lloyd described as "long poles with double hooks on one end—hooks made of steel—and a sharp steel point on the other end." Their high-altitude food supplies included bacon, beans, flour, sugar, dried fruits, butter, coffee, hot chocolate and caribou meat. To endure the subzero cold, they simply wore bib overalls, long underwear, shirts, parkas, mittens, shoepacs (insulated rubber boots), and Indian moccasins. (The moccasins that the pioneer Denali climbers wore were like Eskimo mukluks: tall, above-the-calf footwear, dry-tanned, with a moose-hide sole and caribou-skin uppers. Worn with insoles and at least three pairs of wool socks, they were reportedly very warm and provided good foot support.)

Even their reading material was limited. The climbers brought only one magazine, which they read from end to end. "I don't remember the name of the magazine," Lloyd later commented, "but in our estimation it is the best magazine published in the world."

Other essentials included wooden stakes for trail marking and poles for crevasse crossings. The poles were placed across crevasses too wide to jump; the men then piled snow between the poles, which hardened and froze to create a bridge over which they could travel in snowshoes.

The team reached the site of its third and final camp on March 17, at the head of the Muldrow Glacier. Lloyd estimated the elevation at "not less than 15,000 feet," though later explorers determined the camp's altitude could have been no higher than 11,000 feet. The climbers spent the next several days digging a protective tunnel into the snow, relaying supplies from lower camps, cutting steps into the ice along what is now called Karstens Ridge, and enduring stormy weather.

On April 1, the Sourdoughs made their first summit attempt, but stormy weather turned them back. Two days later, they tried again. Outfitted with a bag of doughnuts, three thermos bottles of hot chocolate (plus caribou meat, according to some accounts), and their fourteen-foot spruce pole, Taylor, Anderson, and McGonagall headed for the summit at

3:00 AM. Lloyd apparently had moved down to the Willows Camp; exactly why isn't clear, but he may have been suffering from altitude sickness.

Unroped, without the benefit of any climbing aid other than their crude homemade crampons and ice axes, the three climbers ascended Karstens Ridge, crossed the Grand Basin—later to be named the Harper Glacier—and headed up a steep couloir now known as the Sourdough Gully.

A few hundred feet below the summit, McGonagall stopped. Years later, in a conversation with alpine historian Francis Farquhar, he explained, "No, I didn't go clear to the top—why should I? I'd finished my turn carrying the pole before we got there. Taylor and Pete finished the job—I sat down and rested, then went back to camp." It has also been suggested that McGonagall fell victim to altitude sickness.

Taylor and Anderson continued on, still hauling their spruce pole. And sometime late in the afternoon, they concluded their unprecedented ascent by standing atop the North Peak's summit. Twenty-seven years later, in an interview eventually published in the *American Alpine Journal*, Taylor recalled that he and Anderson spent two and a half hours on top of the mountain, though the temperature reached as low as –30°F that day. "It was colder than hell," he reported. "Mitts and everything was all ice."

Before descending back to camp, the Sourdoughs planted their pole, complete with American flag. Said Taylor, "We . . . built a pyramid of [rocks] about fifteen inches high and we dug down in the ice so the pole had a support of about thirty inches and was held by four guy lines—just cotton ropes. We fastened the guy lines to little spurs of rock." Though they'd planned to leave their flagpole at the summit, the climbers were forced to plant it on the highest available rock outcropping, located a few hundred feet below the top.

Taylor and Anderson returned to the high camp late that night, completing their speed climb in eighteen hours. The next day, all members of the party were reunited at the Willows Camp. They made no attempt to climb the South Peak.

Their mission accomplished, Taylor, Anderson, and McGonagall returned to Kantishna. Lloyd, meanwhile, traveled to Fairbanks with news of the history-making ascent. Unfortunately, the Sourdough Expedition's team leader decided to mix fantasy with fact, and the team's true feat was transformed into an Alaskan tall tale. Returning to a hero's welcome on April 11, Lloyd proclaimed that the entire party had reached the summits of both the North and South Peaks. Furthermore, they'd found no evidence to substantiate Cook's claims.

Word of the team's success quickly spread. On April 12, the *Fairbanks Daily Times* published an account of the historic climb, and the story quickly made headlines around the country. Congratulations included a telegram from President William Howard Taft.

Not everyone took Lloyd's word at face value, however. On April 16, *The New York Times* ran a story in which naturalist/explorer Charles Sheldon challenged Lloyd's claims:

> It is clearly the duty of the press . . . not to encourage full credibility in the reports of the alleged ascent until the facts and details are authoritatively published. Only Tom Lloyd apparently brought out the report, the other members of the party having remained in the Kantishna District 150 miles away; so we haven't had their corroborative evidence.

Despite such published doubts, *The New York Times* successfully bid for first rights to a detailed report of the climb. And on June 5, the newspaper devoted three pages of its *Sunday Magazine* section to the Sourdough Expedition; the package included a story of the ascent written by W. F. Thompson plus Lloyd's own firsthand account, which featured entries from his daily record. A day later, the story ran in London's *Daily Telegraph*.

Even as Thompson was preparing his *New York Times* article, the challenges to Lloyd's account increased. Other evidence of the ascent was demanded, but photos taken during the expedition proved unsatisfactory. Lloyd felt enough pressure that he asked Taylor, Anderson, and McGonagall to repeat the climb and secure additional photos. In a little-known but fascinating adventure, the three climbers reascended Denali in May. They reached Denali Pass (elevation about 18,200 feet) and took additional photographs of the mountain. Nearly forty years later, McGonagall recalled: "We didn't camp—we just kept going for three days—it was light enough and we were all skookum [an Indian word meaning strong or heroic]." The photos resulting from the second climb remain one of the Sourdough Expedition's many mysteries, because apparently they were never published.

With no solid proof to back up Lloyd's boasts, skepticism continued to build, such doubts being reinforced in part by the Sourdough leader's age and overweight condition; according to Taylor, Lloyd was "awful fat." Before long, the Sourdoughs were looked on no more favorably than Cook, the man they'd hope to discredit. According to historian Cole:

> The contradictions in [Lloyd's] story and the fact that he supposedly admitted in private to some of his friends that he had not climbed the mountain himself, eventually discredited the entire expedition. Soon the Sourdoughs and their flagpole were regarded as just one more fascinating frontier tale, about as believable as an exploit of Paul Bunyan.

Back in Kantishna, the other Sourdough team members were unaware that Lloyd's false claims had caused their mountaineering feat to fall into disrepute. When interviewed in 1937, Taylor said, "He [Lloyd] was the head of the party and we never dreamed he wouldn't give a straight story. I wish to God we hadda been there. . . . We didn't get out till June and then they didn't believe any of us had climbed it."

Taylor also said he gave no prior approval to Lloyd's account of the climb in *The New York Times*. Yet on June 11, each of the Sourdoughs signed a notarized statement that "a party of four in number known as the Lloyd party" had reached the North Peak at 3:25 PM on April 3, 1910. Whether they knew in advance of Lloyd's fictitious account, or chose to go along with his claims because of some misplaced loyalty, none of the Sourdoughs publicly challenged their leader's story until years later.

(There's an interesting historical sidenote to the Sourdough Expedition. At least partly because of embarrassment about its role in the promotion of Lloyd's story, the *Fairbanks Daily Times* organized its own Denali expedition in 1912. Led by Ralph Cairns, the newspaper's telegraph editor, the party reached Denali's base in late February. The climbers failed to find McGonagall Pass, which provides the easiest access to the Muldrow Glacier, and instead set up base camp on the Peters Glacier. The expedition was turned back at about 10,000 feet by apparently unclimbable ice walls, and on April 10, 1912, the *Times* ran a front-page story reporting the team's failure.)

A final blow to the Sourdoughs' believability was struck in 1912, when Belmore Browne and Herschel Parker reported that they saw no evidence of the fourteen-foot flagpole during their attempt to climb Denali. Because Browne and Parker carefully documented their own ascent, great credibility was given to their point of view. In his report of the 1912 climb, Browne wrote:

> On our journey up the glacier from below we had begun to study the North Peak. . . . Every rock and snow slope of that approach had come into the field of our powerful binoculars. We not only saw no sign of the flagpole, but it is our concerted opinion that the northern peak is more inaccessible than its higher southern sister.

Though Browne intended only to disprove the Sourdoughs' claims, he ultimately paid them a great compliment by noting the greater difficulty faced in climbing the North Peak. Parker, meanwhile, was quoted as saying, "Dr. Cook didn't have anything on the Lloyd party when it comes to fabrications." Case closed. Or so it seemed at the time. The Sourdough story became generally accepted as nothing more than an Alaskan tale, until the following year.

In 1913, after a decade of unsuccessful attempts to reach the pinnacle of North America, an expedition led by Episcopal missionary Hudson Stuck placed all four of its members on Denali's 20,320-foot summit. And en route to the top, they spotted the Sourdoughs' flagpole.

The climbers made their exciting discovery from the Grand Basin, located between the North and South Peaks. In his mountaineering classic *The Ascent of Denali,* Stuck recalls:

> While we were resting . . . we fell to talking about the pioneer climbers of this mountain who claimed to have set a flagstaff near the summit of the North Peak—as to which feat a great deal of incredulity existed in Alaska for several reasons—and we renewed our determination that if the weather permitted when we had reached our goal and ascended the South Peak, we would climb the North Peak also to seek for traces of this earlier exploit on Denali. . . . All at once Walter [Harper] cried out: "I see the flagstaff!" Eagerly pointing to the rocky prominence nearest the summit—the summit itself covered with snow—he added: "I see it plainly!" [Harry] Karstens, looking where he pointed, saw it also and, whipping out the field glasses, one by one we all looked, and saw it distinctly standing out against the

sky. With the naked eye I was never able to see it unmistakably, but through the glasses it stood out, sturdy and strong, one side covered with crusted snow. We were greatly rejoiced that we could carry down positive confirmation of this matter.

When Stuck returned to Kantishna and told members of the Sourdough party about his team's sighting, "there was a feeling expressed that the climbing party of the previous summer [Belmore and Parker's group] must have seen it also and had suppressed mention of it." But Stuck concluded:

> There is no ground for such a damaging assumption. It would never be seen with the naked eye save by those who were intently searching for it. Professor Parker and Mr. Belmore Browne entertained the pretty general incredulity about the "Pioneer" ascent, perhaps too readily, certainly too confidently; but the men themselves must bear the chief blame for that. The writer and his party, knowing these men much better, have never [doubted] that some of them had accomplished what was claimed, and these details have been gone into for no other reason than that the honor may at last be given where honor is due.

It's especially worth noting that Stuck's party was the only group ever to verify the flagpole's existence. The next expedition to climb the North Peak, two decades later in 1932, failed to find any evidence of the pole.

Except for the one chance sighting, the Sourdoughs' story might always have been regarded as a tall tale. But thanks to the efforts of the 1913 expedition this group of skookum miners was finally and deservedly given credit for what Stuck called "a most extraordinary feat, unique—the writer has no hesitation in claiming—in all the annals of mountaineering."

Eighty-six years later, the Sourdoughs' achievement is still recognized as extraordinary. And certainly unique.

The Ascent of Denali

– HUDSON STUCK –

By 1912, eight expeditions had ascended Denali's slopes, but none had yet reached the summit of North America's highest mountain. Among those to fail were two of America's premier explorers and climbers: Dr. Frederick Cook (whose claims of reaching the top had been disproven) and Belmore Browne. Enter Hudson Stuck (1863–1920), a man unknown in mountaineering circles and, by his own admission, "no professed explorer, or climber or 'scientist,' but a missionary, and of these matters an amateur only." This amateur mountaineer would, in 1913, lead a team of four Alaskans to the mountain's top, a remarkable achievement recounted by Stuck in The Ascent of Denali.*

Stuck had climbed in Great Britain, the western United States, and the Canadian Rockies. But before Denali, the greatest height he'd reached was the top of Washington's 14,410-foot Mount Rainier. More concerned with men than mountains, he came to Alaska in 1904 to work as an Episcopal missionary with Alaska's Natives. As archdeacon of the Yukon, he visited Native settlements throughout Interior Alaska year-round.

Stuck's passion for mountain climbing was rekindled in 1906 by a view of Denali from Pedro Dome, near Fairbanks. "Dominating the whole scene...it shimmered in its pearly beauty and grew clearer and brighter as I gazed. What a glorious, broad, massive uplift that mountain is!" Five years later, he resolved to reach Denali's summit, or at least make a serious attempt. For companions, he picked three men experienced in dealing with ice and snow, though none was a mountaineer. Stuck's first choice was Harry Karstens, who'd been lured north from Illinois by the Klondike gold rush; he'd built a reputation as a first-rate explorer, woodsman, and backcountry traveler. The other two were Robert Tatum and Walter Harper, both twenty-one years old. Tatum, from Tennessee, worked with Stuck at the Episcopal mission in Nenana, while Harper, part Native, had served as Stuck's attendant, interpreter, dog team driver, and boat engineer. The team began its expedition at the village of Nenana—about ninety miles northeast of Denali—in mid-March and began moving up the mountain's north side, via the Muldrow Glacier, on April 18. They would reach the summit fifty days later, on June 7.

Two excerpts from Hudson Stuck's book are included here. One shows the logistical demands of an early twentieth-century expedition; the other describes the party's stay on the summit. The Ascent of Denali: A Narrative of the First Complete Ascent of the Highest Peak in North America *was first published by Scribner's in 1914 and reprinted in 1989 by the University of Nebraska Press's Bison Books.*

I: Preparation and Approach

. . . THE RESOLUTION TO ATTEMPT the ascent of Denali was reached a year and a half before it was put into execution: so much time was necessary for preparation. Almost any Alaskan enterprise that calls for supplies or equipment from the outside must be entered upon at least a year in advance. The plan followed had been adopted long before as the only wise one: that the supplies to be used upon the ascent be carried by water as near to the base of the mountain as could be reached and cached there in the summer, and that the climbing party go in with the dog teams as near the 1st March as practicable. Strangely enough, of all the expeditions that have essayed this ascent, the first, that of Judge Wickersham in 1903, and the last, ten years later, are the only ones that have approached their task in this natural and easy way. The others have all burdened themselves with the great and unnecessary difficulties of the southern slopes of the range.

It was proposed to use the mission launch *Pelican*, which has travelled close to twenty thousand miles on the Yukon and its tributaries in the six seasons she has been in commission, to transport the supplies up the Kantishna and Bearpaw Rivers to the head of navigation of the latter, when her cruise of 1912 was complete. But a serious mishap to the launch, which it was impossible to repair in Alaska, brought her activities for that season to a sudden end. So Mr. Karstens came down from Fairbanks with his launch, and a poling boat loaded with food staples, and, pushing the poling boat ahead, successfully ascended the rivers and carefully cached the stuff some fifty miles from the base of the mountain. It was done in a week or less.

Unfortunately, the equipment and supplies ordered from the outside did not arrive in time to go in with the bulk of the stuff. Although ordered in February, they arrived at Tanana only late in September, just in time to catch the last boat up to Nenana. And only half that had been ordered came at all—one of the two cases has not been traced to this day. Moreover, it was not until late the next February, when actually about to proceed on the expedition, that the writer was able to learn what items had come and what had not. Such are the difficulties of any undertaking in Alaska, despite all the precautions that foresight may dictate.

The silk tents, which had not come, had to be made in Fairbanks; the ice-axes sent were ridiculous gold-painted toys with detachable heads and broomstick handles—more like dwarf halberds than ice-axes; and at least two workmanlike axes were indispensable. So the head of an axe was sawn to the pattern of the writer's out of a piece of tool steel and a substantial hickory handle and an iron shank fitted to it at the machine-shop in Fairbanks. It served excellently well, while the points of the fancy axes from New York splintered the first time they were used. "Climbing irons," or "crampons," were also to make, no New York dealer being able to supply them.

One great difficulty was the matter of footwear. Heavy regulation-nailed alpine boots were sent—all too small to be worn with even a couple of pairs of socks, and therefore quite useless. Indeed, at that time there was no house in New York, or, so far as the writer knows, in the United States, where the standard alpine equipment could be procured. As a result of the dissatisfaction of this expedition with the material sent, one house in New York now carries in stock a good assortment of such things of standard pattern and quality. Fairbanks was ransacked for boots of any kind in which three or four pairs of socks could be worn. Alaska is a country of big men accustomed to the natural spread of the foot which a moccasin permits, but we could not find boots to our need save rubber snow-packs, and we bought half a dozen pairs of them (No. 12) and had leather soles fastened under them and nailed. Four pairs of alpine boots at eleven dollars a pair equals forty-four dollars. Six pairs of snow-packs at five dollars equals thirty dollars. Leather soles for them at three dollars equals eighteen dollars; which totalled ninety-two dollars—entirely wasted. We found that moccasins were the only practicable foot-gear; and we had to put *five* pairs of socks within them before we were done. But we did not know that at the time and had no means of discovering it.

All these matters were put in hand under Karstens's direction, while the writer, only just arrived in Fairbanks from Fort Yukon and Tanana, made a flying trip to the new mission at the Tanana Crossing, two hundred and fifty miles above Fairbanks, with Walter and the dog team; and most of them were finished by the time we returned. A multitude of small details kept us several days more in Fairbanks, so that nearly the middle of March had arrived before we were ready to make our start to the mountain, two weeks later than we had planned.

Karstens having joined us, we went down to the mission at Nenana (seventy-five miles) in a couple of days, and there two more days were spent overhauling and repacking the stuff that had come from the outside. In the way of food, we had imported only erbswurst, seventy-two four-ounce packages; milk chocolate, twenty pounds; compressed China tea in tablets (a most excellent tea with a very low percentage of tannin), five pounds; a specially selected grade of Smyrna figs, ten pounds; and sugared almonds, ten pounds—about seventy pounds' weight, all scrupulously reserved for the high-mountain work.

For trail equipment we had one eight-by-ten "silk" tent, used for two previous winters; three small circular tents of the same material, made in Fairbanks, for the high work; a Yukon stove; and the usual complement of pots and pans and dishes, including two admirable large aluminum pots for melting snow, used a number of years with great satisfaction. A "primus" stove, borrowed from the *Pelican*'s galley, was taken along for the high work. The bedding was mainly of down quilts, which are superseding fur robes and blankets for winter use because of their lightness and warmth and the small compass into which they may be compressed. Two pairs of camel's-hair blankets and one sleeping-bag lined with down and camel's-hair cloth were taken, and Karstens brought a great wolf-robe, weighing twenty-five pounds, of which we were glad enough later on.

Another team was obtained at the mission, and Mr. R. G. Tatum and the two boys, Johnny and Esaias, joined the company, which, thus increased to six persons, two sleds, and fourteen dogs, set out from Nenana across country to the Kantishna on St. Patrick's day.

Travelling was over the beaten trail to the Kantishna gold camp, one of the smallest of Alaskan camps, supporting about thirty men. In 1906 there was a wild stampede to this region, and two or three thousand people went in, chiefly from the Fairbanks district. Town after town was built—Diamond City, Glacier City, Bearpaw City, Roosevelt, McKinley City—all with elaborate saloons and gambling-places, one, at least, equipped with electric lights. But next summer the boom burst and all the thousands streamed out. Gold there was and is yet, but in small quantities only. The "cities" are mere collections of tumble-down huts amongst which the moose roam at will. Interior Alaska has many such abandoned "cities." The few men now in the district have placer claims that yield a "grub-stake" as a sure thing every summer, and spend their winters chiefly in prospecting for quartz. At Diamond City, on the Bearpaw, lay our cache of grub, and that place, some ninety miles from Nenana and fifty miles from the base of Denali, was our present objective point. It was bright, clear weather and the trail was good. For thirty miles our way lay across the wide flats of the Tanana Valley, and this stage brought us to the banks of the Nenana River. Another day of twenty-five miles of flats brought us to Knight's comfortable road-house and ranch on the Toklat, a tributary of the Kantishna, the only road-house this trail can now support. Several times during these two days we had clear glimpses of the great mountain we were approaching, and as we came out of the flat country, the "Sheephills," a foothill range of Denali, much broken and deeply sculptured, rose picturesquely before us. Our travel was now almost altogether on "overflow" ice, upon the surface of swift streams that freeze solidly over their riffles and shallows and thus deny passage under the ice to the water of fountains and springs that never ceases flowing. So it bursts forth and flows *over* the ice with a continually renewing surface of the smoothest texture. Carrying a mercurial barometer that one dare not intrust to a sled on one's back over such footing is a somewhat precarious proceeding, but there was no alternative, and many miles were thus passed. Up the Toklat, then up its Clearwater Fork, then up its tributary, Myrtle Creek, to its head, and so over a little divide and down Willow Creek, we went, and from that divide and the upper reaches of the last-named creek had fine, clear views not only of Denali but of Denali's Wife as well, now come much nearer and looming much larger.

But here it may be stated once for all that the view which this face of the mountains presents is never a satisfying one. The same is true in even greater degree of the southern face, all photographs agreeing with all travellers as to its tameness. There is only one face of the Denali group that is completely satisfying, that is adequate to the full picturesque potentiality of a twenty-thousand-foot elevation. The writer has seen no other view, no other aspect of it, comparable to that of the northwest face from Lake Minchúmina. There the two mountains rise side by side, sheer, precipitous, pointed rocks, utterly inaccessible, savage, and superb. The rounded shoulders, the receding slopes and ridges of the other faces detract from the uplift and from the dignity, but the northwestern face is stark.

One more run, of much the same character as the previous day, and we were at Eureka, in the heart of the Kantishna country, on Friday, 21st March, being Good Friday.

We arrived there at noon and "called it a day," and spent the rest of it in the devotions of that august anniversary. Easter eve took us to Glacier City, and we lay there over the feast, gathering three or four men who were operating a prospecting-drill in that neighborhood for the first public worship ever conducted in the Kantishna camp. Ten miles more brought us to Diamond City, on the Bearpaw, where we found our cache of food in good condition save that the field-mice, despite all precautions, had made access to the cereals and had eaten all the rolled oats.

Amongst the Kantishna miners, who were most kindly and generous in their assistance, we were able to pick up enough large-sized moccasins to serve the members of the party, and we wore nothing else at all on the mountain.

Our immediate task now lay before us. A ton and a half of supplies had to be hauled some fifty miles across country to the base of the mountain. Here the relaying began, stuff being taken ahead and cached at some midway point, then another load taken right through a day's march, and then a return made to bring up the cache. In this way we moved steadily though slowly across rolling country and upon the surface of a large lake to the McKinley Fork of the Kantishna, which drains the Muldrow Glacier, down that stream to its junction with the Clearwater Fork of the same, and up that fork, through its canyon, to the last spruce timber on its banks, and there we made a camp in an exceedingly pretty spot. The creek ran open through a break in the ice in front of our tent; the water-ousels darted in and out under the ice, singing most sweetly; the willows, all in bud, perfumed the air; and Denali soared clear and brilliant, far above the range, right in front of us. Here at the timber-line, at an elevation of about two thousand feet, was the pleasantest camp of the whole excursion. During the five days' stay here the stuff was brought up and carried forward, and a quantity of dry wood was cut and advanced to a cache at the mouth of the creek by which we should reach the Muldrow Glacier.

It should be said that the short and easy route by which that glacier is reached was discovered after much scouting and climbing by McGonogill and Taylor in 1910, upon the occasion of the "pioneer" [Sourdough Expedition] attempt upon the mountain, of which more will be said by and by. The men in the Kantishna camp who took part in that attempt gave us all the information they possessed, as they had done to the party that attempted the mountain last summer. There has been no need to make reconnaissance for routes since these pioneers blazed the way: there is no other practicable route than the one they discovered. The two subsequent climbing parties have followed precisely in their footsteps up as far as the Grand Basin at sixteen thousand feet, and it is the merest justice that such acknowledgment be made.

At our camp the Clearwater ran parallel with the range, which rose like a great wall before us. Our approach was not directly toward Denali but toward an opening in the range six or eight miles to the east of the great mountain. This opening is known as Cache Creek. Passing the willow patch at its mouth, where previous camps had been made, we pushed up the creek some three miles more to its forks, and there established our base camp, on 10th April, at about four thousand feet elevation. A few scrubby willows struggled to grow in the creek bed, but the hills that rose from one thousand five hundred to two thousand feet around us were bare of any vegetation save moss and were yet in the main covered with snow. Caribou signs were plentiful everywhere, and we were no more than settled in camp when a herd appeared in sight.

Our prime concern at this camp was the gathering and preserving of a sufficient meat supply for our subsistence on the mountain. It was an easy task. First Karstens killed a caribou and then Walter a mountain-sheep. Then Esaias happened into the midst of a herd of caribou as he climbed over a ridge, and killed three. That was all we needed. Then we went to work preparing the meat. Why should any one haul canned pemmican hundreds of miles into the greatest game country in the world? We made our own pemmican of the choice parts of this tender, juicy meat and we never lost appetite for it or failed to enjoy and assimilate it. A fifty-pound lard-can, three parts filled with water, was set on the stove and kept supplied with joints of meat. As a batch was cooked we took it out and put more into the same water, removed the flesh from the bones, and minced it. Then we melted a can of butter, added pepper and salt to it, and rolled a handful of the minced meat in the butter and moulded it with the hands into a ball about as large as a baseball. We made a couple of hundred of such balls and froze them, and they kept perfectly. When all the boiling was done we put in the hocks of the animals and boiled down the liquor into five pounds of the thickest, richest meat-extract jelly, adding the marrow from the bones. With this pemmican and this extract of caribou, a package of erbswurst and a cupful of rice, we concocted every night the stew which was our main food in the higher regions.

Here the instruments were overhauled. The mercurial barometer reading by verniers to three places of decimals was set up and read, and the two aneroids were adjusted to read with it. . . .

Meanwhile, the relaying of the supplies and the wood to the base camp had gone on, and the advancing of it to a cache at the pass by which we should gain the Muldrow Glacier. On 15th April Esaias and one of the teams were sent back to Nenana. Almost all the stuff we should move was already at this cache, and the need for the two dog teams was over. More-over, the trails were rapidly breaking up, and it was necessary for the boy to travel by night instead of by day on his return trip. Johnny and the other dog team we kept, because we designed to use the dogs up to the head of the glacier, and the boy to keep the base camp and tend the dogs, when this was done, until our return. So we said good-by to Esaias, and he took out the last word that was received from us in more than two months.

The photograph of the base camp shows a mountainous ridge stretching across much of the background. That ridge belongs to the outer wall of the Muldrow Glacier and indicates its general direction. Just beyond the picture, to the right, the ridge breaks down, and the little valley in the middle distance sweeps around, becomes a steep, narrow gulch, and ends at the breach in the glacier wall. This breach, thus reached, is the pass which the Kantishna miners of the "pioneer" expedition discovered and named "McPhee Pass," after a Fairbanks saloon-keeper. The name should stand. There is no other pass by which the glacier can be reached; certainly none at all above, and probably no convenient one below. Unless this pass were used, it would be necessary to make the long and difficult journey to the snout of the glacier, some twenty miles farther to the east, cross its rough terminal moraine, and traverse all its lower stretch.

On the 11th April Karstens and I wound our way up the narrow, steep defile for about three miles from the base camp and came to our first sight of the Muldrow Glacier, some two thousand five hundred feet above camp and six thousand three hundred feet above the sea. That day stands out in recollection as one of the notable days of the whole ascent. There the glacier stretched away, broad and level—the road to the heart of the mountain, and as our eyes traced its course our spirits leaped up that at last we were entered upon our real task. One of us, at least, knew something of the dangers and difficulties its apparently smooth surface concealed, yet to both of us it had an infinite attractiveness, for it was the highway of desire.

V: The Ultimate Height

We lay down for a few hours on the night of the 6th June, resolved to rise at three in the morning for our attempt upon the summit of Denali. At supper Walter had made a desperate effort to use some of our ten pounds of flour in the manufacture of "noodles" with which to thicken the stew. We had continued to pack that flour and had made effort after effort to cook it in some eatable way, but without success. The sour dough would not ferment, and we had no baking-powder. *Is* there any way to cook flour under such circumstances? But he made the noodles too large and did not cook them enough, and they wrought internal havoc upon those who partook of them. Three of the four of us were unwell all night. The digestion is certainly more delicate and more easily disturbed at great altitudes than at the lower levels. While Karstens and Tatum were tossing uneasily in the bedclothes, the writer sat up with a blanket round his shoulders, crouching over the primus stove, with the thermometer at –21°F outdoors. Walter alone was at ease, with digestive and somnolent capabilities proof against any invasion. It was, of course, broad daylight all night. At three the company was aroused, and, after partaking of a very light breakfast indeed, we sallied forth into the brilliant, clear morning with not a cloud in the sky. The only packs we carried that day were the instruments and the lunch. The sun was shining, but a keen north wind was blowing and the thermometer stood at –4°F. We were rather a sorry company. Karstens still had internal pains; Tatum and I had severe headaches. Walter was the only one feeling entirely himself, so Walter was put in the lead and in the lead he remained all day.

We took a straight course up the great snow ridge directly south of our camp and then around the peak into which it rises; quickly told but slowly and most laboriously done. It was necessary to make the traverse high up on this peak instead of around its base, so much had its ice and snow been shattered by the earthquake on the lower portions. Once around this peak, there rose before us the horseshoe ridge which carries the ultimate height of Denali, a horseshoe ridge of snow opening to the east with a low snow peak at either end, the centre of the ridge soaring above both peaks. Above us was nothing visible but snow; the rocks were all beneath, the last rocks standing at about 19,000 feet. Our progress was exceedingly slow. It was bitterly cold; all the morning toes and fingers were without sensation, kick them and beat them as we would. We were all clad in full winter hand and foot gear—more gear than had sufficed at 50° below zero on the Yukon trail. Within the writer's No. 16 moccasins were three pairs of heavy hand-knitted woollen socks, two pairs of camel's-hair socks, and a pair of thick felt socks; while underneath them, between them and the iron "creepers," were the soles cut from a pair of felt shoes. Upon his hands were a pair of the thickest Scotch wool gloves, thrust inside huge lynx-paw mitts lined with Hudson Bay duffle. His moose-hide breeches and shirt, worn all the winter on the trail, were worn throughout this climb; over the shirt was a thick sweater and over all the usual Alaskan "parkee" amply furred around the hood; underneath was a suit of the heaviest Jaeger underwear—yet until nigh noon feet were like lumps of iron and fingers were constantly numb. That north wind was cruelly cold, and there can be no possible question that cold is felt much more keenly in the thin air of nineteen thousand feet than it is below. But the north wind was really our friend, for nothing but a north wind will drive all vapor from this mountain. Karstens beat his feet so violently and so continually against the hard snow to restore the circulation that two of his toe-nails sloughed off afterward.

By eleven o'clock we had been climbing for six hours and were well around the peak, advancing toward the horseshoe ridge, but even then there were grave doubts if we should succeed in reaching it that day, it was so cold. A hint from any member of the party that his feet were actually freezing—a hint expected all along—would have sent us all back. When there is no sensation left in the feet at all it is, however, difficult to be quite sure if they be actually freezing or not—and each one was willing to give the attempt upon the summit the benefit of the doubt. What should we have done with the ordinary leather climbing boots? But once entirely around the peak we were in a measure sheltered from the north wind, and the sun full upon us gave more warmth. It was hereabouts, and not, surely, at the point indicated in the photograph in Mr. Belmore Browne's book [*The Conquest of Mount McKinley*], that the climbing party of last year was driven back by the blizzard that descended upon them when close to their goal. Not until we had stopped for lunch and had drunk the scalding tea from the thermos bottles, did we all begin to have confidence that this day would see the completion of the ascent. But the writer's shortness of breath became more and more distressing as he rose. The familiar fits of panting took a more acute form; at such times everything would turn black before his eyes and he would choke and gasp and seem unable to get breath at all. Yet a few moments' rest restored him completely, to struggle on another twenty or thirty paces and to sink gasping upon the snow again. All were more affected in the breathing than they had been at any time before—it was curious to see every man's mouth open for breathing—but none of the others in this distressing way. Before the traverse around the peak just mentioned, Walter had noticed the writer's growing discomfort and had insisted upon assuming the mercurial barometer. The boy's eager kindness was gladly accepted and the instrument was surrendered. So it did not fall to the writer's credit to carry the thing to the top as he had wished.

The climbing grew steeper and steeper; the slope that had looked easy from below now seemed to shoot straight up. For the most part the climbing-irons gave us sufficient footing, but here and there we came to softer snow, where they would not take sufficient hold and we had to cut steps. The calks in these climbing-irons were about an inch and a quarter long; we wished they had been two inches. The creepers are a great advantage in the matter of speed, but they need long points. They are not so safe as step-cutting, and there is the ever-present danger that unless one is exceedingly careful one will step upon the rope with them and their sharp calks sever some of the strands. They were, however, of great assistance and saved a deal of laborious step-cutting.

At last the crest of the ridge was reached and we stood well above the two peaks that mark the ends of the horseshoe.

Also it was evident that we were well above the great North Peak across the Grand Basin. Its crest had been like an index on the snow beside us as we climbed, and we stopped for a few moments when it seemed that we were level with it. We judged it to be about five hundred feet lower than the South Peak.

But still there stretched ahead of us, and perhaps one hundred feet above us, another small ridge with a north and south pair of little haycock summits. This is the real top of Denali. From below, this ultimate ridge merges indistinguishably with the crest of the horseshoe ridge, but it is not a part of it but a culminating ridge beyond it. With keen excitement we pushed on. Walter, who had been in the lead all day, was the first to scramble up; a native Alaskan, he is the first human being to set foot upon the top of Alaska's great mountain, and he had well earned the lifelong distinction. Karstens and Tatum were hard upon his heels, but the last man on the rope, in his enthusiasm and excitement somewhat overpassing his narrow wind margin, had almost to be hauled up the last few feet, and fell unconscious for a moment upon the floor of the little snow basin that occupies the top of the mountain. This, then, is the actual summit, a little crater-like snow basin, sixty or sixty-five feet long and twenty to twenty-five feet wide, with a haycock of snow at either end—the south one a little higher than the north. On the southwest this little basin is much corniced, and the whole thing looked as though every severe storm might somewhat change its shape.

So soon as wind was recovered we shook hands all round and a brief prayer of thanksgiving to Almighty God was said, that He had granted us our hearts' desire and brought us safely to the top of His great mountain.

This prime duty done, we fell at once to our scientific tasks. The instrument-tent was set up, the mercurial barometer, taken out of its leather case and then out of its wooden case, was swung upon its tripod and a rough zero established, and it was left awhile to adjust itself to conditions before a reading was attempted. It was a great gratification to get it to the top uninjured. The boiling-point apparatus was put together and its candle lighted under the ice which filled its little cistern. The three-inch, three-circle aneroid was read at once at thirteen and two-tenths inches, its mendacious altitude scale confidently pointing at twenty-three thousand three hundred feet. Half an hour later it had dropped to 13.175 inches and had shot us up another one hundred feet into the air. Soon the water was boiling in the little tubes of the boiling-point thermometer and the steam pouring out of the vent. The thread of mercury rose to 174.9° and stayed there. There is something definite and uncompromising about the boiling-point hypsometer; no tapping will make it rise or fall; it reaches its mark unmistakably and does not budge. The reading of the mercurial barometer is a slower and more delicate business. It takes a good light and a good sight to tell when the ivory zero-point is exactly touching the surface of the mercury in the cistern; it takes care and precision to get the vernier exactly level with the top of the column. It was read, some half-hour after it was set up, at 13.617 inches. The alcohol minimum thermometer stood at 7°F. all the while we were on top. Meanwhile, Tatum had been reading a round of angles with the prismatic compass. He could not handle it with sufficient exactness with his mitts on, and he froze his fingers doing it bare-handed.

The scientific work accomplished, then and not till then did we indulge ourselves in the wonderful prospect that stretched around us. It was a perfectly clear day, the sun shining brightly in the sky, and naught bounded our view save the natural limitations of vision. Immediately before us, in the direction in which we had climbed, lay—nothing: a void, a sheer gulf many thousands of feet deep, and one shrank back instinctively from the little parapet of the snow basin when one had glanced at the awful profundity. Across the gulf, about three thousand feet beneath us and fifteen or twenty miles away, sprang most splendidly into view the great mass of Denali's Wife, or Mount Foraker, as some white men misname her, filling majestically all the middle distance. It was our first glimpse of her during the whole ascent. Denali's Wife does not appear at all save from the actual summit of Denali, for she is completely hidden by his South Peak until the moment when his South Peak is surmounted. And never was nobler sight displayed to man than that great, isolated mountain spread out completely, with all its spurs and ridges, its cliffs and its glaciers, lofty and mighty and yet far beneath us. On that spot one understood why the view of Denali from Lake Minchúmina is the grand view, for the west face drops abruptly down with nothing but that vast void from the top to nigh the bottom of the mountain. Beyond stretched, blue and vague to the southwest, the wide valley of the Kuskokwim, with an end of all mountains. To the north we looked right over the North Peak to the foot-hills below, patched with lakes and lingering snow, glittering with streams. We had hoped to see the junction of the Yukon and Tanana Rivers, one hundred and fifty miles away to the northwest, as we had often and often seen the summit of Denali from that point in the winter, but the haze that almost always qualifies a fine summer day inhibited that stretch of vision. Perhaps the forest-fires we found raging on the Tanana River were already beginning to foul the northern sky.

It was, however, to the south and the east that the most marvellous prospect opened before us. What infinite tangle of mountain ranges filled the whole scene, until gray sky, gray mountain, and gray sea merged in the ultimate distance! The near-by peaks and ridges stood out with dazzling distinction, the glaciation, the drainage, the relation of each part to the others all revealed. The snow-covered tops of the remoter peaks, dwindling and fading, rose to our view as though floating in thin air when their bases were hidden by the haze, and the beautiful crescent curve of the whole Alaskan range exhibited itself from Denali to the sea. To the right hand the glittering, tiny threads of streams draining the mountain range into the Chulitna and Susitna Rivers, and so to Cook's Inlet and the Pacific Ocean, spread themselves out; to the left the affluents of the Kantishna and the Nenana drained the range into the Yukon and Bering Sea.

Yet the chief impression was not of our connection with the earth so far below, its rivers and its seas, but rather of detachment from it. We seemed alone upon a dead world, as dead as the mountains on the moon. Only once before can the writer remember a similar feeling of being neither in the world or of the world, and that was at the bottom of the Grand Cañon of the Colorado, in Arizona, its savage granite walls as dead as this savage peak of ice.

Above us the sky took a blue so deep that none of us had ever gazed upon a midday sky like it before. It was a deep, rich, lustrous, transparent blue, as dark as a Prussian blue, but intensely blue; a hue so strange, so increasingly impressive, that to one at least it "seemed like special news of

God," as a new poet sings. We first noticed the darkening tint of the upper sky in the Grand Basin, and it deepened as we rose. Tyndall observed and discussed this phenomenon in the Alps, but it seems scarcely to have been mentioned since.

It is difficult to describe at all the scene which the top of the mountain presented, and impossible to describe it adequately. One was not occupied with the thought of description but wholly possessed with the breadth and glory of it, with its sheer, amazing immensity and scope. Only once, perhaps, in any lifetime is such vision granted, certainly never before had been vouchsafed to any of us. Not often in the summertime does Denali completely unveil himself and dismiss the clouds from all the earth beneath. Yet we could not linger, unique though the occasion, dearly bought our privilege; the miserable limitations of the flesh gave us continual warning to depart; we grew colder and still more wretchedly cold. The thermometer stood at 7° in the full sunshine, and the north wind was keener than ever. My fingers were so cold that I would not venture to withdraw them from the mittens to change the film in the camera, and the other men were in like case; indeed, our hands were by this time so numb as to make it almost impossible to operate a camera at all. A number of photographs had been taken, though not half we should have liked to take, but it is probable that, however many more exposures had been made, they would have been little better than those we got. Our top-of-the-mountain photography was a great disappointment. One thing we learned: exposures at such altitude should be longer than those below, perhaps owing to the darkness of the sky.

When the mercurial barometer had been read the tent was thrown down and abandoned, the first of the series of abandonments that marked our descent from the mountain. The tent-pole was used for a moment as a flagstaff while Tatum hoisted a little United States flag he had patiently and skilfully constructed in our camps below out of two silk handkerchiefs and the cover of a sewing-bag. Then the pole was put to its permanent use. It had already been carved with a suitable inscription, and now a transverse piece, already prepared and fitted, was lashed securely to it and it was planted on one of the little snow turrets of the summit—the sign of our redemption, high above North America. Only some peaks in the Andes and some peaks in the Himalayas rise above it in all the world. It was of light, dry birch and, though six feet in length, so slender that we think it may weather many a gale. And Walter thrust it into the snow so firmly at a blow that it could not be withdrawn again. Then we gathered about it and said the *Te Deum*.

It was 1:30 PM when we reached the summit and two minutes past three when we left; yet so quickly had the time flown that we could not believe we had been an hour and a half on top. The journey down was a long, weary grind, the longer and the wearier that we made a détour and went out of our way to seek for Professor Parker's thermometer, which he had left [from a previous expedition] "in a crack on the west side of the last boulder of the northeast ridge." That sounds definite enough, yet in fact it is equivocal. "Which is the last boulder?" we disputed as we went down the slope. A long series of rocks almost in line came to an end, with one rock a little below the others, a little out of the line. This egregious boulder would, it seemed to me, naturally be called the last; Karstens thought not—thought the "last boulder" was the last *on* the ridge. As we learned later, Karstens was right, and since he yielded to me we did not find the thermometer, for, having descended to this isolated rock, we would not climb up again for fifty thermometers. One's disappointment is qualified by the knowledge that the thermometer is probably not of adequate scale, Professor Parker's recollection being that it read only to 60° below zero, F. A lower temperature than this is recorded every winter on the Yukon River.

A thermometer reading to 100° below zero, left at this spot, would, in my judgment, perhaps yield a lower minimum than has ever yet been authentically recorded on earth, and it is most unfortunate that the opportunity was lost. Yet I did not leave my own alcohol minimum—scaled to 95° below zero, and yielding, by estimation, perhaps ten degrees below the scaling—there, because of the difficulty of giving explicit directions that should lead to its ready recovery, and at the close of such a day of toil as is involved in reaching the summit, men have no stomach for prolonged search. As will be told, it is cached lower down, but at a spot where it cannot be missed.

However, for one, the writer was largely unconscious of weariness in that descent. All the way down, my thoughts were occupied with the glorious scene my eyes had gazed upon and should gaze upon never again. In all human probability I would never climb that mountain again; yet if I climbed it a score more times I would never be likely to repeat such vision. Commonly, only for a few hours at a time, never for more than a few days at a time, save in the dead of winter when climbing is out of the question, does Denali completely unveil himself and dismiss the clouds from all the earth below him. Not for long, with these lofty colds contiguous, will the vapors of Cook's Inlet and Prince William Sound and the whole North Pacific Ocean refrain from sweeping upward; their natural trend is hitherward. As the needle turns to the magnet so the clouds find an irresistible attraction in this great mountain mass, and though the inner side of the range be rid of them the sea side is commonly filled to overflowing.

Only those who have for long years cherished a great and almost inordinate desire, and have had that desire gratified to the limit of their expectation, can enter into the deep thankfulness and content that filled the heart upon the descent of this mountain. There was no pride of conquest, no trace of that exultation of victory some enjoy upon the first ascent of a lofty peak, no gloating over good fortune that had hoisted us a few hundred feet higher than others who had struggled and been discomfited. Rather was the feeling that a privileged communion with the high places of the earth had been granted; that not only had we been permitted to lift up eager eyes to these summits, secret and solitary since the world began, but to enter boldly upon them, to take place, as it were, domestically in their hitherto sealed chambers, to inhabit them, and to cast our eyes down from them, seeing all things as they spread out from the windows of heaven itself. . . .

The South Buttress of Mt. McKinley

– RICCARDO CASSIN –

On the south side of Denali rises a steep, 9,000-foot-high granite and ice spine that dissects the mountain's South Face and leads directly from the glaciers below to its summit. Early mountaineers had labeled this precipitous route impossible to climb, but while conducting aerial photographic surveys of Denali in the 1930s and 1940s, visionary mountaineer and cartographer Bradford Washburn became convinced it could in fact be done.

Years later, in the 1956–57 issue of Mountain World, Washburn proposed several new routes to Denali's summit and wrote that "probably the most difficult and dramatic of all potential new routes on Mount McKinley is the great central bulge on the fabulous 10,000-foot South Face of the mountain. . . . This route may be classed as unequivocally excellent climbing from start to finish." Despite Washburn's inspired commentary, the South Face's great central bulge remained untested until 1961, when a climbing party representing the Italian Alpine Club paid a visit to the mountain.

The Italian expedition had been organized by Carlo Mauri, a talented climber and mountaineering guide who three years earlier had made the first ascent of Gasherbrum IV, a 26,000-foot Himalayan peak. In planning for the *trip, Mauri recruited the legendary Riccardo Cassin to spearhead the most difficult and dangerous route yet attempted in Alaska. During the 1930s, Cassin had built a reputation as one of Europe's most brilliant alpinists, becoming the first climber to ascend three of the Alps' most difficult and dangerous north-face routes: the Grandes Jorasses, Piz Badile, and Cima Ovest di Lavaredo. By 1961, Cassin was in his fifties, but he was still greatly respected for his toughness and mountaineering intelligence. As Italian climber Fosco Maraini put it, "There is something indestructible about this man; Paleolithic and Neanderthalish. Climbing with him you sense an inner force utterly alien to our complicated, mechanized, intellectualized world."*

Cassin was eventually named the expedition's leader; Mauri, meanwhile, dropped out after suffering a severe injury while skiing. Joining Cassin were five young Italians belonging to the elite Spider climbing club based in the town of Lecco. Of the six, only Cassin and Giancarlo (Jack) Canali had high-altitude experience. Also invited was Bob Goodwin, a noted American mountaineer.

Riccardo Cassin's account, "The South Buttress of Mt. McKinley," is taken from his book 50 Years of Alpinism, *published in 1981 by The Mountaineers in Seattle.*

IN 1961, I MADE MY FIRST VISIT to North America, with the ambitious plan of mounting a bid to climb the South Face of Mt. McKinley. North America is a land which for us Europeans still represents something fabulous, in terms of its history, its men, its level of progress, and its spirit of freedom. Mt. McKinley (20,322 ft./6,194 meters), the highest mountain in North America, is located in the remote and mysterious, yet rich and splendid land of Alaska. It was Carlo Mauri who fired the imagination of our CAI section with the idea of the expedition, but a serious skiing accident prevented his participation. With Pietro Meciani's valuable help, we contacted Dr. Bradford Washburn, director of the Museum of Science in Boston. He knew the mountain well, and suggested the magnificent and unclimbed South Face.

The news that a French expedition had the same project in mind compelled us to act fast. The five mountaineers whom I was to lead were chosen. They were young climbing friends whose technical ability and commitment I valued: Giancarlo (Jack) Canali, Gigi Alippi, Romano Perego, Luigino Airoldi, and Annibale Zucchi. As soon as the equipment had been prepared and shipped off, I went on ahead of the other members of the expedition for organizational reasons. Romano Perego and I left from Malpensa on June 5 and we reached Boston after a few hours' stopover in New York.

Dr. Washburn showed me his magnificent collection of maps and photographs of Mt. McKinley, and gave us first hand information that immediately clarified the potential difficulties of the face. His hospitality was both cordial and handsome: after dinner, he showed me his stereo-scopic pictures of McKinley, which enabled me to assess the steepness of the various facets of the mountain. Our friends were arriving in Anchorage five or six days later, so our host advised us to take advantage of the time by visiting New York. We wandered through the streets of this immense city, stopping a little confused in the squares, raising our eyes to the impressive walls of its skyscrapers, fascinated by these man-made spires and towers.

On June 9 we reached Anchorage, and were met at the airport by Mr. Dinielli, an Italian resident. In his house we felt the atmosphere of our own distant homes, and again I was touched by the warmth of our reception.

On June 11, I met the intrepid pilot Don Sheldon who was going to fly us to an area near the base of the East Kahiltna Glacier, in his small plane equipped with snow skids. I also contacted Gianni Stocco, a building contractor from home who lived and worked in Anchorage, and enlisted his help to locate our equipment. Both Stocco and Armando Petrecca, an Italian-American from New York, declared themselves passionate climbers and wanted to join our expedition; but I withheld judgment for a couple of days to see what they could do before agreeing to this. By previous agreement, Bob Goodwin, a well-known North American mountaineer, should have joined us, but we had heard no news from him and thought him unable to come. Because of this, I decided to take Stocco and Petrecca with us.

I then flew to Talkeetna, the last small centre of habitation on our journey, in Don Sheldon's plane. Passing over the Mt. McKinley area, I saw close up for the first time our South Face, a grand and imposing sweep of rock and ice. I returned to Anchorage and the following day the other members of the expedition arrived. The equipment, however, was still in transit. In New York, they told me, they had met my dear old friend, Ernani Faé, a rock climber and worthy protagonist in our younger years. I promised myself to say hello to him on the way back.

In the days that followed, we managed to transfer the men and equipment, first to Talkeetna, and then to a glacier near the foot of the face, at the spot I had chosen with Dr. Washburn's help. This could be reached with Sheldon's plane and was the closest point to the actual climb. Bob Goodwin, who had just returned from an ascent on Mt. Russell, now joined us, so our group comprised nine members. Sheldon's experience and ability allowed us to transfer everything gradually to the field of operations. Some of the equipment was dropped four kilometers higher up to ease our movements as much as possible and lessen our work. But the spot where Sheldon left us was not quite where we had calculated from the topographic map, for we could not land at the right place because of the snow conditions. Naturally, this created a more difficult situation for us because, from the North-East Kahiltna Glacier where we were, with the equipment deposited four kilometers higher, we had to move to the East Kahiltna. Jack Canali, Gigi Alippi, and Bob Goodwin began the work of moving the equipment while Don Sheldon and I returned to Talkeetna, where the others had remained. The weather was so bad that flying was impossible; we had to wait until the 24th, before Sheldon could both fly and land again.

Preparations at Base Camp were now in their most active phase: provisions, equipment, climbing materials, tents, and fuel had been accumulated there. We worked until 9 PM because at that latitude it never really gets dark in summer. In a spirit of self-sacrifice and enthusiasm, each one of us did what he could: we knew that everything now depended on us and only on us. A small, inhabited world came to life, a miraculous contrast to our savage frozen surroundings. Above us loomed McKinley's South Face, which I studied frequently, weighing it up, learning its tiniest secrets.

In these first days before the attack, I quickly became aware that whilst Bob Goodwin was totally competent, Petrecca and Stocco were completely unready for such a hazardous enterprise. Bluntly I tried to convince them to withdraw because they were unprepared physically, technically, and psychologically. It would have been an unforgivable weakness on my part to take them with us. They gave no impression of being able to look after themselves, especially under those particular environmental conditions. On this subject, I should like to stress that a real mountaineer, properly prepared, must always be potentially able to help others when difficulties overcome them.

We were ready to attack the face but the weather remained unfavourable. On the first three days of July it snowed and we were forced to wait: we only managed to reach the landing strip to gather some equipment for our tents at Base Camp. But as well as making our preparations for the thrilling prospect of climbing Mt. McKinley by such a difficult route, we were kept busy by a multitude of simple everyday chores like sweeping tents, shovelling snow, cooking, keeping our personal gear in order, and writing home. In addition, as head of the expedition, I had to act as head of the family and keep everyone's spirits high, be a doctor if necessary, keep the diary, and correspond with our club and our friend Ernani Faé, who had to be kept up to date with the expedition's progress for the newspapers. Cooking also provided a diversion. Pressured by Gigi and Luigino, I cooked a dinner with some fat trout we had caught during our enforced wait in Talkeetna. We had been able to preserve them in our glacial "refrigerator," and they now provided a spectacular and morale-boosting feast that was greatly appreciated by everyone.

Goodwin, an excellent fellow, shared a tent with me. It was a pity we didn't understand each other, for we were unable to talk and keep each other company; my companion spent all his free time asleep. With the weather still bad we couldn't start on anything constructive. One development, not unwelcome considering the serious nature of our objective, was that Stocco and Petrecca eventually understood that the difficulties were too much for them and decided to return to Anchorage. On July 4 they descended to the landing strip to wait for Don Sheldon to pick them up while we, at the end of another day spent transporting equipment to Base Camp, converged on the tents, where Airoldi and Goodwin had prepared another good dinner. We discussed our programme for the following days, praying for some decent weather.

At noon on Wednesday July 6, as soon as we saw some sunshine, we decided to attack the big couloir that led up to the foot of the ridge, taking it on the right where there were some exposed rocks. But we had barely reached a small couloir among the broken rocks when it started to snow. Nevertheless, we managed to fix ropes on all the completed section. The evening was spent in the usual conversations and discussions; it was a pity that none of us could sing and draw the others in. On Gasherbrum,

Mauri, Bonatti, Gobbi, and Zeni often sang, and nothing seemed better able to raise our spirits.

The weather was beautiful the next day, but a huge dark cloud at the bottom of the valley seemed to be warning us against boldness: we feared that the weather might still be unsettled. We climbed the couloir on the fixed ropes, heavily loaded, passed the previous day's high point, and attacked a new section of rock covered in verglas: Jack was leading and had to work exhaustingly hard to get over it. Gigi then took the lead on a section which was even more difficult. In the meantime, as we expected, it started to snow, but we kept on climbing. Gigi found himself faced with first an overhang which he climbed with a point of aid, then an enormous granite bulge. He told us it was impossible to go any further that way.

I told Perego to cross over to the left, where the chances seemed better, and when he stopped, I joined him to check for myself. We were at a col on the ridge but the mist had meanwhile thickened, and it was late: better to go down and try again next day.

By now I had realised that the couloir we had climbed was not the one marked on the map by Dr. Washburn, at an altitude of 11,690 ft., but an adjacent one which started 200 meters further up the glacier.

Reaching Base Camp, we found Luigino, who had recovered from a slight indisposition, and Goodwin, who had just returned from the landing site with a heavy load of food and a tent. When we began climbing again Goodwin joined us, while Luigino went to the landing site to wait for Sheldon. As it turned out he was too late: Sheldon had dropped the mail and left. We quickly reached the previous day's high point, on the col. The route from here was not obvious. As planned, Annibale, Gigi, Jack, and Romano went on, keeping to the left. In the meantime Goodwin and I found a suitable spot, cached a small supply of food and equipment, and returned to Base. This lower section of the ridge was proving to be very difficult and complex. Until we had overcome it and broken out to the snow ridges and the glacier above, it was useless and dangerous to continue climbing all together. It was better to divide ourselves up and alternate attack with rest, taking into consideration the physical condition of each individual climber. On our way down to Base Camp, while the others were trying to force the route to the left, I thought I saw another possibility. Annibale, Romano, and I went to check it out, but unfortunately it was not feasible. The South Face of McKinley was presenting all the uncertainty and difficulty I had foreseen as soon as I had set eyes on it.

We planned to try again in the place we had previously given up. However, the weather still refused to clear, and it was still snowing. Our "lil-ion" equipment was even more precious under those conditions: snow slid off the material, while the ropes did not absorb moisture and so did not freeze. Once again we went down to Base Camp without any noticeable progress.

On the morning of July 8, Jack Canali, Gigi Alippi, and Luigino Airoldi were back on the face again and managed to reach a diedre to the left of a prominent rock prow with some Grade 4 and 5 climbing. The diedre was out of the question, being very steep, but they finally saw a solution to the problem: it was possible to climb down into a steep couloir which led directly to a col behind the obvious tower on the ridge above, just below the sharp snow crest that led directly to the small glacier halfway up the ridge. This could be seen clearly even on the topographic map which Dr. Washburn had kindly given us. First they rappelled down, crossed the couloir, which was vertical at that point, then climbed up some icy rifts and short walls to rejoin the couloir above the steep section. Suddenly, thanks to a brief clearing in the sky—doubly lucky since it was still snowing—they could see above the new col to the end of the big couloir and, though they considered the difficulties not less than Grade 4, realized they could reach it.

Next day Jack and Gigi were climbing again, for Annibale had slight conjunctivitis and Romano a mild infection on his hands. Goodwin joined them, jumping enthusiastically at my suggestion. I had to stay at Base Camp to finish several letters and reorganize the film shot in the previous days.

That night a violent wind made us fear for our tents: the sun finally appeared on the horizon, but at the bottom of the valley were the usual clouds symptomatic of unstable weather. Nevertheless, my three companions left at 7 AM. The wind howled on while I was finishing the correspondence, and even increased. By 5 PM it was so strong that it almost flattened the Pamir tent. Inside the tents the continuous flapping gave the impression of a deafening barrage of machine gun fire. I went out for a moment to check the food tent, and a gust of wind almost knocked me over. But as soon as the wind died down, it started to snow heavily again. I was worried about the boys being on the mountain in such terrible conditions and kept nipping out to peer at the first couloir, straining my ears to catch the slightest noise that might herald their arrival. Around

9:30 PM, to my great relief, all three of them returned, completely encrusted in ice.

The following morning I went up with Annibale Zucchi and Luigino Airoldi, the latter leading. Annibale was carrying the Pamir tent to pitch at Camp 1. Following what had become a normal pattern, I was completely preoccupied with filming and taking photographs. After climbing the fixed ropes we gained the ridge where we found a flat place under the large granite tower, where I thought of pitching Camp 1. We went on to see if it were possible to reach the snow crest I mentioned before. Luigino tried first, but unsuccessfully, and on my advice Annibale tried again, keeping more to the right where I thought I had seen a couloir. Committing himself to a traverse on thick ice, he reached its base; I followed immediately, and he went on to attack the couloir, which turned out to be quite difficult due to a layer of fresh snow; he had to use a number of pitons on it. After 40 meters, he stopped, telling me he could only see ice and snow.

When I joined him the situation was not clear to me either. Annibale climbed on towards the crest: the steep face was covered knee-deep with a soft blanket of snow. I barely dared breathe, feeling that everything might crumble at a moment's notice. But once we had reached the crest, we couldn't see the glacier for the thick mist. It seemed to be clearing slightly to the north, which prompted us to wait, but it was late and Luigino, who had been waiting in the freezing couloir for almost an hour, was calling us. We arranged all the gear brought up by us and our companions the day before under the grey tower, at the place where we wanted to pitch Camp 1, and then went down the fixed ropes. It seemed a never ending descent, and we finally reached Base Camp around midnight. I immediately gave instructions to Romano Perego, Jack Canali, and Gigi Alippi, who were to climb next morning, alternating leads: they had to organize Camp 1, on the second col, pitch the tent, and study the crest formation carefully to work out the best way to reach the glacier.

On the 13th, all six of us were busy: Perego, Canali, and Alippi left from Camp 1 as previously arranged, while Annibale Zucchi, Luigino Airoldi, and I followed, after a rest, with heavy loads to refurbish Camp 1. Just before we went back down, Jack, Gigi, and Romano returned with the results of their reconnaissance: the crest was about one kilometer long, and composed entirely of floury unstable snow, under which they could feel a thick sheet of ice. They told me that they had reached the wall of the first bergschrund of the glacier, below which they had pitched a tent for Camp 2.

While Romano came down to Base Camp with us, Gigi and Jack stayed, intending to supply Camp 2, and sleep up there, so as to be ready to attempt the face above the glacier. Meanwhile, Zucchi and Perego were climbing up to Camp 1, with all the gear they needed to go on up to join the others.

Luigino and I on the other hand went down to the landing strip on the 14th to collect the mail Sheldon had left. We saw several distinct marks that we thought were those left by the aeroplane, but when we arrived we found it was Goodwin, who had left Base Camp a few days earlier because his vacation was over and he had to return to work. Sheldon had not yet arrived, and the "landing strip" that had deceived us was a bunch of little flags Bob had placed to show him the landing site in case of poor visibility. We gave Bob our mail, and left him with profound regret that the pressure of work would not allow him to go on with us.

It was a superb day, and with my binoculars I could see every detail of the South Face, its sweep of ice alternating with enormous overhanging walls, crevasses, and protruding diedres. I carefully followed the projected route that separated us from the summit and at one point I could clearly see Jack and Gigi climbing the first bergschrund of the hanging glacier and going towards the centre of the spur, keeping on its right. From our point of view, it looked more logical to climb the ice couloir on the left to avoid some dangerous sections.

We were now entering the most committing phase of the expedition, that preceding the final attack. I concentrated on studying the plan of action in great detail so as to create conditions that would guarantee our success. So far the rhythm of work we had adopted allowed us all to give our maximum output with the possibility of recuperating our energies afterwards by taking turns resting.

Thus, while Luigino and I got ready to go to Camp 1 the day after we had been to the landing strip, Annibale and Romano were climbing the crest towards Camp 2. Once at the hanging glacier, they made for the chimney climbed by Jack and Gigi who, meanwhile, were returning to Base Camp.

Annibale and Romano continued climbing an icy diedre with Grade 5 difficulties and, at an altitude of 5,200 meters, found a suitable site for Camp 3; they then returned to sleep at Camp 2, while Luigino and I reached Camp 1 with the high altitude equipment and the usual provisions, including a Pamir tent. At the beginning of the second couloir, where there were fixed etriers, we met Gigi and Jack heading towards Base Camp for their rest.

On the following morning, the 16th, while we were climbing to Camp 2, we ran across Annibale and Romano, whom I asked to go down to the first col for the food and gear we had left in various improvised caches, and take everything to Camp 1: we were to take the Pamir tent to Camp 2 and then try to reach Camp 3 with the Nepal tents. But the weather turned foul and when we reached Camp 2 it was snowing. The snow fell ceaselessly all night, which made us postpone any attempt. Meanwhile, Jack and Gigi had reached our two other companions at Camp 1 and bivouacked with them. Next morning it was still snowing and given the persistent bad weather Luigino and I decided to go down and join the others at Camp 1. Forced to rest, the boys passed the time chattering in their characteristic Lecco dialect: I preferred to lie down in another tent after drinking a mug of milk. But I could not sleep for the thought of this enforced inactivity, while there were so many problems to solve higher up. In the late afternoon, the sky cleared and we all set out enthusiastically for Camp 2; we decided to head for Camp 3, if at all possible, in two ropes of three, the next day.

In the morning, we realized this plan, and half way up the hanging glacier, heard Sheldon's aeroplane: in fact, we watched him manoeuvering to land and take Goodwin back to work. Then he was in the air again, making some acrobatic turns trying to say hello to us. We went on to the highest point reached by Jack and Gigi, passed it, and reached the place where we intended to pitch Camp 3, at the site identified by Annibale and Romano. In an icy wind, buffetted by continuous blasts, we flattened a small terrace and pitched the two tents of Camp 3 at 5,200 meters. The cold was intense and we felt really confined in the tiny tents, but we were so tired that we slept anyway. It snowed during the night, but in the morning the weather seemed favourable.

We prepared the necessary gear for the final assault and all six of us left, divided into two ropes. The first team comprised Zucchi, Perego, and Airoldi; the second, Alippi, Canali, and me. Our plan was to attempt to reach the summit, and then go back without stopping to Camp 3. I was aware of the risks but, because of the bad weather, could see no other way.

Each of us knew the strains, sacrifices, and commitments we were to take on this decisive day. The boys were truly magnificent in their complete dedication to the ascent, though a certain nervous tension showed on their faces. As a matter of fact, they were all, except for Canali, on their first expedition outside Europe.

We climbed straight up the spur, to the last outcrop of rock, took a brief rest, and conferred on the route: before us everything was difficult and deceptive. I proposed trying on the left, where in fact we found the route leading to the snow and ice couloir which ended under the summit rocks. We were delighted to have found the key, but we had to fight very hard against the technical difficulties and the weather. The snow was succeeded by a tremendous wind from the south-east, which made it impossible to continue along the ridge, where the ideal route lay. The temperature was savage, the icy spindrift whipping our faces. In these conditions I could not take movies or photographs, but we continued to the bottom of the rocks on the last section. The altitude made itself felt here and the climb became extremely tiring, the more so because of the particular types of ground we were covering: now rock-hard ice, now powdery snow alternating with a frozen crust that often gave way under our feet, giving us a sensation of continual instability. It was delicately poised: our mountaineering skills now demanded an equally important contribution from the will to survive. Even the summit rocks presented serious difficulties: we were tired and completely numb with cold, for the temperature was around 30–35° Centigrade below zero.

Suddenly, unexpectedly, we heard the roar of a reconnaissance plane which circled above us two or three times at close range, seeming to want to comfort us in our weariness, which had become unbearable at times. Our stiff boots seemed to have solidified with our feet: Jack, in particular, complained of cold feet. But our goal was near and at 11 PM, on July 19, we were all on top of Mt. McKinley!

It was almost dark and it was dangerous not to wear gloves, but I took two pictures anyway with Gigi's camera, almost sure that they wouldn't come out. But at least one picture, admittedly not perfectly clear, was to record that we had reached the summit.

We tied to an ice screw little flags, pulled laboriously out of our packs. The wind blew them together, uniting the colours of Italy, the United States, Alaska, Lecco, and our Spiders: it looked like an invitation to the brotherhood of nations. We hugged each other emotionally, barely able to speak. Each of us spent these moments in our private, personal thoughts. Faces glowed with that particular radiant smile that comes right from the heart. Ours was a beautiful success for Lecco and for Italian alpinism!

The boys, wanting to surprise me, had brought a little statue of St. Nicholas, patron of our city, to leave on the summit. We had to return immediately: the cold was extreme and only when we were safe would we be fully able to appreciate our achievement.

As soon as we were under the summit rocks Jack complained of nausea. At first, I jokingly asked him what he wanted to vomit: we had been moving for 17 hours and had eaten only a can of fruit and syrup in the afternoon. But when we reached the couloir, which was quite steep, I heard a sound beside me, and saw Jack falling towards the valley. Belaying with my ice axe, I managed to stop him. My dear friend, who had generously given his all in the interests of our success, was racked by continuous vomiting. I was really worried about his condition and, to watch him in the most difficult sections, I went last on the rope and stayed near him during the descent: he slipped several times but fortunately I always managed to hold him. When we reached the traverse, we abandoned the now useless pitons and karabiners. The descent was particularly painful for Jack, who, even though he seemed a bit better, complained all the time that his feet were terribly cold. The wind stopped, but it began to snow and our descent became increasingly risky. It took a tremendous effort to reach the chimney. Here we were forced to rappel. Annibale and Jack went down first and we followed taking great care to ensure the safe retrieval of our ropes. These manoeuvres were not easy as we all had frozen hands and feet except for Gigi, whose boots were made from reindeer leather. At six in the morning on July 20 we all finally reached Camp 3. Exhausted, we fell into the two tents and made something hot to eat.

Worried about Jack, I took care of him, massaging his feet with Foille cream. We all did our best to cheer him up. I tried to hide my fears so as not to upset the boys, but in Gigi's eyes I seemed to see the same anxious questions that nagged inside me. With Jack in this condition how were we to reach Base Camp? And what if he went on getting worse? Outside it snowed incessantly. The night was long and the tents overcrowded. At first I could not sleep because I was afraid that Jack might need something: he was moaning, his speech confused, his feet swollen and blue. On this expedition, I was acting as doctor and that, because of my companion's worrying condition, increased the strain on my nerves. But later, physical exhaustion finally overcame me and I fell asleep. My feet were very cold but I did not move for fear of disturbing my friends, and as a result, suffered slight frostbite under both my big toes.

It was not until around 11 AM on the morning of July 21, that we decided to go on down. Jack's feet would not go into his boots. All our boots were stiff and frozen but, with a little effort, the rest of us managed to put ours on; for Jack it was impossible. Gigi generously offered him his reindeer boots, which left him with only four pairs of socks and a pair of inner boots: it also meant he could not use crampons, so that getting down to Camp 2 became a torture for him too. On the ice slopes we had to hold his full weight because he had broken his inner boots and only had his socks left. We were about half way down the glacier when he fell towards the valley: Romano's belay could not hold him; somehow I managed to grab both their ropes and stop them. Luigino, meanwhile, was striving to find a way over the bergschrund in practically nil visibility because of the sleet and thick mist. Finally, after groping around in the snow, he found the anchors and sling that we had left. Even Romano, tired out by constantly helping Gigi, took a fall, a great flight ending below the bergschrund on a flat place which was fortunately covered with soft snow: we all ended up laughing!

We reached Camp 2: Romano, Luigino, and Gigi wanted to stop, but I insisted on going on to Base Camp with Jack and Annibale since Jack's condition was really frightening. I was in fact afraid that if we waited any longer he would not be able to put his feet on the ground, and we still had to cross the steep ridge, upon which it would be impossible to carry a man. The trek was exhausting: groping in ever-thickening mist and near-darkness we reached Camp 1, where we could at last stop and sleep. Annibale's stamina seemed inexhaustible and Jack, despite his condition, was a real prodigy of moral and physical strength. We had very little food or fuel, so we resigned ourselves to melting snow with sugar and Ovaltine. With the drop in altitude, Jack improved. I massaged his feet with Gelovit, which hurt him terribly. We all spent a horrible night. Only at dawn did we manage to rest a little, while it went on snowing outside.

In the morning, around 11 AM, we decided to go down. The fixed ropes were all covered in snow and encrusted with ice; small avalanches fell in a continual succession, but fortunately they were of very soft snow, and gave us little trouble. On the rock slabs I lost a crampon and could not catch it. Towards the end of the first couloir I was hit by a big avalanche which completely buried me, but although it had come from high up, it only stunned me a little: I was still holding the fixed rope, and everything ended all right because the snow was extremely light. Unfortunately, however, I had lost the other crampon too, so the descent became even more tiring. At the end of the big couloir, the snow was so soft and deep that we sank all the way into it and had to swim our way out. It was a great relief to arrive at Base Camp!

It was another horrible night for all three of us: Jack constantly moaned because of the unbearable pain and that made us suffer too. After 75 hours of continuous snow, we finally saw the sun on the morning of July 23. Avalanches started to pour down the mountain: I thought of my friends still up there. In the evening, we were all finally united at Base Camp. After days of tension, we finally entered a state of grace, really a total relaxation of our nerves, which allowed us to savour to the full the joy of our success. From a piece of canvas with four handles on the corners we improvised a sled to carry our brave and unlucky Jack to the landing strip where Sheldon, having seen us, was waiting. He was overjoyed to discover that all six of us had climbed the route and returned safely. We immediately loaded Jack on to the plane and asked the pilot to mail the telegrams announcing our victory!

Sheldon came back next day to pick up Romano and Luigino, while Gigi, Annibale, and I stopped for another day to salvage as much gear as possible. We were all reunited in Anchorage a few days later. At the hospital Luigino, Romano, and I were treated for slight frostbite, and I also had a thorough medical check. However, for Jack the period of medical care was to be long and painful. Nevertheless he recovered fully, which was most important as he was able to continue his work as a guide and ski instructor in the mountains. While I remember and write these memoirs, now that he is no longer among us [Canali died in a skiing accident at Sestrieres], I can see his fine, calm face again, and feel the warmth of his friendship and his generous enthusiasm for mountaineering.

Gigi, Luigino, Annibale, and Romano returned to Italy before me. Whilst waiting to accompany Jack home, I went to Kotzebue to visit the incomparable Padre Spolettini. I thus had the chance to see and admire the lifestyle of the Eskimos: simple, but very impressive. Back in New York I met my dear old friend Ernani Faé. We eventually got home to Lecco on September 1.

I shall always remember the hospitality of so many friends in that distant land, the moments of beauty and suffering during the climb, the magnificent episodes of brotherhood and human solidarity in the realization of a marvellous dream: the conquest of the South Face of McKinley.

It was a superb victory for Lecco, and a marvellous success to mark the 15th anniversary of the formation of the "Spiders." It was also one of my greatest satisfactions in my long life as an alpinist, brought about by my five young companions through their dedication, their spirit of sacrifice, their discipline, and their unquestioned technical ability. I would be quite prepared to join any one of them on a major mountaineering expedition.

The expedition received far wider acclaim than just in our native city. Among other congratulations I received the following telegrams, one from the President of the United States, the other from the Italian President:

I send my warmest congratulations to you and to the other members of the Italian team, who have achieved such a splendid mountaineering feat on Mt. McKinley. This outstanding accomplishment under the most hazardous of conditions is a fine testimonial to your superb skill and fortitude. Our nation is proud to have witnessed within its own borders this conquest which has served to strengthen the ties between the United States and Italy and to earn the admiration of all the world.
—John F. Kennedy

To you and to your courageous companions comes admiring applause and deep congratulations from all Italians, and myself personally, for this successful and arduous mountaineering feat.
—Giovanni Gronchi

EDITOR'S AFTERWORD: *Cassin and his Spider teammates returned from Denali as heroes. While their many honors included telegrams of congratulations from two presidents, perhaps their greatest accolade was Washburn's postclimb observation that Cassin and his five teammates had pulled off what up to that time was "without question the greatest climb in North American mountaineering history."*

Though Cassin labeled his team's route the South Buttress, it was later renamed in his honor. Now known as the Cassin Ridge, the South Face's "central bulge" is widely revered as one of Denali's—and North America's—classic alpine challenges.

Minus 148°:
The Winter Ascent of Mt. McKinley

– ART DAVIDSON –

By the mid-1960s, nearly all of Denali's mountaineering secrets had been revealed. Improved access, equipment, and techniques had made it possible to ascend each of its major faces and ridges, including those once considered impossible. No longer was North America's highest peak such a mysterious place to climb—except in winter. No one had even seriously considered a winter ascent, until Art Davidson and Shiro Nishimae came along.

A Colorado native, Davidson had been introduced to climbing in high school. Despite some initial trauma, mountaineering soon became his passion, and in 1964 that passion brought him to Alaska. A year later he helped the Osaka Alpine Club put in a new route up Denali's South Buttress; three Japanese climbers reached the summit, including the twenty-nine-year-old team leader, Shiro Nishimae.

During the expedition, Nishimae and Davidson tried to imagine Denali in winter. Their imaginings infected them with a desire to visit the mountain during this still-unknown season. At age twenty-two, Davidson began preparing for the challenge he'd dreamed of since his childhood: a journey into unexplored territory. By December 1966, an eight-man team had been assembled.

Members included team leader Gregg Blomberg, a mountaineering instructor from Denver; George Wichman, an Anchorage orthopedic surgeon who signed on as the team doctor; John Edwards, a biologist from Ohio; Dave Johnston of Anchorage, a self-described climbing bum with a degree in forestry; Frenchman Jacques "Farine" Batkin, one of Europe's most powerful climbers; and Swiss-born Ray Genet, a future Denali legend who talked himself onto the team despite minimal climbing experience.

Flown into the Alaska Range in late January 1967 by renowned bush pilot Don Sheldon, the climbers suffered an early tragedy: on their third day in the mountains, Batkin fell into a crevasse and died. The team decided to continue, however, and Davidson, Johnston, and Genet reached Denali's summit on February 28. Forced to descend in darkness, the three chose to bivouac at 18,200-foot Denali Pass, rather than continue to high camp at 17,200. That night, a severe storm struck the mountain. Exposed to 100-mile-per-hour winds and –100° (or colder) wind chills, the men retreated into a snow cave.

The following excerpt is taken from Art Davidson's book Minus 148°: The Winter Ascent of Mt. McKinley, *originally published in 1969 and reprinted in 1986 by Cloudcap Press in Seattle. It recounts two of the days that he, Johnston, and Genet spent in the cave. To give a more complete picture, he also included diary entries from teammates lower on the mountain.*

March 3: "Pieces are coming off my bad ear!"
DENALI PASS: ART, PIRATE, DAVE

THE INFERNAL NOISE FILLED our heads.

The wind's vicious, I told myself. It's diabolical. Silently cursing it became a pastime. I tried to think of all the words that described its evil nature—fiendish, wicked, malicious. I called it a vampire sucking the life out of us.

But the wind didn't hear me, and I knew my words were irrelevant anyway. The wind wasn't malevolent; it wasn't out to get us; it had no evil intentions, nor any intentions at all. It was simply a chunk of sky moving about. It was a weather pattern, one pressure area moving into another. Still, it was more satisfying, somehow more comforting, to personify the wind, make it something I could hate or respect, something I could shout at. I wished I were an old Eskimo shaman, seeing devils and demons in the storm and understanding the evil spirits that lived in the mountain. I thought that a good shaman would know a chant that would chase away the wind. But I didn't know any magic, and I knew all my cursing was only an attempt to escape the simple facts; we had to descend, we couldn't descend in the wind, and the wind showed no sign of letting up.

We needed water most desperately. There was very little gas left in the stove; I wanted Dave to melt ice with it. I tried to think of the most pleasant ways of reminding him that we needed to drink, but whatever I said he growled at. I knew he felt the strain of having to do all the chores for Pirate and me. I felt too thankful, too dependent, almost too much at the mercy of Dave to pester him about the water. He told me that "later" he would melt some ice and thaw the bacon or peas, but gradually the day slipped by without our eating or drinking. Yet, if my hands had been all right, I would have put off the cooking the way Dave did because the altitude had cut away our motivation; it was so much easier to say "later" because, though we didn't really believe it, we always thought the wind might suddenly stop, letting us run down to the cave at 17,200 feet.

It was toward the middle of the afternoon when I heard Dave beginning to coax the stove back to life. He fiddled with it for several minutes without any luck, then decided to let it sit while he opened one of the large cans of bacon, ham, or peas.

It was the moment I had waited for all day.

"Which one do we want first?" he asked.

"Mix 'em all together," Pirate suggested.

Dave scraped the ice off the can of bacon with his knife, clearing the top so he could open it. I could already taste the bacon.

"Damn!" Dave swore in disgust. "Holes in the can! We can't eat the bacon! It's rotten!"

He reached for a can of peas.

It could certainly not happen again. Those holes had been an accident. Nevertheless, Pirate and I listened intently as Dave cleared the ice from the can of peas.

When only about half the ice was off, he swore again. More holes! Then he tried the ham, our last can. It was the same!

We sank back into a numb depression. For two days we had anticipated the flavor of the bacon. We had let ourselves dream of the juice of the peas in our mouths. Suddenly the food we had counted on was gone. The gnawing cramps in our stomachs weren't going to be quieted.

Immediately we were angry for being so cruelly cheated, but only after several minutes did we realize how the spoiled food had transformed our trial with hunger into a confrontation with starvation. We had almost nothing left to eat—three bags of gorp, a dozen slices of cheese, some hard candies, a little coffee, a three-ounce can of chopped pork, and maybe a dozen cookies. The combined calorie count of our remaining food was probably adequate for one person for one day. Solemnly, Dave divided a little less than half of the remaining food into three equal portions.

Although Dave battled with the stove long after his fingers were insensitive from handling the cold metal, he failed to get it going. There was so little gas left that he couldn't build up enough pressure to vaporize it. At thirty below the gas was sluggish—he had to give up. Just like the punctured cans of food, our last drops of gas mocked us with their uselessness.

Our one hope was a gallon of gas Dave had cached on the far side of Denali Pass when he had climbed McKinley in the summer three years earlier. It might still be there; Dave had spotted the bottle of gas the first day we had tried for the summit. He thought we should take a look, but no one volunteered to go out. He said he had originally cached the gas only about two hundred feet from where we lay. No one moved. Dave was the most fit to go out, and the most certain of the place it was cached, but the horror of entering the wind overcame the slightest inclination Dave might have had to go after it.

We tried to imagine what the others at 17,200 were doing. They had shelter, but only a limited supply of food. I remembered how a week or two before we had been concerned for the strength of John and George, about Shiro's cough and hemorrhoids, and about Gregg's unpredictable emotions in a crisis. Now they were entirely dependent on their own resources; and the three of us who had once been the strongest might soon come to depend on their judgment and strength to be rescued.

We hoped the others would not attempt anything rash for our sake—that the strain of their fear for us wouldn't break them. We thought of the gallon of gas. We imagined how delicious a cup of water would taste.

We shifted our hips and shoulders to relieve the hard cold beneath us.

We talked very little. The grayness inside the cave faded into darkness.

17,200 FEET TO 14,400 FEET: GREGG AND JOHN

John's journal:

We decided that today, the third, Gregg and I should go down to 14,400 feet and then on to the radio to call for a helicopter overflight, or for Sheldon to fly over Denali Pass to drop fuel, etc. George and Shiro will stay at 17,200 feet to determine what is at the top of the pass as soon as the weather allows getting up there. We had a miserable breakfast, cleared the snow off our gear, and slowly prepared for the descent. Set out about noon into heavy wind. Said thanks to Shiro and good-by to George. Not a great deal of response from either—dozing.

Not too cold, much blowing sandy snow in eyes. Severe, buffeting winds down buttress made going very difficult. As usual, concern that the crampons would come loose, but they held.

Just near the gendarme above sixteen thousand feet Gregg wrenched his ankle. We encountered terrible winds here and had to cling to the ridge rocks to save from being blown off our feet. Sometimes the wind blew up, sometimes down, unpredictable. Very difficult to maintain balance. On hands and knees to the fixed ropes in a screeching wind. I anchored Gregg, but this was not much use since I had Dave's ice axe, which had lost its point. Shiro is using mine. A crosswind and a driving snow made traveling down the fixed line difficult, but we got down the line without many problems. . . . Gregg moved slowly on his bad ankle. The pace was just right. Both exhausted by the time we reached the igloos.

Pieces are coming off my bad ear.

Shoveled out the entrance, listening to the roar of the wind up at the pass. Went to sleep standing up, leaning against the door of the second igloo. But felt much better after meal. Sorted gear for descent. Crevasse problem worrisome, but only a few wicked places. Weather down here contrasts—whiteout, gentle snow, occasional wind.

Compare the three on the pass. They must be getting near the end now.

And George and Shiro in the gusty snow cave are only a little better off than if in a tent at the same place. Tonight the sack is damn wet from all the snow that came into the snow cave. . . . This lousy weather cannot continue much longer.

Gregg's journal:

John and I are at 14,400 feet. They didn't come down last night. Nasty weather. Shiro got up to fix the hole over the tent three times. Really miserable. I was hoping I would find Dave, Pirate, and Art here; that somehow, descending, they had missed the high camp.

I pity all those above. At least a plane could land here. We can hear the wind above. We must try for the radio at seventy-five hundred feet and get help. I hope the others are still holding out. Shiro and George will make it. If it is clear tomorrow they will try to get to the pass. We have no idea how long the others can hold out.

We had a good meal with plenty of liquid. Didn't realize how badly off we were above. It was such a problem to cook that we let it go too much. With only two to cook for they will be better off. I wonder if the weather will clear tomorrow. Inside this igloo we are oblivious to what is going on outside. With a reasonable day and God's help we can make it to seventy-five hundred feet tomorrow. Descending seven thousand feet with a screwed-up ankle is quite a day. I dread the crevasses. They are my only worry at this point. I only know we must try to get help for those above. If we don't soon it will surely be too late. This is their fourth night.

The trip down today was quite windy and our eyelashes were caked up with ice, but it was a warm south wind, thank goodness, and when we got here we were astonished at how warm it was: –10°. I don't know how cold it was at 17,200 feet the last few nights, but it must have been about –30°. Maybe it was just because the wind wasn't blowing here that made the difference. If John and I make it to 7,500 feet tomorrow we will be safe. Then we will radio out, and as soon as Sheldon can come and get us, we can get a rescue in progress.

Edi, I hope you're not too worried. We have no way of knowing whether the outside world knows anything of what is going on. Ray had been contacting Radio Anchorage every night and then stopped. So chances are that people are worried about us.

I hope the light isn't too flat tomorrow. It was hard descending with my ankle because I couldn't see where I was putting my feet. One minute the ground was steep and hard, then flat and soft, then a dropoff, etc.

Shiro and the others are more optimistic about the chances of those up at the pass than I am. If only they had made a break for it the first day, they would have been all right. Every minute they wait, they become weaker and have less resolve to make a run for it. Yet they are all tough, and if Ray, as usual, takes the initiative, they could make it yet. Tonight the weather might clear. They have only a thousand feet to descend to safety. . . . A hell of a mess, and yet climbing McKinley in the winter is no harder than we anticipated. We just got a mess of bad weather breaks.

Well, honey, it's time to get to sleep. Big day tomorrow. Wish us luck. If we are careful and God is with us, we will make it.

March 4: Delusion
DENALI PASS: ART, DAVE, PIRATE

I woke elated. The wind had stopped. I heard a helicopter.

Just outside the cave I heard the steady whir. Gregg must have gotten a rescue started. It sounded as if the copter had already landed. People must be searching the pass for us. I was afraid they wouldn't find our cave; it was such a small hole in the ice. Maybe they'd give up and leave.

"Dave!" I rolled toward him. "Dave, do you hear the helicopter? We'd better get outside right away."

"Go to sleep . . . it's the wind."

"No! It can't be. It's too steady, too constant. It's a copter. . . . Dave. . . . "

He didn't answer.

"It's a copter," I repeated to myself. "It's the steady whir of a copter." I listened to be certain; but I wasn't certain. Maybe it was the wind; it couldn't be. I almost asked Dave to listen, but I knew he was right; yet I strained my ears for a voice, any sound that would let me believe there were rescuers outside.

There was only the wind.

After a long silence Dave admitted that he had been susceptible to my delusion; he had convinced himself for several minutes that the sound of the wind really was a rescue helicopter.

"But you know," Dave said, looking toward me, "it makes you feel kind of humble to know a helicopter couldn't possibly get to us."

Dave went on to explain how he felt good to know that no device of technology nor any effort on the part of our companions could conquer the storm, or even reach through it to help us. He said the three of us were alone in this sanctuary of the earth's wilderness, and that our only security lay in ourselves, in our individual abilities to endure, and in our combined capacities of will-power and judgment.

I said, "Dave, it may sound funny, but I feel closer to you than ever before."

Dave beamed and said, "Yeah, I know what you mean. If we can't fight our way out of this storm, at least we can stick together, and try to live in harmony with it."

I thought to myself how the storm itself was helping to protect us from its own fury. Ever since the McKinley massif had been thrust upward out of a flat land, the wind had been packing the snow and ice of Denali Pass into contours of least resistance. We were sheltered inside ice that conformed to the pattern of the wind. We had suffered and nearly succumbed to the storm that first morning when we had fought it head-on in the open, but now all the force of the wind only pounded more stability into the roof of our cave as it swept across the slope above us.

The altitude riddled our attention span into fragments of thoughts. Discomfort was the only thing on which my mind seemed able to concentrate. My lips were deeply cracked in several places. Moving my tongue along the roof of my mouth I felt clumps of dried-up mucus; other experiences with dehydration had taught me that if I didn't get water soon, the rawest areas in my mouth would begin bleeding. The ligaments in my legs ached as they dried up. It was especially painful to stretch or change positions; unfortunately, the hardness of the ice made my hips and back sore whenever I remained still for more than a few minutes. I complained very little, not because I was naturally stoic, but because there was no one to complain to—each of us experienced the same discomforts; pain had become a natural condition of our life under the ice.

I was probably warmer than either Dave or Pirate because their sleeping bags were icing up faster than mine. Every time Dave had cooked, steam from the warm liquid had been absorbed into his bag, where it soon froze. As the down had matted together, its resilience had disappeared. It was particularly unsettling when Dave pointed out a number of lumps of ice mixed with the down. I didn't see how his bag could retain any warmth. Pirate's bag was a little better, but his down was fast becoming clogged with moisture from his breath because, against Dave's advice and mine, he persisted in burying his head in his bag, where his exhaled moisture had no escape. All of us sorely missed the foam pads. Without them, we were only able to place a spare wind parka or pair of wind pants under our buttocks and shoulders, leaving the rest of our sleeping bags on bare ice.

Pirate's hands were swollen, but he said he was worried most about his feet. He asked about my down booties. Though he didn't say it outright, I could tell he wanted to wear them. I tried to ignore him, acting as if I hadn't heard. My feet were cold with the booties; without them I thought they would surely freeze while I slept, or even while I lay awake. I avoided thinking about it, but that was exactly what was happening to Pirate's feet. He knew I didn't want to give them up, and didn't ask again. As he kicked his feet inside his bag to relieve their numbness, I knew he must be thinking of the warmth of my booties. Pretending to be asleep, I tried to forget about Pirate's feet.

I couldn't remember how many days we had been in the cave. The day we had gone to the summit, then that first day of the wind, the day we ate ham, then a day without water—it must have been the fourth day, but I was uncertain.

Sometime during the middle of the day Dave rationed us each a fig bar and two hard candies. Sucking on the candies brought a few minutes of relief to the rawness in my mouth. I put the fig bar aside. I wanted to save it for later in the afternoon as a break in the monotony of hunger. After about an hour I couldn't wait any longer. I had looked forward to saliva coming back into my mouth as I chewed the fig bar, but the crumbs only stuck to the gums and roof of my mouth. With some effort I swallowed the sticky wad, feeling it tumble into my stomach, where it set off a series of cramps. The pain constructed a morbidly amusing picture of four or five hands in my stomach grabbing for the fig bar, fighting each other for it, tearing and ripping at it. After a few minutes the cramps died down and the usual steady ache returned.

Silently I cursed the punctured cans of food. Some careless climbers must have punched holes in them with their ice axes as they tried to chip away the ice that covered them. We all wished we had never seen the cans. Without them we might have been able to accept our hunger, but knowing that ham and peas, rotten as they were, lay within arm's reach while we were gradually starving was almost unbearable. The cruelest twist to the irony was the uncertainty; the canned food might still be good. Perhaps the food had remained frozen ever since it had been brought to Denali Pass. It was doubtful that there were any bacteria living at 18,200 feet. At least a portion of the ham, peas, and bacon might not be rancid, but to find out would be risking food poisoning.

Early in the afternoon it became obvious that we were going to spend another night in the cave. Even if the wind let up toward evening, we wouldn't have the time, nor perhaps the strength, to descend. We knew our dehydration was critical. We hadn't drunk a cup of liquid for more than thirty-six hours. Because our circulation was down we were all chilly inside our bags with all our parkas and wind pants on. Occasionally, I could feel Dave's body tense and shake with shivers. We needed water, which meant we needed gas—which we didn't have.

The only possibility was the gas Dave had cached at Denali Pass three years before. If one of us went for the gallon of gas, he might not make it back through the wind to the cave. The gruesome reality of this possibility had kept us from retrieving the gas, but there was no longer any alternative. One of us had to go for the gas! Who? I couldn't go because of my hands, so I lay quietly in my bag, letting my silence ask someone else to go.

Dave resisted the thought of his going. He had dug the cave. He had cooked for us when there had been gas. He knew his efforts had kept Pirate and me alive. And we knew it.

It wasn't right that Dave go out into certain misery to possibly disappear in the wind. Yet, knowing Dave, I sensed he was struggling with his weariness and fear to find it in himself to go out. Since he was the only one of us who knew for certain where the gas should be, it was logical that he go. Neither Pirate nor I could ask him. Semiconscious from the altitude and the numbing hypnotism of the wind, we retained a sense of justice.

There was another reason we weren't anxious for Dave to go. He was our hands! We needed him to cook if we ever got some gas. We would need him to tie the rope around us and hold us on belay when we descended, whenever that might be.

Quietly—I don't remember hearing him say he would go—Pirate got out of his sleeping bag. When he started to pull on his boots, he found it difficult and painful to force his swollen feet into them. I offered him the use of my down booties. He took them and quickly had them tied on. Dave described the rocks among which the gas had been cached. Pirate pulled down his face mask.

The wind had become more erratic: there were gusts and then short—ten- to thirty-second—lulls of comparative calm. Pirate lay on his stomach, facing the entrance, listening for the lull that sounded right to him. A resigned determination seemed to be all that was left of his former fierceness. Suddenly, he gave a short and not too loud "Arahhaa!" and began squirming out the entrance, uphill, through loose snow. Dave and I cheered, not loudly, but with all our remaining enthusiasm. For a moment we heard Pirate placing the pack across the entrance again. Then the lull ended abruptly, and all we heard was the wind.

For the longest time Dave and I listened without saying a word. Ten, fifteen minutes passed. We knew Pirate should have returned, but we said nothing. He might call for help only ten feet from the cave and we'd never hear him. I couldn't help imagining what we'd have to do if he failed to return. Maybe Dave would make a try for the gas. Maybe the two of us would attempt to dash down from the pass. If Pirate didn't return within a few minutes there would be no reason to go looking for him. Maybe Dave and I would simply lie in the cave, waiting until Gregg, Shiro, George, and John could reach us, or until we passed into delirium.

We heard a movement at the entrance. Two immediate whoops of sheer joy expressed our relief. A flurry of snow, then a plastic jug shot into the cave, followed by an exhausted Pirate.

"Bad!" He was gasping. "I couldn't stand up, even in the lulls. Something's wrong with my balance." I had never before heard Pirate say anything was rough or dangerous. "I crawled all the way, clawing into the ice with two ice axes. I can't feel my feet now."

We had gas! We could drink water!

With a merriment we'd forgotten ever existed Dave melted chunks of ice and piles of snow. The first can of water, especially, smelled and tasted sweet; we did not remember that the sweetness was the scent of urine. Dave heated can after can of water till they became hot. We drank, and drank, and always waited for yet another canful. For the first time in five days we went to sleep with full stomachs. That we were only full of water mattered not at all—or so we thought.

My feet had become colder. I had to constantly wiggle my toes to keep them from becoming numb. Still, I was glad I had not asked Pirate to return my booties after his trip for the gas.

14,400 FEET: GREGG AND JOHN

John's journal:

Foul and filthy day. No chance to move when we got ready the first thing, with the intention of using all available light to get to seventy-five hundred feet. I feel very restless and anxious to communicate with O.M. [John's wife] who will be concerned and worried with no information.

Pent up in igloo, I stood around almost all day, going out every half hour to look at the weather. I am unable to read, unable to do anything constructive. Gregg's ankle is bad. There is a whiteout, so we can't get down to give word of our situation. We go about our private tasks with little conversation, but are both preoccupied with the three up top and now with George and Shiro since today is a whiteout and they can neither go up nor down.

Hell. Late afternoon, wind drops hope for tomorrow. Crevasses will be a bad problem. How I want to be off this mountain. This PM we talked nonsense conversation for a couple of hours, and felt better for it. We should have been doing it all day.

Gregg's journal:

Damn, we are still here. . . . It is just too nasty out to move. If there were four of us it might be different. If a man falls into a crevasse with four around he is out and down the slope in no time. With two it is easily a three- or four-hour ordeal.

The route from here to Windy Corner has only a half dozen wands at best, which makes them of little or no use. If only the route were properly wanded from here we could go. We didn't get unpacked till 1:30 PM, hoping for the slightest break in the weather. We will even go tonight if the weather is clear. Though the wind is still blowing, it does seem to be getting a slight bit brighter outside. A good sign, I hope. John thinks we may be able to move in an hour, which would put us in the dark, but that's O.K. if it is clear. I would at least like to be past Windy Corner in the light. . . . I told you I'd call you on the fifth, and I intend to try to keep that promise.

John is nervous, but then so am I. I am only afraid that I won't sleep well until I am home with you. I hope we can seclude ourselves for a few days then. God, but I hope we can get to seventy-five hundred feet tomorrow. If tomorrow is a day like today, we will just have to try regardless. I'd like to see Shiro and George show up. With four of us I feel positive we could get down, no matter what the weather. . . . It is harder to sit than it is to move at this point. The waiting is more terrible than moving. But to move now might complete the destruction of the party. No, we must wait until we are reasonably sure we can make 10,200 feet at least.

I try hard to forget the situation that the three above are in, but it is a gnawing, sickening thought that won't go away.

The weather took a slight turn for the worse, but the wind has died. It is snowing heavily. I hope we are not in for a five-day snowstorm. That's all we need. I just can't describe how anxious I am to get down and out, but I know the others feel the same way.

Edi, I feel sorry for you. The injustice and worry this venture has caused you. All the work you did for it. If I do get safely back to you, the least I can do is not go on another. I promise you will be along on anything I do from here on. I think I've said earlier that this climb is a real lead into that simple, uncomplicated life we want. I do hope you are not too worried for me. . . . I will be safely home to you in no time. I love you and am full of good hope for the future. All my love. Good night.

EDITOR'S AFTERWORD: *The wind finally died enough to allow Davidson, Johnston, and Genet to leave their cave and, on March 7, resume their descent. Approaching Windy Corner (elevation 13,200 feet), they were surprised, thankful, and a bit annoyed to discover that a massive rescue mission had been launched to save them. After all they'd been through, the three men felt the rescue operation was unnecessary; they could descend under their own power. They didn't like the idea of being responsible for such a big commotion. Still, it was reassuring to know that others had been concerned enough to risk their own safety to help save the missing climbers. And there was the frostbite to consider. The three were descending on half-frozen feet. Each step brought excruciating pain.*

Picked up by helicopter, the men abandoned their climbing rope. Seeing it on the ice, Davidson felt a twinge of regret: "It seemed unfair that the rope which had tied the three of us together over so much ice had to remain on the mountain. Only now that we were leaving did we begin to fully realize how isolated we had been and how closely the three of us had been bound together; it would never be that way again."

Davidson, Johnston, and Genet were reunited with Edwards and Blomberg in Talkeetna, while Nishimae and Wichman later joined their teammates in Anchorage. Afterward, all team members except Nishimae (who returned to Japan) went to Fairbanks for some postclimb medical testing. Scientists conducting the tests "just shook their heads in disbelief at the human wrecks the mountain had sent back to them," Davidson wrote. During their five weeks on the mountain, the three who'd reached the summit had lost an average of thirty-five pounds each. Five of the seven surviving climbers suffered some degree of frostbite. And for periods ranging from a few hours to several days, all expedition members experienced a sense of isolation and unreality that is normally associated with severe psychosis.

The team later learned that its estimates of the extremes of the incredible storm they had experienced were conservative. Government scientists determined that winds on Denali's upper slopes had exceeded 150 miles per hour, with temperatures of –50°F. So the resulting wind-chill temperature during those life-threatening days at Denali Pass had been considerably colder even than –148°F.

Hunter and Foraker

– MICHAEL KENNEDY –

Seen from Anchorage, the Alaska Range's northern skyline is dominated by twin mountain giants that appear nearly identical in height. But their long-distance sameness is an illusion. The giant on the right is 20,320-foot Denali, the continent's tallest mountain. The giant to Denali's left is not nearly as high, or well known. At 17,400 feet, Mount Foraker is North America's sixth-highest peak, and the third highest in Alaska. Tanana Indians knew Foraker by two names: Sultana, "The Woman," and Menlale, "Denali's Wife." Both are far more appropriate than the name chosen in 1899 by Army Lieutenant Joseph Herron, that of Joseph Benson Foraker, a U.S. senator from Ohio who would later retire from politics in disgrace.

Caught in the shadow of her taller mate, Sultana (the more commonly used Native name) has historically been overlooked or perhaps ignored by pioneering climbers and the mountaineering masses who later followed. Not until 1934—twenty-one years after Denali was climbed—did a team even attempt Sultana. And while Denali has lured more than 16,000 people to its slopes, Sultana's suitors have numbered in the hundreds. Yet those who've climbed the mountain have discovered challenging and often awe-inspiring routes. The

French Ridge, Pink Panther, and Highway of Diamonds, for example, are considered a match for any on the continent. So is the Infinite Spur, widely regarded as one of the most audacious routes ever done in Alaska. Even in ideal circumstances, the central spur of Sultana's south face would have been a grand accomplishment. But Colorado climber Michael Kennedy and Californian George Lowe pioneered the route after losing teammate Jeff Lowe (no relation to George)—the expedition's driving force, as well as its strongest climber—who'd earlier broken his ankle as the trio ascended nearby Mount Hunter.

Now the editor of Climbing *magazine, Kennedy was the group's designated "young upstart and tiger." Looking back, he says the 1977 ascent of Sultana's Infinite Spur "probably was the most important and best route I've ever done. It showed me the possibilities inherent in big mountains." Indeed, both he and George Lowe went on to do a string of notable big-mountain ascents. Almost lost in the glow of their Infinite Spur triumph was Kennedy and Lowe's ascent of Hunter's unclimbed Northwest Face, via what is now called the Kennedy–Lowe Route.*

Michael Kennedy's account, "Hunter and Foraker," first appeared in 1978 in The American Alpine Journal.

SITTING NEXT TO OUR BIG TENT we were unlikely candidates for the Alpine Hall of Fame. Jeff Lowe looked quite natty in a white shirt, glacier hat and army-surplus woolies, and kept us amused with his Don Juan fantasies and ribald jokes. George Lowe tried to inject a note of seriousness into the proceedings by playing the elder statesman, veteran of many harsh epics in the great ranges of the world . . . after all, he *was* over 30, mumbling about quitting, and had certain rights as the nominal "leader" of the "team." Meanwhile, I attempted to play down the role of young upstart and tiger that I had been relegated to, although my compulsive organizational efforts merely reinforced this misrepresentation.

Jim Sharp had landed us on the southeast fork of the Kahiltna Glacier several hours before, and since then we had managed to do nothing more than drag ourselves and what little food and gear we possessed fifty yards from the airstrip. Jeff had taken a reconnaissance flight to check out the routes and had returned bubbling over with enthusiasm. The weather was clearing, the tent was up and a brew on, and we lay about in a happy confusion of tattered ropes, bent pitons, worn slings and two large boxes of food more suitable to a convention of Winnebago owners than a "lightweight" climbing expedition.

We had come to Alaska with two routes in mind, and our ideas on climbing them, while not new, were perhaps a bit radical. Major Alaskan climbs have traditionally been undertaken in ponderous Himalayan style, with large teams of climbers, fixed ropes and camps, and extended siege tactics. But in recent years this has been changing to a more classical alpine approach; speed, commitment and technical competence have become the new idiom of Alaskan climbing. Such climbs as those on the Moose's Tooth, the Cathedral Spires, Devils Thumb, Mount Dickey, Mount Deborah and particularly Charlie Porter's solo ascent of the Cassin Ridge on McKinley stand out as landmarks in this development. This type of climbing involves a certain amount of risk, and we were well aware of the chances we took: a storm high on the mountain could leave us stranded without the comforting umbilical cord of fixed ropes to safety, and with only three climbers, every step would count even more than usual. Accident or illness would create serious problems of retreat and evacuation. In addition, all supplies for the climbs would have to be carried along, and we couldn't afford to take an ounce too little or too much.

I wonder even now how we ever hoped to complete our program, for it was a very ambitious one. The north face of Mount Hunter (14,573 feet) was our first objective; it would give us all a chance to acclimatize and would at least give us one good climb should our other plans fail to materialize. This face had been tried two or three times previously. Rising 7000 feet from the glacier in full view of the landing strip, it was a tempting prize. The initial section consists of a moderate snow and ice rib in the center of the face, after which a steeper ice-face (the Triangle) is encountered. At the apex of the Triangle comes what would be the crux of the route, a horizontal ridge, extremely steep on both sides and heavily corniced. This is followed by an ice cliff, then easy snow slopes continue to the summit. We planned to descend via the four-mile-long west ridge, which Fred Beckey and Heinrich Harrer had climbed to make the first ascent of the peak in 1954.

Hunter was appealing enough, but our main objective was the central spur on the south face of Mount Foraker (17,400 feet). This lies between the ridge climbed by Alex Bertulis and party in 1968 and that climbed by the French in 1976; Bertulis' party had originally intended to do the spur from the Lacuna Glacier, but turned back after a few hundred feet in the face of rockfall. Another party, this time approaching via the Kahiltna Glacier (as we intended to do), had intentions on the route in 1975 but hardly reached the base due to avalanche danger.

This route had an entirely different character from that on Hunter. Instead of being almost all snow, it is almost all rock; the initial third of the route looked the steepest, largely bare rock with some ice mixed in, the second third consisted of a prominent ice rib with a very steep mixed section at the top, and in the last third a corniced ridge led back to a hanging glacier below the south summit. From the glacier to the south summit is a vertical rise of almost 9000 feet, at an average angle of 54°. From here we would have to follow an easy ridge one-and-a-half miles and another 1000 feet to the main summit, and then down the southeast ridge (Adams Carter and party, 1963). Due to its length and classic beauty, we had christened the route the Infinite Spur.

On the evening of our arrival we skied up the glacier to visit Tom Bauman and Wayne Errington, who were about to leave for the north buttress of Mount Hunter, a magnificent 4000-foot rock spur rising left of the central snow and ice slopes that we planned on. After wishing them luck, we returned to camp and slept. The next day in perfect weather we prepared food and gear for the climb: a small tent, full-length sleeping bags, winter clothing, food and fuel for five days, two ropes and a small selection of pickets, deadmen and ice-screws.

We planned to climb the lower slopes by night, for the cold would solidify the snow and reduce the avalanche hazard. At 10:30 PM on June 14 we left camp and skied to the bottom of the face. By midnight we were climbing, roped in case of crevasses but moving simultaneously for speed. The climbing itself was mostly moderate snow, although George did lead one pitch past a steep sérac. By 6 AM we had reached a flat area below the Triangle.

After a short rest and a bite to eat, we continued on, belaying now on higher-angle ice. Pitch followed pitch. As soon as the leader had put in his anchors, the second climbed through, as the third came up, using a Gibbs ascender as a belay. We could thus climb as quickly with three people as with two, but the slope still felt endless.

Following the line of least resistance, we hoped to intersect what had appeared to be an easy ridge leading left to the apex of the Triangle. Unfortunately it was anything but easy: steep and dangerously corniced. The sun made the snow wet and unstable. George teetered over several cornices before dropping back down on the face and traversing below them. Jeff continued traversing. Then I led the last pitch of the day to the apex. I was in for a shock.

We had expected a flat area to bivouac on; there was nothing. No decent anchors, no place to sit, let alone set up the tent, and after almost 18 hours of climbing, no energy left to think straight. But the worse was yet to come: the ridge ahead looked impossible or, at best, suicidal. It was not just steep and corniced, but *horribly* steep and corniced. Huge snow mushrooms sat on top of a knife-edge of ice, in places overhanging on both sides. In no condition to make any rational judgment, we left the anchors at the last stance, wrapped the rope around a lump of snow at the apex for additional security and chopped a small ledge for a bivouac.

We discussed the position that our over-confidence had placed us in. The crest of the ridge seemed impossible, but going down 4000 feet was unthinkable. The only alternative, a 300-foot rappel down the left side of the ridge and a traverse below the threatening cornices, was too danger-ous. Sleep that evening was restless and short, punctuated by the dull rumble of ice falling and the contortions necessary for the three of us to stay on the ledge. Two AM saw us awake and ready to go. By the time I had returned with the ice-screws from the last stance, Jeff was ready to start.

He made rapid progress along the top of the ridge; it looked as if we might actually have an easier time of it than expected. After one rope-length I started out. With few anchors and stances available, it would be safer and faster for both of us to move together. George belayed us from the bivouac.

I had gone perhaps twenty feet and was waiting for the gentle tug that was my cue to move on. But this time it wasn't so gentle. Suddenly, the rope came tight, jerking me into the air; blue and grey flashed by, all was a blur, and just as suddenly I came to a halt, bent over and straddling the ridge with 4000 feet of space on either side. Jeff had fallen almost 60 feet. As he came to a halt, the front-points of his crampons had snagged in the ice, shattering his left ankle.

The whole complexion of the climb changed drastically. All of our fine concepts of light and fast were dust in the face of an all-too-real situation: we were 4000 feet up a hard route with one member seriously injured, with no backup, no fixed ropes, no radio and no one to depend on but ourselves. Even in the best of conditions, there would have been no chance of a rescue. The weather was taking a turn for the worse. Fortunately Jeff managed to hobble, using his one good leg and an ice axe for support.

We immediately set off down the Triangle. George went first, setting up the rappel anchors, then Jeff, and myself last. I took out the extra anchors at each stance, leaving one behind; we hadn't enough to leave the normal doubled anchors. Many hours later we reached the flat area where we had stopped the day before. Thick mist obscured everything, and we were tired and wet as we set up the bivouac.

The next morning we splinted Jeff's leg. He could put some weight on it now, not much, but enough greatly to speed progress. We would lower or rappel on the steeper sections, and where the angle wasn't so great Jeff would hobble along, occasionally sinking into the snow when the pain became too great. The only suitable anchors we had were deadmen; we had but two and so the last man had to climb down.

Early in the afternoon of June 17 we reached the glacier, and within a few hours Jeff had flown out to the Anchorage hospital for treatment. It was a sad parting. We were all glad to be alive and relatively unscathed, but these climbs were Jeff's idea. He had provided most of the energy and drive behind them, and now he was gone. How much I wished that I had been leading that day!

George and I were left. A day of storm depressed us even further. Late that afternoon, Bauman and Errington came down, having climbed only 1500 feet of their route and survived an epic retreat in the storm. Things looked bleak; I wondered if yet another great climbing trip was about to go down the drain. All signs seemed to point south, back to Colorado and the safety of home.

We were still determined at least to finish the route on Hunter. Having been up a large part of the hard climbing, we almost had to complete it in Jeff's honor. The accident had shaken us badly, but oddly enough had also given us a great deal of confidence. There were no ego-games between George and me, no competition, and the experiences of the last few days had brought us very close.

June 19 it started to clear, and once again we made a midnight start. The fresh snow hampered us, but our old tracks often helped. This time we took a more direct line up the center of the Triangle. It was steeper, but we avoided the bad ridge which had slowed us so much before, and by 1 PM on June 20 we had regained the bivouac.

The ridge ahead looked as evil as ever, and we were if anything even more afraid of it. We slept fitfully, warmed by the sun but anxious about the night ahead, and started out at 2 AM on June 21.

The first few feet were the hardest; I felt as though I were going into a totally alien world, each step taking me further and further from home, friends and a life in the past. We moved together, silent, carefully probing the way ahead, separated and bonded by the rope between us. Near the end we shared a stance for a few moments. Ahead lay the most absurd mushroom yet, but we were almost there. A rappel onto the steep ice below was the only answer; I slid down on one rope as George belayed me on the other, and at the end traversed straight left. The ice was very steep, rock-hard and brittle, and I could barely maintain contact. Just as I ran out of rope, the ice ran out into snow, and in a few steps I was on flat ground. The ridge was done.

George rappelled, and I managed to pull him over a good part of the traverse with the belay rope. We were tremendously relieved, and the ice cliff was anti-climactic. An easy ramp led through it onto the upper snow slopes, and we plodded up these to bivouac on flat ground at 13,500 feet.

Sleep came easily, but when we awoke all was white. A storm had set in, and although we were only 1000 feet from the top, we couldn't see enough to move. After the better part of a day, we were blessed with a brief clearing, and another couple of hours saw us on the summit at 3 PM on June 22.

We raced back to the bivouac, packed the gear and set off, but by this time the clouds had closed in again. We had to navigate the broad upper plateau by compass in order to find the west ridge proper. It was slow and nerve-wracking work, plodding along, unable to tell up from down, constantly worried about crevasses and cornices.

The next 24 hours remain a kaleidoscope of imagery as we alternated between the whiteout and stunning views of the glaciers and peaks all around. The climbing was continuous and exposed; although never very difficult, every step required caution, and several sections had to be belayed. George fell when a small cornice broke, and later I plunged into my first crevasse. The sky cleared as night approached, illuminating the fantastic ice forms with the subtle velvet colors of the Alaskan summer twilight. We climbed throughout the night. By mid-morning we had passed the rocky section which was the crux of Beckey's and Harrer's route. A few hours later we reached an impasse; the snow of the obvious easy route was dangerously wet and avalanche-prone, so we bypassed it on the rocks to the left. There was flat ground at the end of the rock and, mercifully, we slept.

The morning of June 24 dawned perfectly clear, cold and windy, and we raced down the concrete-hard snow to the glacier and Base Camp: we had made it!

The possibility of doing Foraker had been on the edge of my consciousness ever since the completion of the corniced ridge. The idea seemed mad even then, but slowly the route began to dominate my thoughts. Could we do it, and should we even try? We were weaker as a team without Jeff, but perhaps two could move quicker than three. We had maps and a Washburn photo of the route, but Jeff had taken the reconnaissance flight. Most importantly, the commitment would be enormous: every act, from packing at the start to our eventual return to Base Camp, would require our fullest attention, concentration on detail and consciousness. We were fully aware of the implications of the climb, and even more aware of our fear, doubts and hesitation.

Finally the risks and uncertainty of Foraker seemed to be too much; we decided on the Cassin Ridge of Mount McKinley instead. It was a relief to have made the decision, but a nagging doubt still persisted. As great a route as the Cassin is, it was not what we had come for. An hour before leaving, we made the final decision: Foraker it would be. Otherwise, we would never know. . . .

George retired to the tent to write to his children. I puttered about, cooked dinner, anxious and relieved at once. Part of me hoped that we could now honorably fail, perhaps burning up enough time and energy in the process to justify a quick consolation romp up the West Buttress; another part could just dimly visualize the possibilities of the route, a fantasy of rock and ice, mist and wind.

Silently skiing through the night, we passed the base of the southeast ridge, leaving a small cache of food and our extra skis. A pass, an icefall, a strange stagnant glacier of dripping séracs, another pass: at 10 AM on June 26 we reached a snow shoulder and our first view of the route.

It looked immense and beautiful, almost powerful in the crystal morning air. This close, features opened up; a huge blank-looking area appeared more reasonable close up than in the photographs, and on the whole the climbing didn't look quite as hard and sustained as we had expected. We set up our tiny tent and spent the day resting and observing the face. No rocks fell, and the weather was still good. It seemed we had no good reason to turn back.

We set out at 3 AM on June 27. Our heavy packs slowed progress, and after a few hundred feet of moving together we started belaying; the climbing was still easy, but at least this way we could rest and take off the packs after each pitch. George led a hard pitch of mixed rock and snow, and then we were on the rock proper.

And very good rock it was, massively fractured, but solid, rough in texture and a delight to climb on. Mist rose as the sun warmed the glacier, enveloping us in a secure grey shroud. Alternating leads, we climbed until 10 PM, then shovelled snow from a ledge and set up the tent.

We were exhausted, but things seemed fine. So far, we were a day-and-a-half ahead of our most optimistic schedule, and had already passed what we thought would be the hardest rock-climbing of the route. The weather remained good, but our elation was tempered with apprehension, for climbing much above this point would commit us totally to going for the top.

The night was clear and cold, but within a few hours the next day the mist had returned. We continued up interesting mixed rock and ice and finally reached the bottom of the ice rib. Mist had turned to snow, but the clouds looked thin; perhaps it was just a small local storm. Several pitches up the ice we bivouacked, cutting small ledges out of the slope on which to sleep. It was a cold and uncomfortable night, and my thoughts turned once again to home and friends. We were really committed now.

Morning brought more clouds and snow. As we continued on, the weather worsened. It got very cold, and often we couldn't see each other at the other end of the rope; snow fell and built up on the slopes above, inundating us with spindrift avalanches. Soon rocks appeared on our left. We were nearing the top of the ice rib and knew that somehow, somewhere, we would have to break through these rocks and onto the ridge leading back to the hanging glacier. But where? The rock here was grim, black, loose and horribly steep.

The ice rib narrowed; I tried one line through the rock in search of a bivouac but gave up after 50 feet. While climbing back down, I slipped and fell a terrifying 20 feet down the ice. The rocks gradually squeezed the ice rib to nothing against the void to the right. We stopped here for a welcome cup of soup and a rest. It was 3 AM on June 30, and we had been climbing for 18 hours straight.

There was no bivouac in sight but a way opened up ahead that would bring us onto the corniced ridge. A steep, rotten traverse over snowy ledges gave access to an intimidating and *very* steep mixed gully; it looked desperate, but the rock all around was even worse. I led the traverse and belayed at the bottom of the gully, which poured almost continually with spindrift. George came across. Weak and exhausted, he felt incapable of leading safely but was willing to follow.

I was tired as well, but still felt strong. My mind was clear and surprisingly calm as I visualized the way ahead, keenly aware of the chalkboard screech of crampons on rock, the rattling thud of an axe in too-thin ice, a sling on a frozen-in spike, the dull ring of a bad piton behind a loose block, calf muscles screaming for relief, choking spindrift in eyes, throat, down the neck. A couple of pitches and we were back on easy ground, and another rope-length brought us to a point 50 feet from the crest of the ridge.

The sun broke over the skyline as I belayed George up this final stretch, and a slight wind stirred the air. The tension of the last few hours ebbed away like the snow crystals dancing in the new light before my eyes. Warmth returned, and with it a need for sleep. We again hacked ledges out of the ice, melted snow and cooked; the day was clear and we could lie in the blessed sun without sleeping bags.

July 1 dawned clear as well. We spent the day making an endless traverse below the cornices to the hanging glacier. It was almost twice as long as we had expected from the pictures; still tired from the previous day, and suffering some intestinal distress, I asked George to take over the lead for several pitches. At long last we reached the end and sat down for a welcome rest.

After a few hundred feet of slogging up deep snow, we found a convenient sérac, under which we collapsed. Soon the tent was up and the food was on. It was an incredible relief to be able to unrope and lie down flat without the constant worry about dropping a boot, or the stove, or something else equally important. It was even possible to fall down without sliding into the abyss.

All good things come to an end sooner or later. We awoke to the sound of wind and snow; another storm had set in, and it had turned bitterly cold. Snow slowly buried the tent as we spent many listless hours resting and trying to conserve our dwindling reserves. Exhausted from the strain of almost 80 pitches of climbing and a series of bad bivouacs, the altitude was beginning to affect us, and we had precious little food with which to build up our strength.

The storm continued through July 2. We began to worry . . . was this one of the legendary ten-day Alaskan blizzards? A closer look at the food bag revealed just how desperate things could become: we had four freeze-dried meals left, but little else; a few scraps of cheese, some margarine and logan bread, a few hard candies. We had already been on slim rations for a couple days, and what we had could be stretched for perhaps five more. But how would we ever make it over the summit and back down after that?

We had stopped in a sheltered spot, but wind-blown snow built up all around; for several hours we couldn't get out to clear the tent or relieve ourselves. Opening the zipper even a half an inch brought a blast of powder inside, soaking our already-sodden gear even more. Lethargy set in, and every movement became an effort. It seemed we would never be able to leave.

The morning of July 3 was good enough for a dash to the summit. "Dash" is hardly the word; it took us three hours just to get going, and we got to the summit at 4 PM. The high wind dropped, but –20° temperatures at 17,000 feet chilled us to the bone and we both worried about frostbite. After a few moments on the summit for the obligatory victory photos we headed down.

The first section of the descent was so easy that we ran, losing a couple of thousand feet in elevation in a couple of hours. Each foot lost gave us new energy as the effects of altitude receded, but the easy going came to an end all too quickly. We did some tricky down-climbing, belaying occasionally, and the weather once again changed its mind. Big black clouds moved in from the north, south and east; Foraker blocked the western view, but we suspected that things would look bleak there as well. We simply couldn't afford to sit out another storm.

All went well until we hit a heavily-corniced section of the ridge, apparently the crux of the route. We were very leery of cornices, and moved slowly and carefully around them, well below the fracture line. But we weren't careful enough. Time slowed down; the next few seconds lasted an eternity. George was ahead, 30 feet from the crest of the ridge; he came across what he thought was a small crevasse, probed it and stepped across. There was a dull cracking sound, and a fracture ran along the ridge for 100 feet. The cornice disappeared, taking George with it, the rope came tight and jerked me off my feet; I flew down one side of the ridge as George plunged down the other in the midst of tons of ice. The rope pulled tighter, arching me up to the crest of the ridge, and I saw myself shooting over the edge and the two of us falling helplessly to the chaotic glacier 8000 feet below.

But we stopped. I was 20 feet from the edge, and rammed in a dead-man within seconds. The rope was still taut. I was sure that George was either dead or very seriously injured. Shouts brought no answers, then the rope slackened. I pulled up a few feet, then another few feet: miracle of miracles, he was at least in good enough shape to climb! We were soon reunited and set about gathering our shattered wits. George was bruised and shaken and had been cut on the nose, but that was it. We had been lucky once again.

We belayed every pitch from this point on, even ones we could walk across. We couldn't take any more chances. Mist enveloped us as we continued down to 11,000 feet and another welcome bivouac. It was 8 AM on July 4. We had completed another long day.

Once again we awoke to a whiteout and were forced to stay in the tent until 11 AM. A short clearing gave us a glimpse of the way down; we had to take advantage of it, for we had only one dinner and a few scraps of food left. Almost as soon as we started the weather closed in, and we descended in a maelstrom of wind, rock, snow and ice. Very nearly at the end of our tether, we were only too conscious of the possibility of a fatal slip. Almost suddenly, it was over. We actually unroped to stumble down the muddy hill at the base of the ridge, laughing and joking about rock crevasses and mud cornices. The skis were only a hundred yards away on the glacier, but we prudently roped up again to get to them.

A quick feast on the cached food revived flagging energies.

It was almost warm, but the mountain gods weren't through with us yet. Mist crept in over the glacier, so we were forced to navigate by compass. The soft snow sucked at our skis, and every step required a conscious effort of will. Only the thought of canned food and banana bread at Base Camp kept us going. We arrived at 3 AM on July 6, gorged ourselves and fell into a deep, dreamless sleep.

The morning dawned clear and warm. We aired our filthy bodies, ate, drank beer, talked to the other parties at the landing area; the sudden transition from the life-and-death struggles of the climb to the world of people, comfort and safety was overwhelming. That afternoon we flew out to the greenery and mosquitoes of Talkeetna.

Denali's Child — 1954
[Mount Hunter]

— FRED BECKEY —

*Between the mountain giants of Denali and Sultana is the Alaska Range's third-highest peak. Like the other two, it stands grandly above the mountain crowd, and at 14,570 feet is easily visible from Anchorage, 110 miles to the south. It would follow, then, that this third giant is "Denali's child." Or so Alaska's Interior Natives believed, calling the mountain **Begguya**. English-speaking mapmakers decided otherwise and named it Mount Hunter. Or rather, misnamed it, as Fred Beckey explains below. The error was finally discovered in 1950, but the mountain has officially remained Mount Hunter.*

Whether Begguya or Hunter, the peak that mountaineering author Jon Waterman calls "the most difficult 14,000-foot mountain in North America" remained unclimbed until the early 1950s. What's even more curious is that no one even attempted it until Bradford Washburn (that man again) described an approach to the summit in a 1953 American Alpine Journal story titled "Mount Hunter Via the West Ridge, a Proposed Ascent."

One year later, a three-man international party flew into the Alaska Range. After a first ascent of Mount Deborah (another Alaska Range gem), Austrian Heinrich Harrer, German Henry Meybohm, and American Fred

Beckey followed Hunter's West Ridge to the top. Already a legendary alpinist, Harrer had achieved lasting fame for his part in the historic 1938 ascent of Switzerland's Eiger Nordwand. Beckey, meanwhile, was well on his way to becoming an American legend. Best known for his pioneering ascents in the Pacific Northwest's Cascade Range, Beckey first gained widespread attention when, as a teenager, he and his brother Helmy did the second ascent of Mount Waddington's South Face, in Canada's Coast Range.

Since his first trip to Alaska in the forties, Beckey has climbed dozens of Alaska mountains, many of them first ascents. But none would match his Denali-Deborah-Hunter triple in 1954 (he and Meybohm had put up a new route on Denali's Northwest Buttress before teaming with Harrer).

Of the Beckey/Harrer Hunter ascent, Jon Waterman has written, "As ice climbers, Beckey and Harrer were decades ahead of their time. . . . This was the first alpine-style climb of a technical route in the Alaska Range. . . . This was also a landmark climb because few climbers had dealt with such steep ice and extensive cornicing."

The account given here, "Denali's Child—1954," is excerpted from Fred Beckey's Mount McKinley: Icy Crown of North America, *published in 1993 by The Mountaineers in Seattle.*

*It is the steepest and most spectacular
of the three great peaks in the Alaska Range.*
—Jonathan Waterman, *High Alaska*, 1988

TO HONOR EXPEDITION SPONSORSHIPS by his aunt in 1903, Robert Dunn had applied the name *Mount Hunter* to a minor uplift on Mount McKinley's western buttress—now Kahiltna Dome—but when maps appeared after the turn of the century, the name mysteriously appeared for the third highest peak in the Alaska Range, on the opposite flank of Kahiltna Glacier. Through a government surveyor's error, a spectacular unnamed, 14,570-foot colossus of rock and ice nine miles south of Mount McKinley became Mount Hunter. As generally was the case, the earlier native name did not survive: the appellation of the natives was *Begguya* (Denali's child). Dr. Cook, who often saw the strategically located mountain, called it Little McKinley, and more than one prospector referred to it as Mount Roosevelt.

Not remotely resembling Mount McKinley or Mount Foraker (Denali's wife), Mount Hunter is a massive, complex bulk with three summits, seamed with cliffs 4,000 to 7,000 feet high—a three-mile-wide high plateau with numerous icy ridges that on a map resemble the tentacles of a spiny octopus. Now considered the most difficult 14,000-foot peak in North America by knowledgeable mountaineers, little was known about the present Mount Hunter until Bradford Washburn made a photographic study flight and in 1953 published a detailed proposal for a probable route via its five-mile-long west ridge. Unlike Mount McKinley, Hunter's highest peak is the northern one, but like McKinley, the western ridge has become the most popular (although not the easiest) route to the elusive summit.

In late spring of 1954, after the expedition to Mount McKinley's Northwest Buttress, Henry Meybohm and I decided to extend our mountaineering forays to Mount Deborah and Mount Hunter, fortunately enlisting the most capable companionship of the famous Austrian mountaineer Heinrich Harrer. The renowned alpinist, who took part in the Eiger's first ascent in 1938, was visiting Alaska for the first time. Harrer drove from New York City in a "beautiful" green Packard and on the graveled Alcan Highway "had countless blowouts and flat tires." Originally, Harrer just wanted to travel about the United States, but he changed his plans when he saw a National Geographic article illustrated with mountain photography, including Mount Hunter and captions indicating the peak was unclimbed. "I tore out these two pages and went to Alaska, where I found you by chance," Harrer recalled recently.

While I was on Mount McKinley, Harrer had climbed Mount Drum in the Wrangell Mountains and was now ready for a more serious challenge. After we met through common friends in Fairbanks, the three of us readied for an attempt on the imposing Mount Deborah—its unclimbed, corniced summit striking a spire into the sky southward. The Austrian's best recalled anecdote related to expedition preparation: "I told you and Henry to buy food for 20 days—one kilo a person a day. I also said, buy what you enjoy to eat, I don't care. After we landed on the glacier and Sheldon had left we sorted out all you had bought: it was the greatest amount of weight with the smallest amount of calories. I learned for the first time the way of American institution."

After the ascent of Mount Deborah, Don Sheldon, who had not yet gained fame as a skilled glacier pilot, flew us directly to Talkeetna.

Inspired by Terris Moore's glacier landings, Sheldon had recently converted his green Piper Super Cub to have ski-wheel capability. Still elated by our quick success on Deborah, the three of us spent an impatient week under cloudy skies in the little town, where we were likely considered bizarre mountain tourists. In the early 1950s the town was merely a boat landing on the Susitna River and a way-stop on the Alaska Railroad. Tourism had not yet made its mark (there was an inn and a trading post), and anyone appearing in alpine attire was probably marked as a bewitched personality who was preparing early for Halloween.

To add to our abnormal appearance, instead of staying at the inn or tenting out, we set up headquarters in Don Sheldon's hangar. Alaskan hospitality reached out quickly. During our first saunter through Talkeetna, we met an outdoorsman who, upon learning our plans, offered to let us stay in his hunting cabin in the Dutch Hills (which we later did). Another resident set us up with the opportunity to fish the river. While waiting for the cloudy weather to move out, we caught three great salmon—the largest weighing fifty-four pounds. Relaxing in Talkeetna turned into a generally good time.

One day Sheldon came over to our corner in the hangar and asked, "Do you get any money for climbing?" Not quite satisfied with our philosophic ramblings on our "inner needs" for alpine challenges, he returned in an hour and asked if we would like to make some money. With Harrer skeptically quizzing the adventurous bush pilot, Sheldon explained that an aircraft had crashed on a mountain (he did not disclose where) and that he needed alpine climbers to get the payroll in the crash and bring it down the mountain. The tentative plan was that Sheldon would purchase an old airplane and land it in the very confined crash area. Because the airplane would never be able to fly out, Sheldon would descend with the mountaineers after retrieving the payroll. We never heard more about the potentially lucrative plan.

In my account in 1955 in the *American Alpine Journal,* our departure from the Talkeetna dirt airstrip is described:

> Finally, on June 29th, the clouds seemed to break up to the west, and on flying toward Mt. Hunter we saw the entire Alaska Range basking in broken sunshine. Our air course took us over the Tokositna country and then over some rugged peaks to the upper Kahiltna Glacier. Again there were busy moments as we

attempted to study the route and at the same time locate an area for a safe landing. We landed about 1½ miles west of Hunter, in the level area (alt. 6700 ft.) between it and the bulk of Foraker. It is best to make these summer glacier landings very early in the morning, while the crust is still hard. Unfortunately, we were delayed, and by the time the craft was ready to leave, the crust had softened to an extent that it required twenty minutes of taxiing on the glacier before the plane gained sufficient momentum for the take-off. For a while, we were certain we would have to feed another man!

With complete confidence in Washburn's proposal, we pitched our single Logan tent on the glacier, "stacked up our food supply, and set out to explore the lower section of the ridge with light packs." Midday in the hot sun is not the optimum time to move along on clumsy snowshoes, but despite the wet "goo" clinging to the webbing, progress would have been slower without them.

There were several potential ways to the ridgecrest at 9,100 feet, none of which were in ideal condition under the blaring early-summer sun. On our first probe to the West Ridge, we chose a minor glacier trough that formed a depression between two granitic rock walls. Although the trough was exposed to some falling ice debris, it seemed generally safe but for one jumbled area. According to my account, "It was necessary to clamber about for a half-hour on some steep slopes to bypass a great bergschrund, but then the glacier sloped back again." We climbed a 200-foot snow wall to where a rock pinnacle blocked progress on the crest; here we made some explorations before finding a way through blocks to the ridge and then made three rappels to a narrow col. Here we left a cache, feeling secure that we had mastered the uncertainties of the first third of the West Ridge.

The morning of July 1 greeted us with a quick storm, which brought a sparkle onto the otherwise dull tone of the glacier. Leaving only some food marked with a pole for the planned outbound trek, we carried clumsy loads along our tracks and then again rappelled to the cache at the col. Adding the additional load to our packs, we continued along the narrow, corniced ridge. Because of our awkward packs, we were barely able to scale a short, vertical snow wall at the peak of a 9,550-foot ridge hump.

The route now traversed the crest to a steep "drop-off" where we had to cut steps in the ice to descend. Our first camp was located at a minor col adjacent to a large rock step. Finding some flat stones here, we laid down a level tent platform. My account continues:

> One of the chief problems of the ridge is the granitic rock wedge that rises for the next 500 feet. We explored it that afternoon in a flurry of snow, leaving a cache at the highest point and putting in three fixed ropes. Generally, we found it best to keep a hundred feet south of the crest, but at the middle section, we had to climb some difficult cracks and a chimney, including some overhang. When it came time to bring up our packs, it was necessary to haul them up a 50-foot chimney, a key point on the climb of this ridge. Needless to say, belays were in order the entire distance. On the final push to the highest camp at 10,600 feet we were fearful of the snow surface atop the glare ice of the steep ridge slopes, so waited until the sun left them in the evening before beginning the ascent. There is ample light to travel all night, for at this latitude the rose-pink sun poises below the rim of the horizon for only a few hours and the sky remains suffused with light. As we had hoped, the steep wall at 10,000 feet was well crusted; we were able to crampon up it with but a few steps, though the points bit into hard glare ice. Even more exposed was the great ridge sweeping to a point at 10,600 feet. Here we had to cut away a swath of drifted snow on a very steep slope, hew out many steps, and place an ice piton for safety. This slope ranges from 45° to 70° for several hundred feet and is best overcome with a fixed rope.
>
> As if to remind us of the cornice danger, a large section of drooping ice broke off almost adjacent to us as we plowed along a level stretch of knee-deep snow on the ridge. Secure in the knowledge that there was no further danger at this exact spot, we decided to place our final camp here. It was midnight and our feet were becoming cold; so the tent was put up, and then without loads we reconnoitered a route over the next ridge hump and along the dangerous cornices to the saddle beneath the final ridge of Hunter. Several tension rifts cracked as we

broke the tracks along the ridge; we carefully stayed as low off the ridge as we possibly could, always keeping on the alert for a break and the necessity of a lightning-quick belay.

Once back at camp, we had a near-catastrophe when my stove blew up just as I was crawling out of the tent. If the blast had occurred just seconds earlier, I might have been engulfed in flames. Fortunately I was not burned and my companions were safely outside. Though it was very small and intended only for bivouac, our spare Borde stove carried through with snow melting and cooking.

In high spirits and with promise of another perfect day, we went to sleep. Our climbing plan was to rest through the day and start late in order to climb on the steep and dangerous slopes after the sun had left them. Accordingly, we packed and dressed for the final ascent—taking down jackets and large lunches—and left the tent at 4:30 PM.

The long and quite exposed ice slope, which extended from 10,700 to 11,500 feet, turned out to be the most taxing on the ascent. Although the front points of our crampons bit well into the ice, so eliminating the need to cut steps, the surface was often unstable and insecure. We deemed it wise to chop bucket-sized belay stances and to place ice pitons between the thirteen belays.

The route continued much like Washburn had predicted: more cornices, steep and short ice pitches, then more cornices. As the sun dropped behind bulky peaks south of Foraker, the temperature plummeted; the wet rope became stiffly frozen, retaining its kinks and curls.

As we gazed toward Mount Hunter's 13,200-foot upper plateau, all that could be seen was a menacing icewall barrier that capped the ridge. Below "tumbled an array of crevasses in every direction." We were concerned that the ice barrier could end our venture rather soon, for no feasible bypass was apparent.

We approached hopefully and kept looking at a large longitudinal crevasse entering the wall directly above the ridge. As we reached its height, we saw that it afforded a route on its sloping side; the "Golden Gate," as we named it, proved a godsend, for it was an avenue to the upper plateau. Any other route to the summit would have been next to impossible; this one worked out readily.

Crossing the half-mile of level névè was tedious because we kept breaking through to the knees. Never had we seen snow conditions such as these. Even on wind-blown ridges one would break through, and only on the steepest slopes was there hard ice. Between midnight and four we plodded across the slope, attempted the corner of the summit ridge, turned back for the west face of the summit pyramid, and climbed a very steep loose snow slope to the final crest. On the last stretch we came into the glorious radiance of the full morning sunshine. Hunter had been climbed! It would be difficult to imagine a more beautiful view than that afforded by the summit. It was warm enough to take off gloves and jackets, and for an hour we rested and photographed. The glittering surrounding summits provided a fascinating study, and of course McKinley and Foraker were resplendent. We agreed that the entire region was one with a great mountaineering future.

Ice pitons and chopped bollards (small pedestals cut out of ice) enabled us to rappel the long, relentless slope, and in twenty hours after leaving the tent we returned for a much-needed rest. We were fatigued. On the 6th we resumed our way back along the long ridge with lighter packs. To reduce error on the steepest rock and ice sections, we resorted to rappels. Descending with packs proved awkward. Below 8,000 feet the snow surface sometimes slid; several times we even found it prudent to begin minor slides in order to make the descent safer. All this required vigilance and patience—always difficult to maintain when nearing the base of a mountain.

Once below the threatening sérac wall, we were out of danger. Fortunately our old steps still appeared, permitting us to take the correct route through and around crevasses to reach the base cache without incident.

After looking in vain for a buried bundle of fresh salmon we had brought on the ski-plane from Talkeetna, we then speculated about the unproven route down Kahiltna Glacier. To get the best possible surface conditions, we began at night, taking nine hours for the first six of the thirty glacier miles. Soft snow reinforced the imminent danger of crevasses: wearing snowshoes, we always kept the rope tight. Pushing hard we continued for nine more hours to reach the "great bend"—some eighteen miles from the cache. Our camp that night was leveled from rocks and ice of a medial moraine. On July 9 we continued on ice ribbons near the glacier's central area. In five miles we were forced to the east by a zone of crevasses, and to exit from the ice we had to ford a deep stream. Meybohm, the lightest man, was swept off his feet and forced to crawl into a thick alder jungle on the far bank.

After ascending the embankment, we followed the stream valley upslope, heading for the hunting cabin near the Dutch Hills. By the time we reached the cabin, we were truly starved. Our last taste of food (cornmeal and an upland bird) had been at breakfast on the glacier. On our last day we struggled along the bushy upland tundra near Dutch Creek (aware that this was grizzly bear habitat), somewhere crossing the Browne–Dr. Cook route of 1906. A last crossing of the Dutch Hills brought us to a placer mine and a crude roadway. The cordial owners welcomed us to a hearty supper and, to enliven the setting, one of the miners poured more gold nuggets onto the table than any of us had ever seen. Harrer could not resist buying a few for souvenirs—they certainly would get some attention in Austria.

As the three of us, sometimes mixing the German and English tongue, chatted about our good fortune with the weather and the ascent of Mount Hunter, the time now went quickly. This was fortunate, for our feet were blistery and sore, and our backs ached from the tiresome tundra hiking. We reflected on how we had planned the ascent (and descent) of much of the West Ridge so that the dangerous passages were undertaken when they were in the shade or during the short Alaska night. Later I wrote:

On Mt. Hunter the cornices were so huge that it was necessary to remain far below the crest in certain places. At point 10,800 feet we kept two rope lengths from the edge, but received a great scare from surface settling—possibly a slab formation on the prevailing windward slope. Three times we heard, and once saw, a cornice loudly crack, but not collapse, almost at our knee level. One fracture crack ran right above the steps of a previous reconnaissance. At one place there was a crest cornice atop a flattened,wide ridge which collapsed almost at our feet, despite the fact the cornice rose only some 15 feet atop a flat ridge. At point 10,600 feet, where one has to climb a great wall and overcome a lateral cornice-wall, one is exposed to the danger of a general collapse of the entire edge of the slope, which acts as a cornice of its own; a small portion of it broke as we maneuvered to belay atop the point.

Since our ascent, skilled mountaineers have sought out numerous other challenging routes on Mount Hunter. There have been some remarkable ascents made on this colossus of rock and ice. Vin Hoeman, who was a member of the peak's second-ascent party, prophesized the future when in the 1960s he compiled a guidebook to Alaska's mountains. In this unpublished work he termed Mount Hunter the "most steep and spectacular of the Alaska Range's three great giants, with a multitude of difficult and dangerous routes awaiting those who would attempt them."

Lone Wolf (The <u>Other</u> John Waterman)
[Mount Hunter and Denali]

– JONATHAN WATERMAN –

*John Mallon Waterman never achieved the widespread national acclaim
of Fred Beckey, Brad Washburn, David Roberts, Royal Robbins, or some other
climbers within these pages—men whose name-recognition would eventually
extend far beyond America's mountaineering community. Yet by the time
Waterman disappeared into the Alaska Range in April 1981, the 29-year-old
climber had become something of an Alaskan legend, an eccentric personality
known for both his climbing brilliance and his sometimes bizarre behavior.*

*"Johnny" demonstrated his genius at an early age. Taken rock climbing at
the age of thirteen by his father, Guy, he quickly became one of the hottest young
talents in New York's Shawangunks. At sixteen he reached Denali's summit,
and soon afterward gave himself totally to mountaineering. By his early twen-
ties he'd climbed extensively within the Alaska Range, as well as in Scotland,
England, Turkey, and the Alps.*

*Of all Waterman's mountaineering pursuits, none was more outrageous
than his 1978 145-day solo ascent of Mount Hunter, a 14,570-foot neighbor of
Denali and the Alaska Range's third highest peak. Other mountaineers were
shocked by this unprecedented mountain marathon. Some still consider it the*

most difficult solo climb ever done in the Alaska Range. Others have used terms like "crazy" and "amazing" to describe it. Certainly, as Anchorage moun-taineering guide Gary Bocarde says, "It's something you have to put into a separate category, all its own." Waterman later described his "vendetta with Mount Hunter" in 1979 in The American Alpine Journal. *Intending to avenge his two previous failures to reach the summit of Hunter, he chose to solo the previously unclimbed Southeast Spur, among the most difficult routes in North America.*

The story of Johnny that's included here was written by another Waterman, Jon. Not related by blood, the two seem nevertheless connected in spirit. An accomplished mountaineer in his own right, Jon Waterman is the celebrated author of several climbing books, most of them tied in some way to Denali. Both Hunter and Denali play central roles in this story, but the essay is more a character study than a mountaineering tale. The portrait, however, is of both the Watermans, Jon and Johnny, whose climbing careers were (and, in the case of Jon, still are) so closely connected to the Alaska Range.

"Lone Wolf (The Other *John Waterman)" first appeared in Jonathan Waterman's book* In the Shadow of Denali, *published in 1994 by Dell Books.*

> *I live not in myself, but I become*
> *Portion of that around me; and to me*
> *High mountains are a feeling, but the hum*
> *Of human cities torture.*
> —Lord Byron

ON APRIL FOOL'S DAY 1981, John Mallon Waterman beelined through a maze of crevasses. He seemed unperturbed that one of these black holes might swallow him alive. His destination—the unclimbed east face of Denali—hung above, bristling with hanging glaciers and avalanche slopes. "Johnny" carried a small pack—and an episodic madness that crippled him in the city. Here in the shadow of Denali, however, with the commitment of a samurai, and a considerable climbing talent, he knew a profound sense of belonging. Within days, Johnny disappeared from the face of the earth.

No soloist committed himself to mountains like Johnny. Where Charlie Porter spent thirty-six hours climbing Denali's Cassin Ridge in

1976, or Reinhold Messner soloed the north face of Everest over three days in 1980, Johnny Waterman spent 145 days soloing the comparatively bantam Mount Hunter in 1978. And his route, the southeast spur, unlike most famous solos, had never been climbed. In one prolonged swoop, Johnny would also complete Hunter's first traverse and its first solo. Mountaineers still murmur of this stunt, with both derision and awe; he remains a primordial myth of Alaskan mountaineering. *Outside* magazine's Tenth Anniversary issue lauded his Mount Hunter solo in a decade's worth of "The Ten Greatest Feats." In the same issue, eight pages later, as if unsure how to catalog Waterman, *Outside* depicted him in "The Ten Strangest Feats" for disappearing on Denali.

I happened to be climbing on Denali at the same time the rangers were searching for Waterman. Climbers to whom I was introduced on the West Buttress Route would raise their eyebrows and celebrate my survival—until I spelled out that I was J-o-n, and the missing J-o-h-n had not been found, despite extensive aerial searches. After two weeks of overflights, the Park Service closed the "Lone Wolf" file that belonged to John Waterman. The news traveled quickly. A nationally syndicated column was released about Waterman's death. In the trailer that served as the Talkeetna post office, the postmaster stamped "return to sender" on any mail addressed to a Waterman with a first name beginning "Jo." She didn't know that two climbers with similar names were sharing the same "General Delivery, Talkeetna" address, so on the back of every Waterman envelope she carefully penciled in "lost and presumed dead." These letters were returned to a score of friends. Some mourned my passing; others took the trouble to call a Talkeetna bush pilot and unravel the mystery.

Although I never met Johnny, my sense of kinship to him and his father would grow until the whole star-crossed event seemed more destiny than coincidence. The odds of two climbers with the same name establishing their reputations in the Far North are unlikely indeed.

Until age twelve, Johnny's obsession had been the Civil War. His older and younger brothers, Bill and Jim, respectively, made friends easily, but middle-child Johnny kept to his soldiers, war books, and complicated battle games. He lived alone on the third floor of the family's huge Stamford, Connecticut, home.

After Johnny turned thirteen, his father took him and his brother Bill up multipitch rock climbs at the Shawangunks ("the Gunks") in New

York. Johnny was hooked. The Civil War was forgotten. Climbing became his sole focus.

Boyd Everett, who engineered new routes on Denali and throughout Alaska, also took note of Johnny. Everett had seldom given Johnny's father, Guy, the time of day, but now he engaged him in long conversations about Johnny's potential, then drove him to New Hampshire for weekend climbs.

Johnny trained every day. He walked the two and a half miles to high school as fast as he could. In the afternoon he'd walk home, tag the front door, walk back to school, then head back home at a brisk pace. Each evening he did forty sets of ten push-ups.

In a letter to me, Guy recalled leading an overhanging Gunks climb called Bonnie's Roof, harder than anything he had ever done before. "It took me a bit to commit myself to the desperate moves," Guy wrote, "with Johnny calling up encouraging exhortations all the while. When I finally pulled myself over the last move of the sequence, it was to the accompaniment of a peal of excited squeaks and squeals: Johnny almost beside himself with pleasure that I had done it. Then when he came up and got his hands on the final holds, I suddenly saw his feet swinging way out from the cliff: in his sheer exuberance and high spirits he just kicked his feet off for the joy of it, before putting them back on the rock and completing the move."

When Johnny was a teenage prodigy in the Gunks, he reached a zenith of ecstasy, soon to fall forever beyond his grasp. On another overhanging barrier of the day, mastered by only a few of the local rock wizards, Johnny finally finessed over the crux. In his elation up above the overhang, he hopped lightly from one foot to the other on a small hold—but missed and fell off. Everyone, including Johnny, swinging on the rope in space, guffawed with laughter.

Another partner recalled that "the sheer power of his enthusiasm for my climbing could inspire me to climb like I'd never climbed before. It was a great gift. Climbing with Johnny was like being inside a grand piece of orchestral music in which all is harmony and there are no wrong notes."

One gifted young climber, Howie Davis, became a fast friend. Howie taught Johnny that surpassing the highest standards (called "5.10 plus" at that time) was easy if you perceived climbing as part gymnastics and part ballet—and then rehearsed it again and again, a notion that preceded the ensuing sport-climbing revolution by two decades. So in a day when teenagers were rare in the Gunks, fifteen-year-old Johnny led one of the area's most difficult climbs, Retribution. When Howie said gently, "Go, Johnny," he committed himself to the overhang. On other days the two could be seen bouncing down Carriage Road beneath the crag just after dawn, heading for their first climb—Howie doing front flips and cartwheels, Johnny matching him all the way.

Shortly thereafter, Johnny's friend became enmeshed in an unhappy love triangle with another climber's wife. One gray morning Howie climbed to the top of a route called Jackie and flung himself toward a giant boulder below. Although he missed the boulder, he was still thoroughly dead once he hit the ground. Howie's theatrical suicide left indelible marks on Johnny.

That winter of early 1969, Everett invited Johnny to his apartment and showed the gathering of young climbers pictures of unclimbed Alaskan routes. Everett undoubtedly sowed the seed of Mount Hunter's south ridge to both Johnny and a medical student, Dean Rau.

A few months later, Everett, Dave Seidman (who first tied a rope on Johnny), and five others were buried alive when an avalanche pulverized the foot of Dhaulagiri in Nepal. Johnny heard the news on a weekday afternoon; Guy rushed home from work to try to console his son, but Johnny fled the house and brooded alone for several hours.

To most young climbers eager to make their mark on the mountains of the world, and filled with the peculiarly adolescent belief in immortality, death seems a most improbable and unlikely outcome. But to the impressionable young Johnny, having three of his most influential friends die while climbing had a devastating impact. Furthermore, at sixteen, Johnny had no girlfriend and knew no social life or sport other than climbing.

Johnny met Chuck Loucks and Ed Nester at the Gunks. Both were old enough to be Johnny's father and soon took over where Everett had left off. Loucks was a carefree imp and Johnny embraced his puckish humor. Loucks taught Johnny how to make huge airy leaps from boulder to boulder at their favorite rock climbing area. And that summer, Nester brought Johnny on his first Alaskan climbing trip; Johnny became the third youngest person to climb Denali, summiting from fourteen thousand feet with Brad Snyder and Tom Frost.

Of course, Johnny had no idea that he would later become the most talked-about soloist in Alaskan climbing, generating more ink and legend than any other soloist. This summer of 1969, the Japanese mountaineer Naomi Uemura wrote to the Park Service, which tried to refuse him permission to solo Denali. Since soloing wasn't illegal, Uemura arrived in August of the following year. After a secluded nine-day climb up the West Buttress Route, he reached the summit on August 26.

Many other soloists would arrive over the years. By the end of the crowded 1970s, dozens had soloed the West Buttress Route. Once the route began to get busy, a solo could be done without any trailbreaking or isolation. At worst, a soloist might have to spend nights alone in his or her tent.

There are other, uncrowded routes where self-sufficiency is paramount to a soloist's survival. In 1976 Charlie Porter made a remarkable thirty-six-hour solo of the Cassin Ridge Route; in 1991, Mugs Stump fired up it in fifteen hours, wearing only a fanny pack. In 1977 Ruprecht Kammerlander soloed the west rib in a week; in 1990, a Russian climber steamed up the route in a long day. All four of these soloists were largely reticent and received little press about their accomplishments.

Women, too, have soloed the mountain. In 1982, after being helicoptered off of Mount St. Elias and thrown into jail for bypassing Canadian Customs, fifty-four-year-old Miri Ercolani of Italy started up Denali. She spent ten days on the West Buttress Route and claimed to reach the summit in mid-July. During a storm at ten thousand feet, she was trapped in a snowcave, and since she didn't remove her boots for five days, she suffered severely frostbitten feet.

Eight years later, Norma Jean Saunders asserted that her climb was the first woman's solo. Saunders fed the voracious Alaskan press with a posed cover photo on *Alaska* magazine, followed by a sixteen-page article titled, "First Woman to Solo Denali?" The garrulous Saunders then told *Climbing* magazine, "There's no documented account. She [Ercolani] was seen roped with other parties; she was never seen above fourteen thousand feet. She has not answered any letters from *Alaska* magazine, the rangers, or myself."

Later, in Florence, when I asked the venerable Ercolani about the controversy, she evoked Johnny Waterman's philosophy: "Some people do it for the publicity," she said with a wink. "I did it for myself."

That summer of 1969, when Johnny Waterman, Ed Nester, and Tom Frost descended Denali and flew back into Talkeetna, they met Dean Rau, who had just finished an unsuccessful attempt on the south ridge of

Mount Hunter. Johnny was impressed nonetheless. Rau drove Johnny back to the lower forty-eight, and the two went climbing together, hatching plans for Hunter a year later.

That winter, Johnny ate, slept, and drank climbing. Guy, who had once led his son up routes, now followed him. He observed that Johnny was the fastest person he had ever climbed with. Guy characterized his son's climbing as "explosive energy and ferocious ecstasy on rock or ice—a masterfully competent but electric, volcanic, creative vitality. When he—or I—got a hard move, his joy was almost uncontainable. He was not grace, he was power," Guy wrote. "He was not beauty, he was energy. He was not control, he was uncontrolled joy. In spite of all the deadly fanaticism of some of today's Eurorock devotees, I have never met anyone to whom climbing (as opposed to gymnastic exercises or competitive triumphs) meant more."

Although divorce would shatter the family like rockfall hitting fine crystal, Johnny and Guy remained close. Guy claims their laughter-filled relationship transcended the normal father-son relationship, particularly when they went climbing together. However, when Duane Soper picked up Johnny en route to Hunter in the summer of 1970, Johnny and Guy said a "distant farewell" to one another. It seemed obvious to Soper that father and son were not getting along. At this point, no one really knew why; Johnny rarely confided in his companions. Guy was receiving the brunt of what most parents perceive as a tumultuous teenage rebellion.

Johnny, Soper, Rau, and Paul Harrison arrived beneath Hunter's south ridge in a blinding blizzard. Rau arbitrarily walked up a snowslope and starting digging a cave; two days later an avalanche stopped within yards of their new home. For the next several weeks they flung themselves on the difficulties above, to no avail, because storms stymied the final bit of climbing. Although Johnny was only seventeen, he did most of the leading.

Ever since Johnny had fallen on climbing, his grades in school improved significantly; he didn't want homework to keep him away from climbing on weekends. But there were penalties to his single-mindedness: Johnny felt he never learned how to interact well with other people, particularly girls.

After graduating from high school, he climbed in England, Turkey, and the Alps. He wrote Guy about "the incredible barriers in my mind toward meeting people and relaxing, the barriers that only let down when

I'm alone in my 'home' in the mountains. I could go on climbing only and try to forget about other things. It would solve itself, only it would have been a very short and hollow life. Not much of a solution."

For a brief period in 1971, he attended Western Washington University in Bellingham. The five-foot, three-inch Johnny loved hard winter climbing, but it was difficult for him to find companions. Potential partners felt alienated by Johnny's increasing temper tantrums and his no-turning-back attitude. (His obituary in the 1982 *American Alpine Journal* read, "He had always had trouble finding partners of equal ability and commitment, and the partners had to cope with his bright ideas that could turn a hard climb into [real suffering].")

On December 20, 1971, he arranged to climb in the Canadian Rockies with America's best Himalayan mountaineer. Johnny wrote to his dad, "He's supposed to be fast. Hope I can keep up." Then on Christmas Day, Johnny wrote again, "Well, another fiasco, I'm down in Spokane with ol' Superman. He wants to spend Christmas with his girlfriend (fine time to decide, fucking fine time)."

Although Johnny would never enter the mainstream of American climbing, his mountain vita established him as a fanatic. In Yosemite he led all the hard pitches on El Capitan's Nose. He made the first solo of the difficult V.M.C. Direct on Cannon Mountain in New Hampshire. He soloed the north face of the Grand Teton in Wyoming. He climbed new routes on the north face of Stanley and the east face of McDonald in Canada. He would travel to Russia and climb in an international exchange. And in 1972 he returned to Alaska to attempt the unclimbed east ridge of Mount Huntington with a resourceful group of mountaineers: Rocky Keeler, Neils Andersen, Roger Derryberry, and Frank Zahar.

In his book, *The Mountain of My Fear,* David Roberts wrote that Huntington's unclimbed east ridge could "put a party in a perpetual state of nervousness." Its "huge hanging glaciers, the most dangerous formations imaginable, sprawled obscenely down the ridge."

Johnny led the crux, a tenacious performance of steep climbing and tunneling into a troublesome cornice while hanging from one arm. When the team summited on July 5, Johnny, according to Zahar, was not resting on the laurels of their difficult climb. There on the final summit cornice, while the rest of the team reveled in a grand event of their lives, Johnny stared obsessively at Mount Hunter, several miles to the west. He considered his climb of the previous summer to be an abject failure. And he began to equate Hunter as an animate being determined to thwart his every effort.

Later that summer, in British Columbia, he completed the third ascent of Mount Robson's north face, with Warren Bleser. And while guiding for his friend Leif Patterson, he took Peter Metcalf up the same mountain. "If I had any problems," Metcalf said, "he was very forgiving. But once I was standing next to him, not watching what he was doing, when I heard this explosion of curses. John was waving his arms, screaming—I thought something horrendous had happened. After a one-minute outburst, he said, 'Oh, I just put a little rip in my windpants.'" Such tantrums began to mark all of his outings.

At nineteen he wrote his father: "As far as John the climber goes, I've already defined my lines. It's John the rest of the time that needs to be found now."

When Guy got divorced, his three sons—Jim, Bill, and Johnny—accepted it, secure in knowing that they held first place in their father's affections. But when Guy remarried in 1972, he felt that they never really forgave him: A stranger now occupied his attention. Furthermore, Guy and his new wife (formerly Laura Johnson) moved to the woods of Vermont, forsaking any modern conveniences such as electricity and the telephone. Guy's self-described "vow of poverty" may well have left Johnny and Bill feeling financially abandoned; Jim had always made his own way without any help from his dad. Johnny and Bill took up permanent residence in Alaska, as if they needed to get as far away as possible from their ruptured family.

Waterman is not a common name, so our parallel desires as climbers made our shared name all the more unusual; then Johnny's father taught me how to ice-climb. In the early 1970s, John Waterman had become an Alaskan legend, as large and phantasmagoric as Denali to a New England teenager like me. His name appeared in the journals, and if the local mountaineers didn't know him, they at least pretended to. Sometimes my presence made other climbers hush, as if Waterman had returned from Alaska—until they realized I was not "the" John Waterman.

Once, in a smoky cabin under Maine's biggest mountain, Katahdin, Guy Waterman entertained me and two dozen other rapt mountaineers by the glow of the lantern. On the other side of the frosted-over windows, it was twenty-five below zero; Guy pantomimed his son outracing an avalanche on Alaska's Mount Huntington. Before I slunk off to my tent, Guy confided under the saffron lantern light that maybe "someday Johnny and 'the other Jon Waterman' could climb Denali together in the winter." I went away transfixed by the power of Guy's stories about his famous son. But I was also vexed that no matter what I did in the mountains, there was another climber greater than I who shared my name.

While Guy seemed the ultimate father for a young climber, my own father was not entirely supportive of my proclivity. So in the same manner in which Johnny spurned Guy after he remarried, I turned and fled from my own parents' divorce, taking solace in the mountains.

Guy's letters followed me everywhere. Whereas Guy and Laura were articulate and full of puns, if my parents wrote at all, their letters were staid and succinct. Moreover, Guy and I frequently got together for mountain outings; my own father played tennis. Guy soon became a mentor.

I knew that he and Laura had completed an early ascent of one of New England's hardest ice-climbing test pieces: the Black Dike. They had even traveled to Alaska and attempted a new route on Mount Hunter; the route was completed half a dozen years later by two of the finest alpinists in North America. But Guy's mountaineering and environmental activism were only glimmers of the talents he had formerly displayed in the city.

At their remote homestead, Guy and Laura built their cabin around a grand piano and several hundred volumes of classic literature; if a visitor pleaded, they might play duets on the piano. Laura was high-powered enough, with or without Guy, and before moving to the woods she had turned her back on a blossoming editorial career in New York City. They both seemed torn from the pages of Helen and Scott Nearing's book about self-sufficiency in the wilderness, *Living the Good Life*, with one crucial difference: They were my friends.

Guy's preservationist philosophy had a profound effect on everything I did in the mountains. As Guy and Laura became renowned as the "Consciousness of the White Mountains," I was secretly pleased when people mistook me for their son. The Watermans never criticized my own actions, but they frequently debated the entrepreneurial and environmentally degrading aspects of the mountain huts I worked in. Consequently I tried to implement change: leading nature walks, minimizing the use of disruptive helicopters, and educating hut users about conservation. Guy had greatly influenced me, and it was not stretching the truth to say that he became a surrogate father.

One day, in a fit of restlessness about our "dinky" four-thousand-foot-high New Hampshire mountains, Johnny's father and I jogged up and down the northern Presidentials until we had gained the equivalent of twenty thousand feet of elevation. I limped back down disappointed that we couldn't finish another nine thousand feet, which—in our minds, anyway—would have equaled Everest instead of Denali. Although our exertions struck other mountaineers as a contrived stunt, to me it was only business as usual with the Waterman family—of which I now seemed half a member.

The following summer I tried to climb Denali for real, but turned around in a storm at nineteen thousand feet, altitude sickness as thick as clouds in my head. I later found a photograph of Johnny from his first visit on Denali; he was wearing the same model and color of Kelty pack that I wore. Although I didn't meet Johnny (who had also experienced altitude sickness as a teenager on the West Buttress Route), his stomping grounds gave my life new clarification. Whereas I had previously experienced mostly adolescent apathy, Denali began to form both my subconscious and actual horizons for the next decade. As a restless middle child, I planned to live in Alaska. Just like Johnny.

That winter he caretook Leif Patterson's home in British Columbia and threw some wild parties. Johnny was constantly talking about girls, but his friends all knew "Johnny's dalliances" to be pure fantasy.

Rau described Johnny's "delayed puberty and a delayed interaction with women. Then all of a sudden there was an explosion." The letters to Johnny's father filled with sexual fantasy. Johnny, however, would never find a steady girlfriend.

In the summer of 1973, accompanying Rau, Don Black, and Dave Carman, Johnny came back to Alaska to settle the score with Hunter. Although Rau thought that his twenty-year-old friend was climbing as well as anyone in the country, he saw that Johnny had changed in the intervening years. "In 1970, you could reason with him, but now Johnny felt that you had to put the climb above everything else. I thought I was with a madman."

While waiting to fly to the mountain, Waterman's companions watched him slam the hardware rack on the floor as hard as he could, or rage at some passing frustration, swearing and screaming like Ahab. On the mountain Johnny often sang strange ditties to himself. Although he became the driving force behind the climb, he was also fast to a fault. At one point Johnny did a sloppy job of hammering in a snowpicket. When he started rappelling, the picket pulled out, and unbeknownst to him, Carman held the rope until Johnny reached the ledge.

"He was your consummate alpine climber on mixed ground," said Carman. "He was very quick, not beautiful, and kind of scary because he was so obsessed."

The climb itself was disastrous, at least in Johnny's mind. After a week of climbing above the col in frequent storm, Black, Carman, and Waterman reached what appeared to be the summit. Both Carman and Black were scared to death of climbing on friable "Coca-Cola ice"; Carman had recurring nightmares about the climb after they got down.

Later, after flying out and examining photographs, standing alone out on the banks of the desolate Susitna River, Johnny studied the distant mountain; it suddenly became clear that they had turned back two hundred feet below the summit. Johnny was crushed.

Then he opened a letter from Leif Patterson. Instead of the expected check, Johnny received a bill for some furniture he'd smashed while caretaking and being a party animal at the Patterson house. Furthermore, the news about his companions from Robson and Huntington reached him through the climbers' grapevine: Warren Bleser and Neils Andersen had died on the Matterhorn.

When bush pilot Don Sheldon told them how much they owed for his services, Johnny burst into tears. No one could speak. Sheldon finally muttered something about accepting credit.

"Johnny knew he was a misfit," says Black. "After a temper tantrum he'd sometimes say, 'I know how difficult I am to deal with.' But you didn't push it after that, because you didn't want to fire him up again."

"The conflict of making money and the higher spiritual beauties in life was tearing him up," said Carman. "Also, the lack of a girlfriend was real painful to him."

His partners posed for a photograph with Johnny, standing nearly a foot shorter than his companions, staring at the camera wearing a court-jester smile entirely inappropriate for his perceived failure on Hunter.

Johnny felt at home in Alaska, famous for its stifling black winters, high suicide rates, eccentric gadflies, and obdurate dipsomaniacs. He shared a cabin with his brother Bill, with whom he was always very close. Although Bill was also passionate about mountains, an accident hopping freight trains left him with one leg. In 1973 Bill wrote a cryptic letter to their father, mentioning a long trip and that he would be in touch when he returned. One friend thought he might have gone to Vietnam; another said South America. To this day, Guy likes to believe that Bill went farther north and became engulfed in the life of some Eskimo village. No body was ever recovered; moreover, no one knew where to begin looking. Bill simply vanished.

Over the coming years, much of Johnny's actions would be interpreted as mad behavior. "Johnny's gone snake eyes," Duane Soper told Dean Rau. Rau himself was confronted at a local fair by "a spaced-out-looking" ticket seller with shoulder-length hair, laughing maniacally and shouting, "Hey, you ratfucker!" Rau barely recognized his former partner. Indeed, Johnny's mother had been diagnosed as psychotic, and such imbalances have been shown to be genetically coded. But the death of Johnny's closest partners and climbing mentors would have slapped even the most well-adjusted climber to rock bottom.

After the deaths of Everett, Seidman, Davis, Bleser, Andersen, and (probably) his brother Bill, Rocky Keeler died in a bicycling accident. Then Leif Patterson died in an avalanche, and Chuck Loucks fell in the Tetons. Finally, even cautious Ed Nester died, rappelling in the Selkirks.

After Guy wrote to Johnny about Loucks, Johnny mailed his father a letter: "What can I say? Your letter said it all. Last person in the world I expected to live longer than. I was really broken up for twenty minutes, and have had recurrences, but the pain is now through. The thing forever removes all legitimacy from climbing to me, but will bring us closer together, I think. I've never been so touched, except maybe by my brother Bill."

One could only imagine how it felt to be cast in the shadow of a father who was as gifted as Guy. He had supported himself through college by playing jazz piano; he published climbing fiction, ragtime pieces, and statistical essays for *Baseball Digest* magazine. And he could recite five hours of *Paradise Lost* from memory. Before he left city life, he was known as a "bright young man" on Capitol Hill during Eisenhower's administration and had written speeches for three different presidents (before or after their terms), and senators such as George Bush's father, Prescott.

Johnny tried to shock and outrage people as a means of gaining attention; he even confided to his friend Lance Leslie that he was trying to win parental approval. But Johnny misread his father. Hearing Guy paint his son's accomplishments, even before the Hunter solo, is to know both great pride and unqualified love.

By the mid-1970s Johnny's reputation was sealed. He drank bottles of salad dressing like soda pop. He strummed on a battered guitar and sang out of key in an amphetamine flow-of-consciousness fashion. He described "airy, sweeping, and lofty" symphonies he would compose about his climbs.

To prepare for his *succès fou* of all climbs, on Mount Hunter, he trained by bathing in tubs filled with ice. When the Talkeetna Motel owner got suspicious and caught Johnny ferrying buckets of ice to his room, he was evicted. Undeterred, Johnny, clad in crampons and floppy mountaineering boots, took long training runs on the snowpacked highway.

Two years before Johnny's climb, Doug Scott and Dougal Haston had demonstrated the "alpine style" ethic, rapid and unencumbered up Denali's south face. Johnny's climb on Hunter almost deliberately defied the new ethic with a dozen packframes and metal boxes and enough spare clothing to outfit several climbers. Lance Leslie and partners, who bumped into Johnny after he was alone for seventeen weeks on Mount Hunter, had never seen a climber with "such a huge pile of shit." Leslie sensed that Johnny was scared, which explained the need to surround and insulate himself with as many possessions as possible.

Many modern climbers, imbued with the ethic of climbing fast and light, came to see his climb as a protracted siege, which was true in terms of the number of days he spent on the mountain. Spending five months on Mount Hunter belied his abilities as an extremely fast and efficient technical climber, particularly with gear placement and belay changeovers. These efficiencies, which had been instilled by his dad on small crags a dozen years earlier and subsequently sharpened during big-wall climbs, have left countless partners impressed to this day. On Hunter, Johnny simply wanted to be left alone, to take his time, and to contemplate the universe.

On Hunter, Johnny freely admitted to bouts of extraordinary loneliness and crying with frustration and rage. While dozens of remote cabin dwellers listened in on their citizens band radios, Johnny begged his pilot to air-drop medication for body lice. "It was some comfort to know at least I was not alone," he later wrote in *The American Alpine Journal.* "My morale was low at this point. I was forty-three days out and was obviously not going to reach the summit plateau with any reserve of food even on two-thirds rations." His bush pilot, Cliff Hudson, rescued him with a big food airdrop on the plateau, and Johnny continued toward the north summit.

Once when Hudson flew by, level with a section of the climb called the perch, Johnny emulated his long-dead friends Howie Davis and Chuck Loucks and flipped into a handspring above the abyss. As the plane shrunk into the skyline, Johnny keyed his radio mike: "Did you see that, Cliff?"

"I'd appreciate it if you wouldn't do that," Cliff replied.

The first time Johnny fell during the climb, he was caught by a shoulder strap attached to his securely driven ice hammer. "The slip made me nervous," he wrote, parodying many understated British climbing writers. "It could have been fatal."

Another time he collapsed a huge cornice and fell forty feet before he was "surprised" that his belay system caught him. Or, matching a miscalculation he'd made on the nearby south ridge five years earlier, a poorly placed anchor pulled while Johnny was rappelling; he miraculously fell upright into his steps below.

The account he published in *The American Alpine Journal* implies that Johnny found Hunter to be an animate force. In addition to referring to his climb as "a vendetta," he wrote how "the mountain and I finally met on our own terms." Furthermore, he named three different pinnacles on the ridge "Judges," as if his performance were being evaluated. Such personification of the inanimate is usually scoffed at by mountaineering literati, but in this case Johnny apparently believed it.

"More than his fellow humans, [the mountains] had become his companions," Ingrid Canfield wrote about Johnny in a chapter from *Skiing Down Everest and Other Crazy Adventures*. "And he invested them with the frailties and duplicities, the enticements and charms of real people, relating to them powerfully and responding only to them with his true essence."

In a conversation with Glenn Randall (who wrote a book about his epic repeat of the route, threaded with Johnny's adventures), Johnny said that something "far more precious would be lost if I lived through it than if I died. Living through it would mean that Nature wasn't as raw as everybody wanted to believe it was. Living through it would mean that Mount Hunter wasn't the mountain that I thought it was."

Bowing to the mountain, Johnny fixed all thirty-six hundred feet of his rope down the north ridge before he went to Hunter's highest summit, believing it more respectful to the mountain to be killed before he put the summit beneath his boot soles. When he finally went to the north summit, he was surprised to make it alive. After descending his ropes, he could have crossed over to the crowded Kahiltna Glacier base camp and been lauded as a hero, but he stayed on the deserted Tokositna Glacier. Johnny spent several days alone—nursing his frostbitten fingers and pondering his newly altered perception of reality—until Hudson flew in to his salvation.

That summer I spent thirty-eight days thrashing up an unclimbed ridge on Mount Logan in the Yukon. My three teammates and I took turns confronting steep water ice, digging trenches up scary snowslopes, kicking off avalanches, and crabbing across rotten rock towers. When I was nearly done with the four-mile ridge, a multiton cornice collapsed beneath my ice ax and thundered off to the glacier several thousand feet below—I quit for the day.

More than once, I tried to imagine how it would feel to solo our route: Getting hurt or killed seemed the lesser danger. The more pressing concern was keeping your sanity in a landscape so utterly unforgiving and so barren of humanity that you would have to scream to hear yourself think—or pretend the mountain was alive and start talking to it. If going mad didn't kill you, and you survived collapsing cornices and tent-ripping storms, you would forever walk twisted among your peers, changed irreparably by a stark and surreal world beyond most people's earthly experience. Just coping with the civilized world again after sharing such intensities with my three partners was all I could handle.

That year's *The American Alpine Journal* came out with articles about two different Watermans on Mount Logan and Mount Hunter. Now I wondered how Johnny felt about another Jon Waterman traipsing up unclimbed ridges. While Johnny faded amid the recluses of northern Alaska, I fled to the mountains of Colorado. Both of us failed to make any lasting niche in society—we were too strung out by our experiences in those hauntingly beautiful mountains of the North.

Several years later, Randall, Peter Metcalf, and Peter Athens cut Johnny's time on the southeast spur of Hunter by more than a hundred days, but they suffered dearly and didn't summit. To date, the reputation of the climb has repulsed further attempts. Despite the extended siege, Johnny's accomplishment equaled Harding and Merry's El Capitan climb or Bates and Washburn's traverse of Lucania and Steele—both climbs were lionized in the mainstream media as well as in mountaineering circles. But beyond the microcosmic Alaskan media and several thousand admirers in the insular mountaineering community, Johnny's achievement gained him less renown than that of a barreler's descent of Niagara Falls.

"The tragedy was that he never got credit for his Hunter climb because he wasn't playing with a full deck," Dean Rau has said. "He should've gone all over the world lecturing."

Instead, Johnny borrowed $20 from Hudson and looked for work in Fairbanks. "To me that was really the ultimate in what was wrong with our society," Johnny said. "After this horrible climb—or, actually, this superb climb—my only societal reward was to be washing dishes at the very bottom of society."

The climb changed him irreparably. Lance Leslie said that before Hunter, "Waterman was odd, but little different than other climbers with his scruffy beard and down feathers clinging to his matted hair. But after Hunter he seemed almost dangerously psychotic."

In Fairbanks, Johnny ran a campaign for the presidency. Although no one took him seriously, he was deadpan about the whole affair. His platform was to feed starving people around the world, legalize drugs for schoolchildren, and promote free sex for everyone. Johnny began kissing acquaintances—male or female—whenever he met them in public. Even the normally unruffled Fairbanksians now wondered if Johnny had gone overboard.

In 1979 Johnny set out to try to climb the south face of Denali. Part of his plan was to gain enough notoriety so Nepalese officials would grant him permission to solo Everest in winter. Hudson flew Johnny into Denali with five hundred pounds of supplies. Johnny planned to climb a dangerous new route alongside (his late mentor's) Dave Seidman's Direct South Face Route. But December is the cruelest, windiest, and blackest period of the Alaskan night. Something in Johnny snapped.

On January 1, after contemplating the route for ten days, Johnny told his pilot, who had dropped off some more supplies, "Take me home; I don't want to die." Back in Talkeetna, he told a reporter, "The mountain defeated me, but he didn't eat me alive."

Two months later, the Talkeetna cabin he was staying in burned down, destroying all his notebooks. "That was the blow," Leslie commented, "which sent Johnny teetering toward the brink." Johnny told several onlookers that the notes he had accumulated over many years were the essence of himself; to lose them meant that he had burned up in the flames.

He convinced the Alaska Psychiatric Institute in Anchorage to admit him. After two weeks he walked out under his own recognizance. Later he told Randall that he was suffering from his Mount Hunter psychosis—fearful of being cold and hungry or lacking shelter.

After he got out he again laid plans to solo Denali. However, with a now-characteristic inability to act on his biggest project, he hung out in Fairbanks for nearly two years, enjoying a cult status and popularity that the community had never awarded a mountaineer. Many Fairbanksians knew him; most tolerated his behavior.

He charged about the Fairbanks campus of the University of Alaska with a flowing black cape and a silver star glued between his glasses. His Mount Hunter slide shows also became the talk of Alaska. At the lectern he would pull off his shirt, talk about the ache of profound loneliness, and then further shock the crowd by confessing to his secret expedition lover, "Rosie." He beamed shamelessly, holding up his right hand.

Finally, in February of 1981, he began walking from the ocean at Anchorage, tracing the frozen and desolate Susitna River, which carved a sixty-mile-long, mile-wide swath from Talkeetna to Cook Inlet. He staggered under a pack almost matching his own gnomelike frame. Ten days later, shortly after midnight, he banged on the door of the Talkeetna Motel and asked for a cup of coffee. Lance Leslie's wife, Lori, let him in. He was thoroughly soaked after breaking through the river ice. He came into the kitchen, and after a few minutes of rambling banter, picked up a carving knife, began various stabbing motions, and asked Lori how to hold a knife if you wanted to murder someone. It was weird, Lori thought, but it was all show.

Afterward he continued marching up the Chulitna, Tokositna, and Ruth rivers, thirty-five miles of forsaken moose and wolf habitat, emerging at the Ruth Glacier. This convoluted highway of ice is difficult walking, so Johnny stopped at two thousand feet. Denali rose as a great blinding citadel, within ten miles of walking and a vertical mile of climbing.

Johnny was yet unable to face the demons of his soul, and blaming the aborted attempt on a faulty stove, he returned to Talkeetna and procrastinated. When he finally summoned the courage to leave, he returned

Cliff Hudson's hand-sized citizens band radio—a gesture that symbolized turning his back on all further communications with the world. Johnny repeated his farewell to Hudson from before Hunter: "I won't be seeing you again."

At six thousand feet on the Ruth Glacier, Johnny met some climbers from Fairbanks, who commented that he looked more run-down and tired than usual. He dallied for weeks up on the glacier, unable to commit himself. Finally, on April Fool's Day, he said good-bye to his friends, and *sans* sleeping bag, cut across the labyrinth of crevasses toward one of Denali's last unsolved routes—a place that the most accomplished mountaineer in the world, Reinhold Messner, rejected as too dangerous.

It would not be difficult to die on Denali while alone on such a route. Even if a climber was playing it safe, the margin between sanity and breakdown would be hard to define in such a chilling and sterile amphitheater, renowned for its fantastic avalanches. There would be temptations to befriend crevasses and hanging glaciers, and during the subarctic night, the only presence to talk to would be the mountain itself.

Two weeks later, everyone presumed Johnny was dead. Some climbers found a box of supplies at six thousand feet on the Ruth Glacier, marked in Johnny's handwriting, "the Last Kiss." A helicopter overflew his route, but with the exception of an old stomped-out tent site at seven thousand feet, there was no trace of his passage.

There are a few Fairbanksians who maintain that Johnny fooled the world and pulled a disappearing act, changing his identity. *Rock and Ice* magazine satirically wrote that he was living in Arizona, anonymously and illegally soloing desert spires on Navajo land; my own letter to the editor protesting the irreverence was answered by another climber's letter insisting that Johnny was a sexual deviant and a madman. Meanwhile, my unknowing high-school chums assumed I was dead and celebrated with a "Jon Waterman Memorial Golf Classic."

Shortly after Johnny's death, Guy wrote to me, "What is really too bad is that you and Johnny never knew each other, or that you could not have climbed together."

Cliff Hudson gave me a suitcase of Johnny's notes and poetry. That winter I kept it with me in my Alaskan cabin, and, falling to the depths of my own depression amid the winter's darkness, I clutched my alter ego's belongings as if they were my own. I also spent many hours that black winter critiquing Guy's proffered book manuscript, dedicated "To

Johnny for whom these forests and these crags were a beginning." But the final time I tried to make sense of Johnny's illegible scrawl on random sheets of paper, I shut the case and never opened it again. I didn't have the heart to send the stormy scribblings to Guy, so when I left the cabin and fled Alaska for good, I abandoned the notes—which found their way to Fairbanks and were sold in the annual John Waterman Memorial Auction.

Six years after Johnny's disappearance, a woman who had lived with Bill and Johnny Waterman in Alaska telephoned me in Colorado, where I had found a job as an editor. She thought that maybe Johnny had survived and written the book *Surviving Denali,* which I had authored. She broke into tears as soon as I answered, because mine was not the high-pitched and reedy voice she had been praying to hear again.

When Guy received more of his son's effects, there were hundreds of pages of writing, mostly indecipherable and overwritten fantasy. One short story of Johnny's, however—remarkably controlled and underwritten—concerned his father's reaction to a telegram describing Johnny's death.

Guy is still trying to accept his son's death. "I found a lot of things along the forty-nine years that preceded the spring of 1981," Guy wrote, "and I can be aware of them even in the midst of the lowest lows. Johnny didn't find enough such things before the spring of 1981." Now in his sixties, Guy still shares a life in the woods with Laura. He actively climbs, sometimes solo, but usually with Laura in the nearby White Mountains.

Guy felt that his son had learned how to survive on difficult climbs in the Alaska Range. He was bothered that some would use Johnny's last climb to illustrate the risks of soloing. On December 29, 1986, Guy wrote, " 'See,' say the conservatives, 'even a super climber was killed when he made the mistake of climbing alone. It always catches up with you, etc., etc.' I trust you know that Johnny knew what he was doing," continued Guy. "He did not want to come back."

On a hidden subridge in New Hampshire's White Mountains, Guy erected a small memorial that contains an old pair of Johnny's boots. Every April, on the anniversary of his son's disappearance, Guy and Laura bushwhack to this aerie. Surrounded by their favorite mountains, Guy remembers earlier times while staring at Cannon—scene of happy epics with Johnny and Laura. Guy then sings three ballads and three poems, including an old Scottish lament played at his father's memorial service:

> *Then here let him rest in the lap of Scaur Donald,*
> *The wind for his watcher, the mist for his shroud,*
> *Where the green and the gray moss will weave their wild tartan*
> *A covering meet for a chieftain so proud.*
> *For free as an eagle, these rocks were his eyrie,*
> *And free as an eagle his spirit shall soar*
> *O'er the crags and the corries that erst knew the footfall. . . .*

I once asked Guy if his son had fooled everyone and simply disappeared instead of dying on Denali. Guy answered: "I wouldn't want to say a 100 percent no, but I really don't think so. In the end, the mountains were the only place Johnny could feel at home, so that's where he went to stay for good." Concerning his son Bill, Guy says, "I never entirely extinguish the possibility of his return."

During a recent visit—no longer a dedicated mountaineer and trying to escape the grim weight of life for a while—I lost the path to the Watermans' rural property. I thought about Johnny a lot that day. I thought that few people indeed can afford to commit themselves irrevocably to their dreams, and I admired him deeply for that. Like Icarus, Johnny had cut off all moorings to his loved ones and flew into the alluring white heat of the sun.

I didn't find Guy until twilight, tending his garden a hundred yards off, under the light of a lantern. When I shouted "Hello!" he ran toward me clutching the lantern, with ecstasy and surprise shining with childlike joy on his face. When his saffron light finally fell on my face, he was plainly crestfallen, even though it had been years since he had seen me.

The next morning, Guy paused in front of a woodpile. He looked into my eyes; he tried a smile. Then he apologized about the way he had greeted me the night before. He explained that once in a while he will greet an unidentified visitor out in the dark and think for just a scant moment that maybe, just maybe, one of his sons has finally come home.

The Mountain of My Fear
[Mount Huntington]

– DAVID ROBERTS –

David Roberts is that rarest of mountaineering breeds: he's received critical acclaim as both climber and writer. Now in his early fifties, the Cambridge, Massachusetts, resident has participated in dozens of expeditions—including several highly praised first ascents—and written dozens of climbing stories (though he's hardly limited himself to the mountaineering genre). Among his most famous ascents, and stories, are those of Alaskan peaks, and one particular account is recognized as a classic of mountaineering literature: The Mountain of My Fear. *Roberts wrote the book in 1966, eight months after he'd participated in the first ascent of Mount Huntington's west face. A 22-year-old first-year graduate student at the University of Denver, he finished it in only nine days, while "enmeshed in a tangle of disturbing emotions, the legacy of our costly victory. . . ." What distinguishes the book from others, in part, is what Roberts calls his "frenziedly poetic passages."*

A 12,240-foot neighbor of Denali, Mount Huntington was named by explorer/mountaineer Belmore Browne in 1910 to honor Archer Milton Huntington, president of the American Geographical Society. Now widely regarded as one of Alaska's most beautiful peaks, this exceedingly steep, tri-

angular pyramid of rock stood in obscurity for nearly a half century after its naming. Only when Bradford Washburn took photographs that "captured the mountain's incredible sharpness, its slender symmetry," says Roberts, did Huntington become "Alaska's hidden prize."

The prize was claimed in 1964, when a French team led by famed alpinist Lionel Terray ascended Huntington via the northwest ridge. One year later, four Americans followed, dreaming of another prize: Huntington's west face, "a magnificent wall of sheer rock . . . the sort of route that had never been done in Alaska." The expedition's driving forces were Roberts and Don Jensen, who'd met in 1962 on a Harvard Mountaineering Club trip. In 1964 they'd spent forty-two days together on Mount Deborah, in Alaska's Hayes Range, but that trip (documented in his 1970 book Deborah) *had been, in Roberts' words, "a failure." For Huntington they recruited two other Harvard students, Matt Hale and Ed Bernd. Neither had been to Alaska, but both were accomplished technical climbers. The four men flew into the Alaska Range on June 29, 1965; one month later, despite extreme climbing and a series of storms, they'd put themselves in position for a summit attempt.*

The following piece is chapters 7 and 8 of David Roberts' The Mountain of My Fear, *first published in 1968 by Vanguard Press and in 1991 by The Mountaineers in Seattle.*

7: The Summit

JULY 29 DAWNED CLEAR. Our fifth perfect day in a row, it was almost more than we could believe. Don and Ed got moving by 7:30 AM. Quickly over the Nose, from there on, they faced unclimbed rock and ice. Ed started to lead the first new pitch. Suddenly he remembered he'd forgotten his ice ax in the rush to get started. It was down by the tent.

"What a dumb thing to do," he said to Don. "You think we should go back for it?"

"No. It would take too much time. We can make do with an icelite."

So Don and Ed took turns leading with Don's ax, while the second man used one of our aluminum daggers for balance and purchase. Although it was awkward, it seemed to work.

To make things more unsettling, they had only five or six fixed ropes and about a dozen pitons. Matt and I had not yet been able to bring up supplies to them; they could expect us to reach the tent sometime today with more of everything, but the beautiful weather couldn't be wasted. They would go as high as they reasonably could.

Ed led the next pitch, a traverse on steep, crunchy snow, quickly and well, needing only a piton at the top to belay from. Don managed the same economy on the next, our thirty-seventh pitch, though the snow was becoming ice in which he had to chop steps. At the top of the 55-degree pitch he found a protruding block of granite, but there didn't seem to be any good cracks in it. At last he hammered a short, stubby piton in about three-quarters of an inch, tied a loop around its blade to minimize the torque if a pull should come on it, and belayed Ed up. The pitch above required another steep traverse, again on the shallow snow-ice that lay uncomfortably close to the rock beneath. Ed led it carefully. Don could see him silhouetted against the sky all the way. The sun was beginning to hit the face, and they welcomed it after their first pitches in cold shadow. To be sure, sooner or later the sun might loosen the snow, but it would be very hard to climb difficult rock without its warmth. And it looked as if they would have to climb a steep cliff very soon.

They left fixed ropes on the first three pitches, then decided to save their few remaining ones, placing them only on the worst pitches, where they would be most helpful on the descent. Don led another pitch, their easiest yet. With excitement he realized at the top of it that he was standing beside the large smooth pillar we had noticed in the Washburn pictures, and which he knew marked the beginning of the last rock barrier. Ed led into a steep couloir, now hard blue ice in which he laboriously and precariously had to chop steps. But he reached rock on the opposite side where he could get in a good anchor. So far they had used only five pitons in five pitches—the absolute minimum, certainly fewer than they would have used had they had plenty to spare. But they had climbed fast. The snow was still solid, but the rock was warming up. It looked as if they might be able to climb the 70-degree cliff above them barehanded. They certainly couldn't climb all of it with mittens on.

Don began the cliff. At least it had a few fine, sharp-edged holds. Trying to save the pitons, he went forty feet before he put one in. It rang solidly as he pounded it—thank God for the fine rock on this route! Thirty feet above that he was faced by a blank section, unclimbable, free. He hammered in a poor piton, one that wouldn't go all the way in, but vibrated noisily as he hit it. But at last it would hold his weight, and with a stirrup he surmounted the blank stretch. Difficult as it was, the climbing exhilarated him, especially knowing, as both Ed and he did, that above the cliff lay only the long, steep summit ice field. Don climbed into a wide chimney, moved up fifteen feet, and found the top blocked by a little ceiling. There was a way out to the left if there was even one handhold at the top of his reach. Except for a thin crack, though, there was nothing. Choosing his smallest piton, he was able to hammer it in about half an inch. He tested it cautiously, putting a carabiner through the piton's eye to hold on to. It felt insecure, but didn't budge; it would probably hold. He was forty feet above the bad piton, seventy feet above his good one. Moving delicately, putting as little weight on the piton as possible, he swung himself up and around the corner. Ed, watching tensely, saw Don step onto the snow above the highest rock. The cliff was climbed. Don quickly brought Ed up. Ed led a short pitch of crusty snow above, which seemed to lie just below the edge of something. Topping the rim, he looked ahead in amazement. The smooth expanse of the summit ice field lay above him, swooping upward at an unbroken 50-degree angle to the summit. After a month of climbing among jagged towers, inside chimneys, up enclosed couloirs, the summit ice field looked nightmarishly bare. It was like hacking one's way out of a jungle suddenly to stand on the edge of an empty desert.

It meant that they might have a chance for the summit that very day. Ed finished the pitch and brought Don up. Together they planned their attack. It was early afternoon, and going for the summit would undoubtedly require a bivouac. Four hundred feet above them stood the only bit of rock in the whole expanse, an outcrop about ten feet high. They decided to aim for it.

Four quick pitches on the unnervingly open slope brought them to it. The last fifty feet before the rock were steeper, and the sun had started to undermine the ice. They reached the rock with a feeling of relief, and agreed that the snow conditions would get worse for the next few hours. Choosing the one small ledge the rock offered, they chopped a little platform on it and pitched the tiny two-man bivouac tent Don had made. It was crowded inside, but consequently warm. Holding a stove on their laps, they could melt ice chips to make water. It was about five in the afternoon. They decided to wait for night, then go all out for the summit. It was still a long way, perhaps five more hours if things went well. But it was within reach. There was still not a cloud in the sky, no wind to disturb even a grain of snow. The afternoon sun gleamed on the mountains around them as they sat, drunk with the excitement of height, looking over the wilderness below them. For the first time they could see all of the Tokositna Glacier, even the dirty tongue sprawled on the tundra in the hazy distance, whose last ice Belmore Browne had crossed sixty years before. . . .

Matt and I had started at 11:15 AM from the Alley Camp. On a hunch, I had suggested that we take our down jackets and an extra lunch, as well as the ropes and pitons we were relaying up to Don and Ed. We made very good time, reaching their tent beneath the Nose in only three and a half hours. It was still early; it seemed pointless to go down at once. We decided to climb above the Nose; at least we could put in extra rope and pitons to safeguard the route behind the leaders for their descent. We were encouraged by the fact that we couldn't hear their shouts; they must be far above.

As we were preparing to climb the Nose, Matt noticed Ed's ax beside the tent. That was very strange; why hadn't he taken it? Unable to think of a more ominous reason, we assumed he had simply forgotten it as he climbed the difficult ceiling and, once above, had decided it wasn't worth going back for. Matt put the ax in his pack so that we could give it to Ed if we caught them, or at least leave it hanging from a piton where they couldn't help finding it on their way down.

At the top of the Nose we saw the newly placed fixed rope stretching around the corner. Without much trouble we followed their steps. Matt led the first pitch, I the second. It was about 3:30 PM; the snow was just beginning to deteriorate in the sun. The steps they had chopped in the ice, therefore, occasionally seemed uncomfortably small; we enlarged a few of them. At the top of the thirty-seventh pitch I saw that the anchor piton was a poor one and looked around for a place to put a new one. About five minutes later I gave up and tied in to the eye of the piton. Since I wasn't sure how long the piton's blade was, I had no way of judging how far into the crack it had been hammered. But there was a fixed rope leading above to the next piton, so it seemed reasonably safe.

Matt started to lead, holding the fixed rope wrapped around his left arm. Only four feet above me he stopped on a steep ice-step to tighten his right crampon, which seemed to be coming off. As he pulled on the strap his foot slipped and he fell on top of me. Not alarmed, I put up a hand to ward off his crampon, holding him on belay with the other. As his weight hit me, I felt the snow platform I had stomped for my feet collapse. But I was tied in with only a foot or two of slack, and I knew that the anchor would catch me immediately, and I would have no trouble catching Matt a foot or two below me. Yet we were sliding suddenly, unchecked. I realized the piton must have pulled out, but wondered in a blur why the fixed rope wasn't holding me; had it come loose, too? We were falling together, gaining speed rapidly. Matt was on top of me. We began to bounce, and each time we hit I had the feeling, without any pain, that I was being hurt terribly. Everything was out of control. I was still probably holding the rope in a belay, but I could do nothing to stop us. The mountain was flashing by beneath us, and with detachment I thought, This is what it's like. . . .

Suddenly we stopped. Matt was sitting on top of me. For an instant we didn't dare breathe. Then we carefully tried to stand on the steep ice.

"Don't move yet!" I said. "We could start going again!"

Now the fear, which we hadn't had time to feel as we fell, swept over us.

"Are you all right?" Matt asked urgently.

I couldn't believe those bounces hadn't broken any bones. I could move all right and I didn't seem to be bleeding. "I think so. Are you?"

"I guess. I lost my ice ax, though."

Then I realized my glasses were missing. As I looked around I saw them balanced on the tip of my boot. I grabbed them and put them on.

"We've got to get a piton in immediately," I said.

I managed to hammer in several poor ones. We could relax a little now, but trying to relax only made us more frightened. Matt had lost the crampon he was adjusting and both mittens. I had lost the dark clip-ons to my glasses. My right crampon had been knocked off, but it hung from my ankle by the strap. We were bruised but otherwise unhurt. The fall seemed to have been selectively violent.

What had stopped us? Matt still had his hand wrapped around the fixed rope, yet we had been falling without any apparent retardation. I looked up. The fixed rope, no longer attached to the anchor I had been belaying from, still stretched in one long chain to the anchor on the next pitch beyond. We saw Matt's ax, too, planted in the ice where his fall had started. Then we saw that the climbing rope had snagged above us on a little nubbin of rock. That was apparently what had stopped us.

It was safer, at least at first, to go up than to go down. I led, soon getting a very good piton in. I traversed back into our steps. As I passed the nubbin that had caught the rope, I looked at it. It was rounded, no bigger than the knuckle of one of my fingers.

Finally I got to a safe anchor above the bad one. As Matt came up, I tried to figure out what had happened. Just after we stopped falling, I had noticed the piton dangling at my feet, still tied to me, but unconnected to the fixed rope. I realized that I had attached myself to the piton's eye, while the fixed ropes had been tied around its blade. When the piton came out, we were no longer connected to the fixed ropes, except by the grasp of Matt's left hand.

We were extremely shaken. We discussed whether to go back or go on. I wanted to go on. The accident, though it had scared us badly, shouldn't affect our general resolve, I said. I had the feeling, too, that if we went back now we might develop an overwhelming, irrational fear and never want to go above the Nose. Matt reluctantly agreed. Fortunately, I had an extra pair of mittens for him. I could get along without the dark glasses, since it was growing late; but the loss of Matt's crampon was more serious. If I led the rest of the pitches, though, enlarging the right-foot steps for him, we thought it would work.

We continued, still shaky and nervous. Now we deliberately overpitoned the route, making it as safe as was humanly possible. As we climbed, we regained confidence. Soon we no longer had Ed's and Don's fixed ropes to follow, but their steps were clear. Wondering where they had climbed the cliff, I caught sight of a fixed rope dangling. The sight was more than exciting; it was reassuring as well.

I led the cliff, marveling at the difficulties Ed and Don had overcome with only three pitons. I put in about five more. As the sun passed over Foraker, low to the west, I emerged on the summit ice field. There was still no sign of Don and Ed, but as I belayed Matt up, I heard Ed shout to us from somewhere above.

"Where are you?" I yelled back.

"In the rock outcrop!"

We couldn't see them, but hearing their voices again was thrilling. Matt and I hurried up the steep ice to join them. The conditions were at their worst now, even though it was 8:00 PM. Twice I had to hammer rock pitons into the ice for anchors, never a dependable technique.

At last we were reunited. It was wonderful to see them. Ed said at once, "You didn't happen to bring my ice ax up, did—you did? What a couple of buddies!" Then, trying not to overstate it, we described our near-accident. Ed, especially, seemed disturbed; but the safety of numbers and the realization that now we could go to the summit together, as a rope of four, made up for all our misgivings. We ate a few candy bars as the sun set behind McKinley and the mountains faded into the dusky pallor of early night. Around 10:00 PM we started.

Since we had only two ropes, we had to tie in at 90-foot intervals instead of the usual 140. Don went first, I second, Matt third, while Ed brought up the rear. In order to save time, I belayed Don above me with one rope and one hand and Matt below me with the other simultaneously. It was growing dark rapidly. Soon I could see Don only as a faint silhouette in the sky, seeming to walk toward Cassiopeia. We were getting tired; the darkness made our effort seem more private, more detached from the mountain beneath us. After five pitches, at half-past midnight, we reached the summit ridge. We could scarcely tell we were there, except by the gradual leveling of the steep slope. We knew the far side was festooned with cornices overhanging the Ruth Glacier, so we didn't go all the way up to the ridge's level crest.

Now all that remained was the quarter-mile across to the summit, a narrow, airy walkway with a 5,000-foot drop on the left and a 6,000-foot drop on the right. This was the first and only part of our climb that coincided with the French route. Although it was such a short distance to the top, we knew we couldn't afford to underestimate it, for it had taken the French four and a half hours to reach the summit from here a year and a month before. For 600 feet we moved continuously, a ghostly walk in the sky. The night seemed to muffle all sound, and I had the illusion for an instant that we were the only people alive in the world. Soon we faced two flutings, short walls of vertical snow carved and crusted by the incessant wind, which spared the ridge only a few days each year. Perhaps we had been lucky enough to hit one of them. Here it was imperative that the four of us spread as far apart as possible. Don started up toward the first fluting as I belayed from a not very solid ice ax. Traversing high, he stuck his foot through the cornice and quickly pulled it back. Through the hole he could see the dull blueness of the Ruth Glacier below. He returned to my belay spot near exhaustion from the tension and exertion of a whole day of leading. We traded places and I started for the fluting, approaching it lower. The light was returning; an orange wall of flame lit the tundra north of McKinley. I could see the contours of the nearby snow now, glimmering palely. As I neared the bottom of the first wall, I thought I saw something sticking out of the snow. I climbed over to it. Stretched tight in the air, a single, frail foot of thin rope emerged from the ice. I pulled on it, but it was stuck solid. The sight was strangely moving. It testified, in a way, both to the transience and to the persistence of man. That bit of French fixed rope was the only human thing not our own that we had found during the whole expedition. It even seemed to offer a little security. I clipped in to it although I knew it was probably weather-rotten.

It seemed best to attack the fluting high, probably even on top of the cornice. If it broke off, at least there would be the weight of the other three on the opposite side of the ridge to hold me. The snow was terrible, made more out of air than anything else. I used one of our longest aluminum daggers in my left hand, my ax in the right, trying to plant something in the snow I could hold on to. At last, by hollowing a kind of trough out of the fluting, I could half climb, half chimney up. Just beyond its top the second fluting began. Don came up to belay me for the new obstacle. It was a little harder, but with a last spurt of energy I got over it. Though things seemed to be happening quickly to me, I took a long time on each fluting, and Matt and Ed grew cold waiting at the other end of the rope. Eventually all four of us were up, however. Then there were only three pitches left, easy ones, and suddenly I stood on top, belaying the others up. The summit itself was a cornice, so we had to remain a few feet below it, but our heads stood higher.

It was 3:30 AM. We'd been going for sixteen hours without rest. Now we were too tired even to exult. The sun had just risen in the northeast; a hundred and thirty miles away we could see Deborah, only a shadow in the sky. As Don looked at it I said, "This makes up for a lot." He nodded.

There was no one to tell about it. There was, perhaps, nothing to tell. All the world we could see lay motionless in the muted splendor of sunrise. Nothing stirred, only we lived; even the wind had forgotten us. Had we been able to hear a bird calling from some pine tree, or sheep bleating in some valley, the summit stillness would have been familiar; now it was different, perfect. It was as if the world had held its breath for us. Yet we were so tired . . . the summit meant first of all a place to rest. We sat down just beneath the top, ate a little of our lunch, and had a few sips of water. Ed had brought a couple of firecrackers all the way up; now he wanted to set one off, but we were afraid it would knock the cornices loose. There was so little to do, nothing we really had the energy for, no gesture appropriate to what we felt we had accomplished: only a numb happiness, almost a languor. We photographed each other and the views, trying even as we took the pictures to impress the sight on our memories more indelibly than the cameras could on the film. If only this moment could last, I thought, if no longer than we do. But I knew even then that we would forget, that someday all I should remember would be the memories themselves, rehearsed like an archaic dance; that I should stare at the pictures and try to get back inside them, reaching out for something that had slipped out of my hands and spilled in the darkness of the past. And that someday I might be so old that all that might pierce my senility would be the vague heart-pang of something lost and inexplicably sacred, maybe not even the name Huntington meaning anything to me, nor the names of three friends, but only the precious sweetness leaving its faint taste mingled with the bitter one of dying. And that there were only four of us (four is not many), and that surely within eighty years and maybe within five (for climbing is dangerous) we would all be dead, the last of our deaths closing a legacy not even the mountain itself could forever attest to.

We sat near the summit, already beginning to feel the cold. I got up and walked a little bit beyond, still roped, down the top of the east ridge, which someday men would also climb. From there I could see the underside of the summit cornice and tell that we had judged right not to step exactly on top. We had touched it with our ice axes, reaching out, but it might not have borne our weight.

Ed, who was normally a heavy smoker, had sworn off for the whole expedition. Now, out of his inexhaustible pockets, he pulled three cigarettes. He had no trouble lighting them; after smoking two, though, he felt so light-headed he had to save the third. One of the things he must have looked forward to, I realized, was that ritual smoke on the summit, partly because of the surprise he knew it would cause. But that was only one of Ed's reasons for being there, a minor one. I thought then, much as I had when Matt and I sat on the glacier just after flying in, that I wanted to know how the others felt and couldn't. Trying to talk about it now would have seemed profane; if there was anything we shared, it was the sudden sense of quiet and rest. For each of us, the high place we had finally reached culminated ambitions and secret desires we could scarcely have articulated had we wanted to. And the chances are our various dreams were different. If we had been able to know each others', perhaps we could not have worked so well together. Perhaps we would have recognized, even in our partnership, the vague threats of ambition, like boats through a fog: the unrealizable desires that drove us beyond anything we could achieve, that drove us in the face of danger; our unanswerable complaints against the universe—that we die, that we have so little power, that we are locked apart, that we do not know. So perhaps the best things that happened on the summit were what we could see happening, not anything beneath. Perhaps it was important for Don to watch me walk across the top of the east ridge; for Matt to see Ed stand with a cigarette in his mouth, staring at the sun; for me to notice how Matt sat, eating only half his candy bar; for Ed to hear Don insist on changing to black-and-white film. No one else could see these things; no one else could even ask whether or not they were important. Perhaps they were all that happened.

It was getting a little warmer. We knew we had to get down before the sun weakened the snow, especially on the summit ice field. Each of us as we left took a last glance back at the summit, which looked no different than when we had come, but for the faint footprints we had left near it.

We put fixed ropes in on all the difficult pitches, refusing to let up or get careless now that we were so tired. For the same reason we didn't take dexedrine tablets, though we carried them. When we reached the bivouac tent, we split into pairs to continue down. Ed and I went first, while Don and Matt packed up the little camp before following us. The sun, high in a still perfect sky, had taken the magic out of the mountain's shapes. Only the soft early light and the tension of our expectancy could have left it as beautiful as it had been. At last, after twenty-five straight hours of technical climbing, we rappelled off the Nose and piled, all four together, into the tent.

Now we could relax at last, but the tent was far too crowded. We felt giddy, and laughed and shouted as the edge of our alertness wore off. We had brought up our pint of victory brandy—blackberry-flavored—and now indulged in a few sips, toasting everything from Washburn to Kalispell. Each of us managed to doze off at some time or other, with someone else's foot or elbow in his face. In the afternoon it grew unbearably hot and stuffy inside, and the Nose began to drip (appropriately enough), pouring water through the roof of the tent. We cooked all our favorite delicacies, robbing the two food boxes rapaciously. By 6:00 PM it had started to cool again, and we saw that, finally, the weather might be turning bad, after six consecutive perfect days, a spell almost unheard of in Alaska. It was as if the storms had politely waited for us to finish our climb. We slept a little more, but still couldn't get comfortable. Around

9:00 PM Ed suggested that he and I go down in the night to the Alley Camp. We were still tired, but it wouldn't be a difficult descent. Once he and I got to the Camp, moreover, all four of us could rest in luxurious comfort, a sleeping bag each, room to stretch out full length, and plenty of food to wait out any storm. We dressed and were ready to go by 9:40 PM.

8: The Accident

The snow was in poorer condition than we liked; it hadn't refrozen yet, and might not that night since a warm wind was coming in. I knew the pitches below better than Ed, having been over them five times to his one, so I tried to shout instructions to him when the route was obscure. It got to be too dark to see a full rope-length. I went down the twenty-ninth pitch, our ice-filled chimney, feeling rather than seeing the holds. But the fixed ropes helped immensely, and since I came last on the two hard pitches (twenty-ninth and twenty-seventh), Ed didn't have to worry so much about not knowing the moves. Despite the conditions, we were moving efficiently.

At the top of the twenty-sixth pitch, the vertical inside corner Don had led so well in crampons, we stopped to rappel. We stood, side by side, attached to the bottom of the fixed rope we had just used on the pitch above. In the dark, we could discern only the outlines of each other's faces. Under our feet, we felt our crampons bite the ice. Just below the little ledge we stood on, the rock shrank vertically away, and empty space lurked over the chasm below. It was too dark to see very far down. Above us, the steepest part of the face, which we had just descended, loomed vaguely in the night. Up there, on another ledge, Don and Matt were probably sleeping. Beside us, in the mild darkness, icicles dripped trickles of water that splashed on the rocks. The fixed rope was wet; here and there ice, from the splashing, had begun to freeze on it.

We didn't have an extra rope, so we untied and attached ourselves to the fixed line, setting up a rappel with the climbing rope. Ed attached a carabiner to the anchor, through which he clipped the climbing rope, so that we could pull it down from the bottom. He wrapped the rope around his body and got ready to rappel. We were tired, but were getting down with reasonable speed. It was ten minutes before midnight.

"Just this tough one," I said. "Then it's practically walking to camp."
"Yeah," Ed answered.

He leaned back. Standing about five feet from him, I heard a sharp scraping sound. Suddenly Ed was flying backward through the air. I could see him fall, wordless, fifty feet free, then strike the steep ice below.

"Grab something, Ed!" But even as I shouted, he was sliding and bouncing down the steep ice, tangled in the rappel rope. He passed out of sight, but I heard his body bouncing below. From the route photos I knew where he had fallen; there wasn't a chance of his stopping for 4,000 feet.

Perhaps five seconds had passed. No warning, no sign of death—but Ed was gone. I could not understand. I became aware of the acute silence. All I could hear was the sound of water dripping near me. "Ed! Ed! Ed!" I shouted, without any hope of an answer. I looked at the anchor—what could have happened? The piton was still intact, but the carabiner and rope were gone with Ed. It made no sense.

I tried to shout for help to Matt and Don. But they were nearly 1,000 feet above, hidden by cliffs that deflected and snow that absorbed my voice. I realized they couldn't hear me. Even the echo of my shouts in the dark seemed tiny. I couldn't just stand there; either I must go up or I must go down. It was about an equal distance either way, but the pitches above were more difficult. I had no rope. There was no point going up, because there was nothing we could do for Ed. His body lay now, as far as anyone could ever know, on the lower Tokositna, inaccessible. An attempt even by the three of us to descend the 4,000 feet to look for him would be suicidally dangerous, especially since we would have only one rope for all of us. If I went up, I should eventually have to go down again. All it could do was add to the danger. I realized these things at the time. Yet the instinct, in my isolation, to try to join Matt and Don was so compelling that for a while I didn't even consider the other possibility. But it became obvious I had to go down.

At least the fixed ropes were still in. I used two carabiners to attach myself to them, then began to climb down the steep pitch we had started to rappel. I moved jerkily, making violent efforts, telling myself to go more slowly. But I had to use the adrenaline that was racing through me now; it was the only thing that could keep the crippling fear and grief temporarily from me.

I managed to get down the hard pitch. The snow on the Upper Park was in poor condition. I broke steps out beneath me, but held my balance with the fixed rope. I realized that I was going far too fast for safety, but slowing down was almost impossible. As I traversed to the Alley, I was sure the weak snow would break under my feet, but it held. At last I arrived at the tent. The seven pitches had taken eighteen minutes, dangerously fast. But I was there; now there was nothing to do but wait alone.

I crawled into the tent. It was full of water. Matt and I had left the back door open! In the dark I sponged it out, too tired to cry, in something like a state of shock. I took two sleeping pills and fell asleep.

In the morning I gradually woke out of a gray stupor. It seemed to be snowing lightly. I felt no sudden pang about the accident; even in sleep I must have remained aware of it. I forced myself to cook and eat a breakfast, for the sake of establishing a routine, of occupying myself. I kept thinking, *What could have happened?* The carabiner and rope were gone; nothing else had been disturbed. Perhaps the carabiner had flipped open and come loose; perhaps it had broken; perhaps Ed had clipped in, in such a way that he wasn't really clipped in at all. Nothing seemed likely. It didn't matter, really. All that mattered was that our perfect expedition, in one momentary mechanical whim, had turned into a trial of fear and sorrow for me, as it would for Matt and Don when they learned, and into sudden blankness for Ed. His death had come even before he could rest well enough to enjoy our triumph.

The time passed with terrible slowness. I knew Matt and Don would be taking their time now that it was snowing. I grew anxious for their arrival, afraid of being alone. I tried to relax, but I caught myself holding my breath, listening. Occasionally a ball of snow would roll up against the tent wall. I was sure each time that it was one of them kicking snow down from above. I would stick my head out the tent door, looking into the empty whiteness for a sign of them. My mind magnified even the sound of snowflakes hitting the tent into their distant footsteps.

I made myself eat, write in my diary, keep the tent dry, keep a supply of ice near the door. But I began to worry about Matt and Don, too. I knew there was no reason to expect them yet, but what if they had had an accident, too?

There were some firecrackers in the tent. We had tentatively arranged on the way up to shoot them off in an emergency. I might have done that now, but there was no emergency. It would be more dangerous to communicate with them than not to, because in their alarm they might abandon caution to get down fast.

I began to wonder what I would do if they didn't come. What if I heard them calling for help? I would have to go up, yet what could I do alone? I calculated that they had at most five days' food at the Nose Camp. I had enough for twenty days at the Alley Camp. I would wait five or six days, and if there was no sign of them, I would try to finish the descent alone. At the cave I could stamp a message for Sheldon; if he flew over, he would see it. If he didn't, I would eventually start to hike out, seventy miles down an unknown glacier, across rivers, through the tundra. . . .

But these were desperate thoughts, the logical extremes of possible action I might have to take; I forced myself to consider them so that no potential course of events could lurk unrealized among my fears.

Already I had begun to miss Ed in a way separate from the shock and loneliness. I longed for his cheeriness, that fund of warmth that Matt, Don, and I lacked. I had wanted so much to relax in the tent, talking and joking with him, reliving the long summit day. I hadn't climbed with him since July 11. Now it was the last day of the month, and he was gone.

I went outside the tent only to urinate. Each time, I tied a loop around my waist and clipped in to a piton outside, not only because I was afraid but because I couldn't be sure that the sleeping pills and the shock (if it was actually shock) were not impairing my judgment or balance. I felt always tense, aware that I was waiting, minute by minute. I could think of very little but the accident; I couldn't get the sight of Ed falling, sudden and soundless, out of my head.

The snow continued to fall lightly, but the tent got warmer as the hidden sun warmed the air. In the afternoon I began to hear a high, faint whining sound. It was like nothing human, but I couldn't place it. Could it be some kind of distress signal from Matt or Don? Impossible. . . . Could it be the wind blowing through a carabiner somewhere above? But there was almost no wind. Was it even real? I listened, holding my breath, straining with the effort to define the sound. I couldn't even tell if it was above the camp or below. I sang a note of the same pitch to convince myself the sound was real. It seemed to stop momentarily, but I couldn't be sure I hadn't merely begun to ignore it. Finally I noticed that when I went outside the tent, I couldn't hear it. Therefore the sound had to come from inside. At last I found it—vaporized gas, heated by the warmth of the day, was escaping from the stove's safety valve! I felt silly but immeasurably relieved.

I tried to relive every moment Ed and I had had together the last day, as if doing so could somehow salvage something from the tragedy. My recollections had stuck on a remark he had made in the Nose Camp as we rested after the summit. I had told him that it had been the best day I'd ever had climbing. Ed had said, "Mine too, but I don't know if I'd do the whole thing again."

I thought he was still upset about Matt's and my near-accident, and suggested so. Ed thought a moment, then said, "No. It's not only that."

We hadn't pursued it, but his attitude had seemed strange to me. For me, there was no question but that it would have been worth doing all over again. Nor for Don. And I thought Matt would have said so, too. But Ed had climbed less than we had; perhaps he wasn't so sure that climbing was the most important thing in his life, as we would have said it was in ours.

Now his remark haunted me. The accident, ultimately inexplicable beyond its mechanical cause, which itself we would never be sure of, seemed that much more unfair in view of what Ed had said. It would have been better, fairer, perhaps, had it happened to me. Yet not even in the depth of anguish could I wish that I had died instead. And that irreducible selfishness seemed to prove to me that beyond our feeling of "commitment" there lay the barriers of our disparate self-love. We were willing to place our lives in each other's hands, but I wouldn't have died for Ed. What a joke we played on ourselves—the whole affair of mountaineering seemed a farce then. But the numbness returned; I told myself to wait, to judge it all in better perspective, months, years from now.

By that night there had still been no sign of Matt or Don. I took another sleeping pill and finally dozed off. Sometime in the night, on the edge of sleeping and waking, I had a vision of Ed stumbling, bloody, broken, up to the tent, yelling out in the night, "Why didn't you come to look for me?" I woke with a jolt, then waited in the dark for the dream to dissolve. I hadn't considered, after the first moments, trying to look for Ed's body. For me alone, without a rope, to try to descend the 4,000 feet would certainly have been suicide. Yet because there was nothing to do, and because I hadn't seen Ed's dead body, a whisper of guilt had lodged in my subconscious, a whisper that grew to Ed's shout in my nightmare.

I took a sip of water and fell asleep again. In the morning I discovered my watch had stopped. An unimportant event, it hit me with stunning force. It was as if one more proof of reality were gone, one more contact with the others, Matt and Don first of all, everyone else alive in the world eventually. I set the watch arbitrarily and shook it to get it started.

That day, August 1, dragged by as the last one had. I was no more relaxed than I had been before. The weather was good for a few minutes in the morning, then clouded up again; but at least it had stopped snowing. I felt surer now that Matt and Don would get to me, but I began to dread their arrival, for it would open the wounds of shock in them, and I would have to be the strong one, at first.

I thought of how rarely an expedition is both successful and tragic, especially a small expedition. Something like 95 per cent of the dangers in a climb such as ours lay in the ascent. But we had worked for thirty-one days, many of them dangerous, on the route without a serious injury before finally getting to the summit. Going down should have taken only two or three days, and it is usually routine to descend pitches on which fixed ropes have been left. I was reminded of the first ascent of the Matterhorn, when only hours after its conquest the climbing rope broke, sending four of Edward Whymper's seven-man party to their deaths. Then I realized that the Matterhorn had been climbed one hundred years, almost to the day, before our ascent. I thought, also, of the ascent of Cerro Torre in Patagonia in 1959, still regarded by many as the hardest climb ever done. On its descent Toni Egger, one of the best mountaineers in the world, had fallen off a cold rappel to his death, leaving only Cesare Maestri to tell of their victory. But thinking of those climbs explained ours no better. I knew that Whymper, after the Matterhorn, had been persecuted by the public, some of whom even suggested he had cut the rope. I knew that, even in an age that understands mountaineering a little better than the Victorians did, vague suspicions still shrouded the Cerro Torre expedition. But even if we could explain Ed's death to mountaineers, how could we ever explain it to those who cared more about him than about any mountain?

Around 4:00 PM I heard the sound of a plane, probably Sheldon's, flying near the mountain. I couldn't see anything through the mist, but perhaps his very presence meant that it was clear up above, possibly that he could see our steps leading to the summit.

Around 10:00 PM I thought I heard a shout. I looked out of the tent, but saw nothing, and was starting to attribute the sound to a random noise of the mountain, ice breaking loose somewhere or a rock falling, when suddenly Matt came in sight at the top of the Alley. He let out a cheery yell when he saw me. I couldn't answer, but simply stared at him. Pretty soon Don came in sight and yelled, "How are things down there?" I pretended I couldn't hear him. Matt said later that they had seen our tracks from high on the mountain and therefore known that Ed and I hadn't completed the descent to the cave. This had disturbed them a little, and their mood had acquired gloominess during the treacherous last descent, on steps covered by new snow, using ice-coated fixed ropes, once belaying in a waterfall that had frozen their parkas stiff. But as they approached, Matt had seen my head poking out of the tent and for an instant had thrown off his worries. Yet my silence made him uneasy again; then, before he got to the tent, he saw that there was only one pack beside it. Then I said, "Matt, I'm alone."

He belayed Don all the way down before either of us said anything to him. When Matt told him, Don stood there frozen momentarily, looking only at the snow. Then, in a way I cannot forget, he seemed to draw a breath and swallow the impact of the shock. He said, "All right. Let's get inside the tent." His voice, calm as ever, was heavy with a sudden fatigue. But once they knew, once I saw that they were taking it without panic, being strong, I felt an overwhelming gratitude toward them: out of my fear, an impulse like love.

Californians in Alaska
[Kichatna Spires]

– ROYAL S. ROBBINS –

The Kichatna Spires are among the world's most spectacularly vertical granite peaks. According to some, they're also North America's most challenging mountains to climb. Yet strangely enough, mountaineers somehow missed these granitic towers—officially known as the Cathedral Spires of the Kichatna Mountains—until the early 1960s. Even stranger, the mountains were misidentified, apparently on purpose, when first presented to the climbing public.

In June 1962, Summit *magazine ran a photograph of fabulous granite spires, on a par with Patagonia's famous towers. Called the Riesenstein, they were said to be in British Columbia. But* Summit's *editors had been duped. Climbers excited by this dramatic new discovery soon found that the Riesenstein didn't exist. So where, everyone wondered, were the peaks located?*

A researcher studying maps at The American Alpine Club's library eventually solved the mystery: these 6,500- to 9,000-foot-high spires belong to the Kichatna Mountains, in the southwestern Alaska Range. Soon after, easterners Alvin DeMaria and Claude Suhl organized a climbing expedition to the Kichatnas, where their six-man team found "the most challenging peaks any of us had ever seen," DeMaria and Peter Geiser reported in the American Alpine Journal.

That 1965 expedition climbed three of the Kichatna Spires' easier rock-and-ice pinnacles, and descriptions of their trip soon triggered other expeditions. By 1980, some twenty climbing parties had completed more than sixty different routes.

Among those drawn to the Kichatnas were many of the nation's best big-wall climbers. David Roberts wrote about the Kichatnas, as did Jim Bridwell, Alan Long, Andy Embick, and others. Steve Roper and Allen Steck included the 1977 ascent of Middle Triple Peak's East Buttress (by Mike Graber, Alan Long, Andy Embick, and George Schunk) in their Fifty Classic Climbs of North America.

The story chosen here is by Royal Robbins, who describes the Kichatnas as "a little bit like Yosemite Valley—and the North Pole; it's a total original, unlike anything else I've been to." Born in 1935, Robbins revolutionized rock climbing with his big-wall ascents of the sixties and seventies, and he gained a reputation as the preeminent rock climber of that period. Most closely connected to Yosemite, Robbins also set new standards in the Colorado Rockies, Utah, Wyoming, and Europe. He climbed in Alaska only twice, both times in the Kichatnas.

Royal Robbins' account of his 1969 trip to the Kichatna Spires, "Californians in Alaska," originally appeared in 1970 in The American Alpine Journal.

I ADMIT TO RESERVATIONS ABOUT the title of this piece. The human proclivity to categorization being relentless, I am not sure I want to be known as a Californian. We read of astonishing Japanese successes in the mountains and dismiss them, subconsciously perhaps, as done by Japanese. After all, they "climb in a more heroic myth than do Americans." Still, California is rather a long way from Alaska, in distance and in climate. One could get further, perhaps. Say, the swamps of Georgia. But the point is that we were scions of the Yosemite–Sierra Mother Earth, offspring of sun-worshippers. Could we do our thing in the rain and snows and glaciers and cold and harsh conditions of the Alaskan mountainscape? Ever since Chouinard wrote that call to arms in 1963 in *The American Alpine Journal*, we have felt obligated to carry the Yosemite banner into hostile arctic regions of the earth. Hence the title.

Our goal is the Cathedral Spires of the Kichatna Mountains of Alaska. We sleep and drive, sleep and drive. On July 7 we pull into the tiny town of Talkeetna. Don Sheldon, the famous bush pilot, will fly us in. He reminds me of a climber—the nervousness, the quick, alert eyes, the energy. He first strikes one as a bit comical, a bit of a country cousin. He looks harmless, friendly, uncritical. But beneath his boyish exterior, beneath that disarming ear to ear grin, is a very hard man. Once or twice when his face is in repose I see he is finely chiseled and strong.

On July 9 we fly in and land on the Tatina Glacier. "The glacier is big enough," says Don, "to land a DC-6." Flowing its sluggard way down a canyon the size of Yosemite, it is surrounded on three sides by savage peaks seven and eight thousand feet high. The easiest route on most of these mountains would be challenging climbs. After the first ascents of these mountains, the story of their great ridges and faces will begin, a tale which promises to be long and exciting.

Don flies off and I am alone. It feels good. Four hours pass before Sheldon returns with my friends. We have done it. We are here, right in the middle of a host of virgin peaks, all waiting to be climbed. We are set to realize our dreams of first ascents in alpine conditions of difficult mountains with hard rock climbing. But the conditions will be even more "alpine" than we expect.

My companions are Joe Fitschen and Charles Raymond. Joe has been a friend from my early climbing days. He was part of that flowering of rock-climbing talent which bloomed in the Los Angeles basin at the end of the Korean War and which dominated California rock climbing until the advent of Charles Marshall Pratt of Berkeley in 1958. Joe achieved notoriety early with his historic 240-foot tumble down the steep slabs of Tahquitz Rock. His route of descent was subsequently climbed and named Fitschen's Folly in his honor. He was ready to climb again as soon as his eyeballs returned to their normal position from one of contemplating his brain. From this stunt he went on to make the second ascents of El Capitan and of the face of Half Dome, as well as a host of fine first ascents in Yosemite and the Tetons. We had climbed much together and made a good team, largely free of the competitive struggle between individuals which often accompanies the struggle against the mountain. Joe has a beautiful wife, a lovely child, a home in the forest, and a secure position as professor of English—eloquent testimony to man's need for something else, for adventure, for experiencing his manhood by facing danger.

I first met Charlie at Krehe's pad in Berkeley. This small, scruffy domicile of Krehe Ritter was once the central meeting place of Berkeley climbers, and for six months housed five in cramped quarters, including Charlie and me. It was a haven for freedom of expression in the uptight world of the late 1950's. We could play Brahms at ear-splitting levels, sing and shout, folk-dance, eat cheese and bread, and down jugs of wine, and bother no one, except perhaps Charlie, the Spartan of our group, who could usually be found studying intensely in the next room. His diligence was duly rewarded with a Ph.D. in glaciology at Cal Tech, and a position at the University of Washington which he would accept upon our return from Alaska.

We marvel at the mountains. This is it—the beginning of our adventure. They don't look too tough. If we can get any break with the weather, we hope to get up quite a few.

Four days later we stagger back to camp drenched by a continuing downpour, all illusions of the accessibility of summits ripped from our minds. We have been out 41 hours with only one of rest, attempting North Triple Peak, an 8400-foot tower standing at the head of the Tatina Glacier. Beset by wind and drizzle on the ascent, we fought our way up difficult rock with freezing fingers to arrive on a fog-shrouded hump of snow we thought was the summit. When the fog cleared we could see the true summit apparently 150 feet higher and 400 feet away, but by then it was too late, for snow was falling heavily and we were fatigued. We fought our way to a lower level, where the snow changed to a very cold rain, and thence hour after hour cautiously down in the demoralizing weather to our storm-flattened camp.

It is a pleasant three days we spend in the tent while the wind, rain, and snow rage against it. Our strength returns and with it our will to climb. The next day, July 17, the sun emerges after a morning rain. We dry our equipment and prepare to attempt Peak 8100. It sits across Monolith Pass from the Triple Peaks and will give us a good view of the peak we tried as well as of the great northwest face of Middle Triple Peak (on which we entertain certain unrealistic designs). Peak 8100 doesn't look difficult, but neither did our first adversary.

All night a gusty south wind tears at our tent. At 2 AM it is at its height, whipping about us with depressing violence. I want to sleep another hour, but Charlie asks, "Why not get up now?" No good reason, so up we get. A vile morning. Early morning ughs. I cannot imagine climbing in such a wind, but events prove Charlie right. We reach the summit 11½ hours after leaving camp. We see now that we were only one rope-length away from the top of North Triple. Of Middle Triple, only the top third is visible. It would be a challenging climb in itself, without the 2400 feet of steep, smooth rock below. The sun is bright and pleasant, but below us is a sea of clouds, into which, after an hour of loitering, we descend, to meet increasing snow and wind until we are fighting our way down in a full blizzard. Snow covers the rocks. We can't see. Traverses that were simple on the way up are serious now. Charlie and I often argue about where the route lies. He is usually right and I am resentfully amazed at the quality of his mind, the sharpness of his memory. Further down my ego is saved by luck as I intuitively select a route which leads us out of the difficulties. We are as long getting off the peak as we were getting on it.

We got one! The second 8000-foot peak to be climbed in three expeditions. [David] Roberts' party got the best: Kichatna Spire—a superb mountain. Our hands are in bad shape, for the rock is more abrasive than Chamonix granite.

Only two days of rest this time. A raven visits our garbage dump. We name him "Nevermore," and name our mountain after the crow. But another mountain is now calling, a big blocky monolith sitting two miles down-glacier with the easiest looking route on its sunny side. It is barely 8000 feet, but Roberts describes it as appearing complicated and tough. It looks bad but is nearly all rock climbing, hence attractive. We hike to its base and climb to a ridge at the beginning of the major difficulties. We pass the twilight here. The wind is now from the north and we think this presages good weather. Not so in the Kichatnas. We rise at six and after two pitches it is snowing. Through intermittent snow we climb all day, traversing a treacherous ridge to stand in fog on the summit at 4:15 PM, 26 hours after leaving camp. On the descent we are struck by blustery winds and heavy snow, but the snow at least, if not the wind, is intermittent. Finally off the ridge and on to straight-forward rappels, one after another for 1000 feet. It is a grind up the glacier back to camp, and eerie, in the subdued morning light. The cold, arctic wind sweeps up-glacier from the north. It is like a dream of a Dali snowscape. Our figures are spectral—black as death against the harsh whiteness. Overhead the dark grey clouds. Plodding and trudging until we are sick of it and long only to be there. At last we are, at 2:15 AM, after a 35-hour round-trip. We name it "Mount Jeffers" after the California poet.

On July 23 we awake at 3 PM to an onslaught of sleet and increasing wind. This continues for eight days with little abatement, sometimes raining, sometimes snowing, often both at once. Trapped in the tent, our spirits begin to flag. Time is running out. Are we to get nothing else done? We dearly want to take back one of the Triple Peaks as our grand prize, but they are receiving heavy snow. Should we again try North Triple Peak? The rappels are set up and we know the route. But go all that way for 50 vertical feet? We finally decide on South Triple Peak, which has the distinction of being rated by Roberts as probably the most difficult mountain in the range. The best route lies on the south side and should clear of snow relatively quickly. We have only a few days left. All hangs on the weather.

At 7:30 AM on July 31 the sky is clear, the temperature 27°. We climb over Monolith Pass and wend a tortuous way down Monolith Glacier. The icefall is nightmarish, and I almost get beaned by falling ice when we venture close to the still self-denuding south face of Nevermore. We camp by the snout of the glacier at the end of our first rainless, snowless day. A northwest wind dissipates the evening clouds. It looks good.

We arise at 3 AM and depart at 5. The air is cool but not cold, the sky mostly clear. After reconnoitering the south face from a glacier at its base we decide on a southwest ridge approach. Contrasting sharply with the light granite above, the dark schists lead us to a notch in the ridge at an elevation of 6300 feet, 3000 feet above our camp at the foot of the glacier. We discover a good ramp on the west side which slashes up and leads to the great south bowl. Charlie leads across to a minor ridge which we in error follow for three pitches, then make three diagonal rappels to the east, partly crossing the bowl. After we scramble down a gully for 100 feet, I lead further east and turn the corner out of the great south bowl. We ascend the ridge between the south and central bowls—superb climbing—moving slowly eastward. Most of the time we are enveloped in thick cloud and have difficulty finding our way. At 9 PM we turn a corner to find a narrow, lonely, snow-covered ledge just as rain begins. Our spirits sag. Are we again to be beaten by the weather? At 3:30 AM the rain has stopped, the eastern sky is bright yellow through ragged clouds. High mountains near Denali are in sight. A break! We are going to get it after all! We traverse east under a formidable wall, with one hard pitch of mixed free and aid climbing to turn a corner into an ice gully leading to the summit ridge. The rain returns, fine and hard-driven by an ever-increasing wind. We cross the gully and ascend to a notch in the ridge where we drop our packs. The weather is quickly deteriorating, the winds ferocious, the rain turning to snow. We think about the descent as we dash for the summit. It means much to us and is worth a little risk. We do the last 500 feet in an hour and stand on the summit at noon in a snowy gale. But now we have got to get down. We quickly descend, gather our packs, and climb westward along the ridge to avoid traversing the central bowl below. A bit of a risk. We could get hung up. After climbing as far along the ridge as possible, we begin our rappels into the mist. It's raining heavily and very cold. We are fatigued and soon soaked to the skin with the cold rain. Shivering continuously, we begin to understand how a man dies of exposure. The last numbed rappel is finished at 10 PM and we reach our tent at midnight.

It is a long haul the next day over Monolith Pass in a heavy rainstorm. Our tent is down and flooded and we pour the water from it. Much of our gear is soaked, but it does not matter now. We are satisfied.

East Face of the Moose's Tooth:
The Dance of the Woo Li Masters

– JAMES D. BRIDWELL –

One of seven Alaskan mountains to be included in Steve Roper and Allen Steck's Fifty Classic Climbs of North America, *the Moose's Tooth is a granite monolith that rises, in spectacular fashion, 10,335 feet above the Alaska Range's Ruth Gorge, about fifteen miles southeast of Denali. It had been named Mount Hubbard in 1910 to honor Thomas Hubbard, then president of the Peary Arctic Club, but was renamed the Moose's Tooth in 1953 to reflect the Native name that Athabascans of the region had given the mountain.*

A pair of British climbers made the first known attempt to scale the Moose's Tooth in 1962, but were turned back well short of the summit. Two years later, Germans Walter Welsch, Klaus Bierl, Arnold Hasenkopf, and Alfons Reichegger became the first to reach its top while following the West Ridge; it was their route that Roper and Steck chose (in 1979) as one of North America's fifty classics. But in March 1981, two of America's best-known alpinists, Jim "The Bird" Bridwell and Terrance "Mugs" Stump, would pull off an even more stunning ascent, via the Moose's Tooth's East Face—a route that, by Bridwell's estimate, had previously stopped at least ten climbing parties, "all very strong teams." It has yet to be repeated. Considered bold and dangerous, their late-winter climb is now widely regarded to be among the all-time Alaskan classics, as is Bridwell's amusingly irreverent account of their alpine-style ascent.

Both mountaineers are classics in their own right. Mugs Stump was among the nation's finest big-wall and ice climbers from the mid-1970s until his freakish death on Denali in 1992. Although he earned acclaim for ascents made in Yosemite Valley, the Rockies, the Alps, Patagonia, and Antarctica, Mugs found his "spiritual home" in the Alaska Range, says friend and climbing partner Michael Kennedy. Among his greatest climbs were ascents of the Moose's Tooth, Mount Hunter, and Denali. Bridwell, too, has long been among the nation's cutting-edge climbers, whether on "extreme rock" free climbs in the States or on Himalayan expeditions. A writer, TV cameraman, and explorer, he's also participated on expeditions to Borneo, the arctic ice pack, and western China.

Jim Bridwell's account of the East Face ascent was first published in 1982 in The American Alpine Journal; *other versions later appeared in* Climbing *magazine and his own anthology,* Climbing Adventures (1992).

A JET. YES, I WAS SURE it was a jet. It was only slightly different, but uniquely so, from the roar of avalanches thundering down everywhere around us. I'd only recently seen huge tongues of boiling snow flickering out from the base of the wall. The plane was probably heading for Oslo or some such place and would arrive in the morning or maybe in the evening. I could figure it out; you are never sure what time it is where they land. My thoughts raced on into relations of time and space. Suddenly my mind focused outwardly and I realized that I was looking down 3000 feet to our tent. The spacious tent looked like Heaven and we were in Hell. What in Hell were we doing here in this inhuman zone? Was it choice, happenstance or fate? Or possibly a combination of all three that brought me to meet my climbing partner, Mugs Stump? Only four months before we were strangers first meeting in an outdoor cafe in Grindelwald, Switzerland. We drank strong coffee and shot the bull about the Eiger and similar experiences on north faces. One cup of coffee equals one hour of bull and before three cups of coffee we were both jawing each other about the east face of the Moose's Tooth. We had both failed on the 5000-foot-high-face, along with a large contingency of other climbers. At least we were in good company! In all, we figured the face had been attempted over ten times by different parties, all very good. We made plans, but *not* for the Moose's Tooth. Maybe that's where fate or coincidence comes to play its part.

In early March Doug Geeting of Talkeetna Air Taxi flew us in his powerful Cessna 185 toward the Great Gorge of the Ruth Glacier, but when we saw our original objective, it looked impossible. The conditions were indeed bad. There was no ice where we had hoped. Instead, a thin veneer of airy ice with a light dusting of spindrift powder clung everywhere. Overhangs bulged with snow clinging incredibly to their undersides. What could we possibly do in these conditions? We had to think of something fast: Doug is a good guy but he wouldn't fly us around forever. The Moose's Tooth was so close that we decided to have a look. The east face looked equally horrendous, but we couldn't impose on Doug's patience any more. This would have to do. These were our cards; we'd have to play them.

The landing was fine, but getting Geeting aloft took some digging and pushing. As the plane sped away, we gazed in awe at the hoary specter before us. It made bones brittle and spirit fragile. Then imagination balked and we set about erecting our beautiful North Face dome tent. At least, home on the glacier would be luxurious and the ogre could wait for inspection when courage was well braced.

The next day was clear and *oh so* cold. In March Alaska still doesn't feel the sun; it passes but doesn't touch. I remembered my hand freezing white like a burn when I touched the metal of the Cessna the day before. They felt the same when I adjusted the focus ring of the spotting telescope. There was no doubt; it *was* cold! The face looked impregnable and the invaders were armed with slingshots. But maybe we could pull off the ol' David and Goliath sketch.

The previous technical-aid routes were hideously plastered with ice and out of the question. Our choice was a more perilous line, but the only plausible one. A lightweight alpine-style approach might be the key. We were bluffing with only a pair. It was grabbing a tiger by the tail: you couldn't let go or you'd be eaten. The lower half of the climb consisted of avalanche chutes and faces which were fed by the whole of the upper wall. If a storm came in, retreat would be suicide. The only way down was to go up. Conquest or death, so to speak. Ridiculous but true! Retreat in good weather would be difficult at best, but we wouldn't retreat in good weather. Unless, of course, there was something up there we couldn't climb.

The barometer rose, but the storms came without caring. We didn't mind. It gave us time to psych up and sort out our gear. The minimum would be the rule: four days of food and fuel to be stretched to six or seven if need be. Food was an austere assortment of gorp and coffee with sugar plus two packets of soup. The hardware rack was skeletal. We trimmed away the fleshy bolt kit and second set of Friends, leaving the bare bones: ten ice screws, fifteen rock pitons, six wired nuts, one set of Friends and the essential Chouinard hook. Of course, we figured to rappel mainly off slings over horns on the descent. We opted for a technical yet swift descent—we hoped not too swift—down a 1500-foot rock face into the east couloir. This would be suicidal in a storm as two huge faces on either side feed the couloir lethal doses of snow. But it did lead directly to the tent, whereas the Bataan death-march down the north ridge led only to the homeless Ruth Amphitheater.

Clear skies came but we spent the first day watching and timing avalanches, attempting to feel for some intuitive glimpse at the secret of its pulsating rhythms. The night was spent consuming large gulps of whisky while deliberating on whether to wait another day. Something inside me—perhaps the whisky—told me to go in the morning. It wields a strong opinion indeed!

We agreed and found ourselves trudging to the base, laboring under packs and hangovers. I didn't want to give myself a chance to know what I was doing until it was too late. Needless to say, Mugs did the leading and I the motivating.

A 55-degree snow slope led into the cauldron, a steep, narrow ice venturi eighty meters long which collected ever minute spindrift slough and amplified it into a blinding, freezing torrent of misery. I was appalled as Mugs without protection led difficult 75-degree to 80-degree ice in waves of gushing spindrift with a 15-kilo pack tugging at his shoulders. It was my turn. At first I thought I could wait out the rushing torrents but soon realized, like Mugs, that it was hopeless and climbed on. I was frozen when I reached the belay. My fingers were wooden. I fiddled with the camera and attempted to feed out the rope.

After one pitch we climbed together to the first traverse. It was steep powder covering sugar snow over rock. Sketchy to say the least, with imaginary belay anchors. Both leader and follower were in fact leading. There was no protection and each became responsible for the other's life. The first traverse was three pitches long and led to a three-pitch, calf-burning ice face and onto another horrid traverse. This one was worse than the first traverse, and longer. Near its beginning we heard a shout. Our minds must be askew! Yet it was true. Some fellow mountaineers, ski-touring up the Buckskin Glacier to the Ruth Amphitheater, were shouting up at us. We shouted back and carried on. The climbing was tenuous. Thin powder snow lay over hidden patches of ice and steep rock. Protection was nearly non-existent and belays were the same. We had to have confidence in each other. In places we were climbing on three to five inches of snow over 60-degree to 65-degree rock. Often, to my distress, these pitches would start with a downward traverse of 40 to 50 feet before going horizontal or upward.

Near the end of the day we reached a steep snow slope on which it was just possible to dig a platform to sleep. Mugs fixed a pitch above for better anchors and we precariously settled in. The North Face Company had supplied me with a space-age sleeping system which I was testing for them. I was warm and toasty, sub-zero temperatures, spindrift and all.

The morning was supremely frigid and we did not dare to move from our cocoons until the sun's rays gave us hope for life. Frostbite was our eminent host if we dared to break the house rules and so we regulated our desires accordingly.

A steep, ice-choked chimney which rose up and out of our field of vision tested our abilities for the rest of the next day. From below I had judged it to be about five pitches long, but it turned out to be seven instead. This chimney and the headwall above would consitute the main difficulties.

I led the first and least steep rope-length. Mugs pressed the attack up the 80-degree to 85-degree gouge. In places he encountered overhanging bulges which the dry, cold winter had turned into airy, unconsolidated granola. Ice axes and hammers became useless weapons. Crampon points barely held, scraping on tiny edges, and we used shaky pitons for hand-holds. My ice-tool picks served as cliff hangers on rock edges or wedged in cracks, nut-fashion. The Forrest saber hammer was especially useful. The assault continued through the day and into the failing light of the evening. I became weak and nauseous from dehydration. In the frigid cold, man's devices cease to function efficiently. The ineffectual stove would boil water only after an hour of coaxing. We were paying for having penetrated into the inhuman zone.

Mugs had fixed the last pitch and I had swung around a corner onto a small 65-degree ice slope, the only posssibility for a bivouac. It took hours to sculpture a precarious perch in the dark. It was nearly 1 AM before we collapsed exhausted in our sleeping bags.

The morning of the third day started with a tedious struggle for liquids before we ascended the fixed rope to our high point. Vertical ice soared upward. Once again Mugs valiantly met the challenge, leading two pitches up the icy serpent. The twisting, curving corridor exited onto an easy 100-meter snow slope which extended to a formidable headwall. Even with the telescope, we hadn't been able to probe the secrets of this section of the climb. Intuition lured us to the right, up an ice runnel and onto a snow rib. I poked my head around the corner to be confronted by a steep rock wall. Its thin cracks were well armored with ice and presented a chilling specter. I tensioned off a nut for which I had chopped a slot in the rock. Thinly gloved fingers searched for usable rugosities, while crampon claws scratched at scaly granite. I laybacked up a steep flake to find its top closed with ice. In desperation I clung on with one hand while I perforated the ice overhead with an ice hammer, hoping it would stick securely. Standing on a shelf of ice, I caught my breath and looked for a possible route up the wall. I moved right to a groove which I climbed on aid and free to where it was possible to swing left onto my ice axe and climb to a small ice ledge. I got some anchors in and brought Mugs up.

Only a portion of the next lead disclosed itself to the eye, but it didn't look promising. Mugs moved off of hooks onto the fragile thinness of precipitous ice. After forty feet of begrudging difficulties, he shouted down that it was blank above. The sky had clouded and snow began to fall. We needed a bivouac site. A night spent exposed and standing would be devastating. He moved only occasionally but made some progress. What was he doing? I could imagine only the worst. He called down for a #3 Friend, and so I climbed up, took out the belay anchor and sent it up. I hung in slings from a tie-off draped over a nub of rock and continued my frigid vigil. The Friend went into a shallow hole, then a hook to a knife-blade behind a half-inch flake and it worked out. Several more technical aid moves, and after two hours of nerve-grinding climbing, Mugs reached an ice tongue that led to easier ground.

I got to Mugs at the belay and started the next pitch as quickly as possible. It was already late in the day and we had to find a place to bivy soon. The snow was coming down heavily, now causing cascading spindrift avalanches. A traverse crossed a slab covered with four inches of snow. I hoped there would be some ice beneath the snow, but no such luck! I splayed my feet duck-style to attain the most surface area. I could not believe they held! It was like climbing on a slate roof thinly covered with snow. I entered a trough filled with bulletproof ice. Mugs came up and found me slumped over; I was weak and nauseous from dehydration. He led the next two pitches of steep mixed ice and rock. It was all I could do to follow in the dark. Fortunately we found a place where we could dig a snow cave. A gift from Heaven!

After two hours the cave was completed and we began brewing tea and coffee, two of the worst drinks possible for dehydration. At 1:30 AM we collapsed in our sleeping bags, secure from the storm.

Life came slowly in the morning. From my vantage point near the cave entrance, I could see the storm was breaking up. Sunshine seeped through the thin clouds, but I kept the vision secret from Mugs, as I just wanted to rest a little longer. When the sun shone into the cave, I could no longer hide the obvious fact that the weather was turning beautiful. We crawled out at 11:30 and commenced climbing. The problems were mainly in route-finding, picking the easiest but not always obvious way, with a talent born of experience and often luck. We were lucky and by 3:30 we stood on top of the Moose's Tooth.

The vantage point was spectacular. The weather was clear in all directions. I took one photograph after another until two rolls had disappeared. Soon it was 4:30 PM, and Mugs coyly asked if I wanted to start down. In reply to Mugs, I said a quick, "No!" I felt a possible ordeal ahead and wanted a full day to cope with any eventuality. It would be a technical and potentially difficult descent and we should give ourselves a full day because once we had started, there would be no place to stop. We agreed and I returned to photography.

Darkness was sneaking over the mountains when our stove begrudgingly produced two cups of sugarless tea. We burrowed deep into our survival cells as the temperatures plummeted to –30° in the night and the wind howled.

It was truly torturous getting ourselves ready to go the next day. All man-made gadgets ceased to work in this inhuman zone; the stove did manage a cupful of cold water each before it died. We climbed down a snow slope and began rappelling over discontinuous snow and rock bands. As we descended rappel after rappel, the snow disappeared, leaving bare, flaking rock, the kind for which the Moose's Tooth is famous. Crumbling and rotten, the face steepened so that it receded below us, making it impossible to see where we were going or what we were coming to. I kept angling left because the couloir we were heading for came up toward our left.

The rock had become blank of cracks but there were a few scabs of very flexible rotten flakes. Survival alarms went off in my head. I rappelled past an overhang and tension-traversed left to a flakelike ledge, pounded two pitons into compressed gravel behind it and wondered what to do next. Looking down I could see nothing to go for. I wished I had brought the bolt kit. I felt like a cat cornered by salivating Alsatians. Then, computerlike, I made a decision and yelled up instructions to Mugs. I asked him to tie off one rope to his anchors and to send the other rope down so that I could see what was below. If I could see nothing, I would have to jümar back up 300 feet to Mugs. Then we would have to climb back to the summit, ten pitches or more, and look for another way down. It would be a devastating course, requiring the rest of the day and part of the next.

I tensioned left again and then climbed up and left. My crampons clawed on the rotten granite, screeching and snarling as I searched for tiny holds. I put in a #3 stopper in the only available place, clipped the rope through and continued rappelling. Near the end of the rope, a small but solitary flake came into view. I stopped and stared at it. Emotions washed over me, visions of people I loved and owed love to. It's sad that we often don't appreciate the commonplace yet wonderful trivial duties of life, like saying hello or washing dishes. I guess you don't miss the water till your well runs dry.

We had to meet our ordeal. I started back up the rope but stopped automatically and turned to take one last look at the flake. Reaching the nut I had placed, I unclipped, swung back right and continued up to the two-piton anchors. I yelled to Mugs to come down. I woke him, as he had fallen asleep, but he could tell that there was uncertainty in my voice. When he reached me, I explained the situation before we pulled the rope so that he could share in the decision. Once we pulled the rope, there would be no choice. He had an easy way of boosting my confidence while accepting my course of action, whatever I might choose.

Casino time; one roll of the dice for all the marbles. I said a prayer and started down. Retracing my traverse, I reached the single stopper I had previously fixed and brought Mugs down to a minimal stance. He surveyed the anchor briefly and then looked at me with wonder. I shrugged my shoulders and said, "That's it!" My heart was trying to escape from my mouth during the 150-foot rappel off the flake until I secured a #1 Friend behind a small flake I had seen from above. I placed another nut while Mugs duplicated the rappel. Mugs later told me that he had almost unclipped from the anchor but quickly realized that a fast death was no more appealing than a slow and agonizing yet inevitable one. After descending half the rope, I gave thanks to the merciful one. Wonder of wonders! The ropes had reached a snow-covered ramp. The chilling grip of death relaxed and a calming peace soothed my quaking soul. The descent became routine and within two hours we were galloping down steep snow toward the security of our tent.

Everything in the tent was frozen. We immediately fired up the stove and began guzzling brew after brew of hot liquids. We laughed and joked until late in the night. We had had five days of intense experience; it takes time to unwind. The cards were played and we had drawn aces. Finally I collapsed into prone paralysis. Just before unconsciousness, the memorable words of the French climber, Jean Afanassieff, came to mind. "This is the - - - - - - - life! No?"

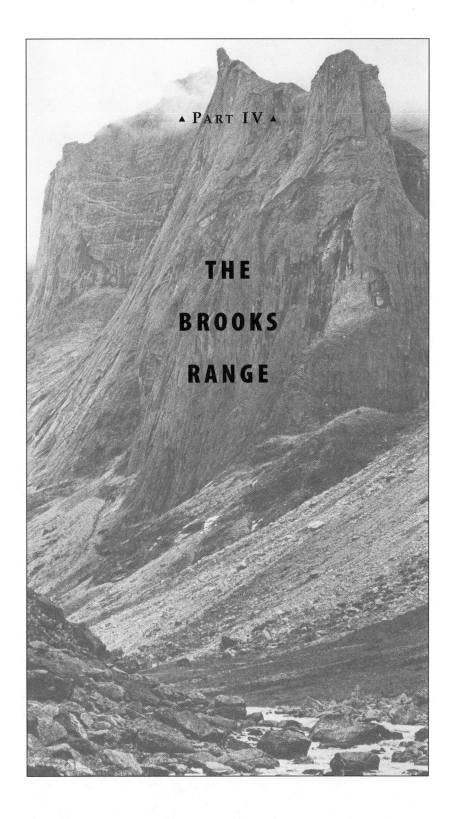

Part IV

THE
BROOKS
RANGE

North Doonerak
[Mount Doonerak]

- ROBERT MARSHALL -

Now recognized as one of our nation's earliest, and greatest, champions of wilderness, Robert Marshall (1901–1939), it could be argued, was destined to be both explorer and wilderness advocate. A city boy by circumstance—he was born and raised in New York City—Marshall felt a lifelong pull to wild and unexplored places. As his brother George once wrote, "Robert . . . was fascinated by blank spaces on maps and was drawn to them from an early age." No wonder, then, that Alaska held such allure; in the 1920s and 1930s much of that vast territory remained unexplored, unmapped.

Trained as a forester, Marshall made four trips to Alaska's Brooks Range between 1929 and 1939. His initial justification was "To add to the scientific knowledge of tree growth at northern timber line." Eventually, Marshall admitted, "an excuse for exploration no longer seemed necessary." His adventures have been chronicled in two books, Alaska Wilderness: Exploring the Central Brooks Range *and* Arctic Village.

While traveling through the Brooks Range, Marshall mapped 15,000 square miles of country and named dozens of mountains, creeks, and lakes. Among the most impressive and enchanting peaks he discovered was a "towering, black, unscalable-looking giant." He calculated the mountain to be 10,100 feet high (later measurements showed it to be considerably shorter, 7,610 feet) and named it Mount Doonerak. "I took [it] from an Eskimo word which means a spirit or, as they would translate it, a devil. The Eskimos believe that there are thousands of Dooneraks in the world, some beneficent, but generally delighting in making trouble."

Not a mountaineer, Marshall nonetheless decided to attempt an ascent of Doonerak, which he incorrectly guessed to be the highest peak in arctic America: "Since I had discovered the mountain, had made the first map of it, and had named it during my trips in 1929 and 1930–31, I wanted to complete the job and make the first ascent."

A series of storms blocked Marshall's first attempt to climb Mount Doonerak, but he returned a year later to try again. His interesting expedition narrative presents a naturalist's, rather than a climber's, perspective, describing in great detail the nature of arctic travel, the landscape, the flowers, and the process of hunting for food. But his was also a milestone climbing expedition: Marshall and his companions were the first to attempt an ascent of any of arctic Alaska's high peaks.

The following excerpt was originally written by Robert Marshall in 1939, in a letter to friends. It's taken from the chapter "North Doonerak, Amawk, Alhamblar, and Apoon" in Marshall's Alaska Wilderness: Exploring the Central Brooks Range, *published in 1970 by the University of California Press (it was originally published as* Arctic Wilderness).

IN JUNE, 1939, NINE MONTHS after our unsuccessful attempt to climb Mount Doonerak, I was fortunate enough to be able to return, for the fourth time, to Alaska. I could not resist the lure of unconquered Doonerak.

As the plane circled the Wiseman landing field it was exciting to recognize each cabin, to observe which of the women had their laundry on the line, to pick out the individual Eskimo children running to the field. We landed at one o'clock in the afternoon on what should have been the longest day of the year, except that for all practical purposes every day for three months was equally long, with twenty-four hours of daylight.

As soon as the welcomes were over and my baggage carried the quarter mile to the roadhouse, Jesse Allen and I retired to his cabin to discuss plans for our next trip. Our foremost objective would be Mount Doonerak. We decided on five days hard back packing overland for another attempt at a first ascent. Afterward we would explore the unknown Arctic Divide at the heads of the North Fork of the Koyukuk and the Hammond River. We would be out for twenty-four days.

We had planned the autumn before, when the previous expedition was not yet completed, that Jesse Allen, Kenneth Harvey, and I would be partners in another attempt at Doonerak. Ernie Johnson was busy with mining and could not come. In his place, Nutirwik, a Kobuk Eskimo, who had the reputation of being the best hunter in the Koyukuk, joined us. Unlike most other Eskimos in the region, he lived alone. This small man—he was scarcely more than five feet tall—with his thin face, high cheekbones, and little gnarled hands, more than held his own with his sturdier-looking companions. His prominent eyebrows were in sharp contrast with his thin eyes. He had a strong, sensitive face and remarkably few wrinkles for a man close to sixty who had lived out of doors all his life. His name literally means blizzard. When he came to live among the whites about 1903 he changed it to Harry Snowden, but we continued to use his Eskimo name on these wilderness adventures. He brought with him his dogs, Coffee and White-eye, while Harvey brought his dog, Moose; they aided materially in dispersing the load.

This load consisted of 285 pounds, of which approximately one-third was photographic and scientific equipment, which would not get lighter; one-third tent, bedding, dishes, packsacks, rifle, ammunition, ax, extra socks and shoes, first aid material, and the like, which likewise would not diminish; and only one-third food, which would gradually decrease until we obtained fresh meat. A few weeks before my arrival, Jesse had packed out staples to a cache on upper Hammond River.

Most of Wiseman was at the roadhouse when we hoisted our packs to our shoulders on the evening of June 23. Harvey, Nutirwik, and I each carried about 55 pounds; one-armed Jesse, who was sixty years old, took 40 pounds; and the three dogs, who were soft from months of inaction, 25 to 30 pounds each. But if dogs get soft from just sitting around and getting fed, so does a bureaucrat, and it was pleasant that for our first day's journey we were taking only the six-mile climb on the road to Nolan Creek. Pleasant also was the chatter of Verne Watts who accompanied us from town with a pack of his own. Pointing to Harvey's advancing baldness, he said: "You'll have to tie a string around your head pretty soon to tell how high to wash your face in the morning." But most pleasant of all was a cold rain which struck us fiercely for a few minutes when we were halfway to Nolan; it put an end to the heat of the evening and to the mosquitoes which had been swarming in great masses around us.

At Nolan Creek we scattered to the cabins of different genial hosts who had invited us to spend the night. I went for nine hours of luxurious sleep to the cabin of George Eaton, now seventy-eight, with whom I had stopped in 1929, 1930, and 1931. Then, although about seventy, he had still been a powerful man, boasting that he could outshovel any man in the Koyukuk, and apparently expecting to be active until he was a hundred years old. Now he was old and unhappy in the realization that active life was over, but still unbroken. He said: "It's terrible to me, Bob, to think my legs is so bad I can't go on a trip like you fellows is going on, but it doesn't bother me a bit that I'm going to die some day soon. I've got to go, and I don't know when, and I'm glad I don't."

We spent the sunny next day on Nolan Creek while I went up and down the valley, chatting with old friends. Almost every one on the creek dropped in afterward to say good-bye as we headed out at eight in the evening.

We planned to travel during the night hours in these days of twenty-four-hour daylight, because the temperature was cooler then and the mosquitoes a little less thick. But on the steep ascent to Snowshoe Pass perspiration and mosquitoes were both profuse until the low sun was temporarily hidden behind the mountainside we were climbing. When we crossed the height of land at ten in the evening we stepped back into the sunlight. Just to the right of the sun, forty miles to the north, black and massive and immense, was old Mount Doonerak, looking utterly unscalable from this angle. But we were not discouraged, knowing a mountain has many angles.

Besides, a person could not be discouraged with bright evening sunshine making flowers and moss fairly glow all around. There was the yellow green of sphagnum, the creamy yellow of reindeer moss, the pure gold of Arctic cinquefoil and poppy, the rich purple of lupine, and the white, cottony tassels of millions of sedge plants waving everywhere.

But these white tassels, for all their beauty, were flags of warning to tell us they waved over sedge tussocks. We avoided them wherever we possibly could as we lugged our packs over the side hills of Glacier River. We made travel as easy as possible by resting at fifty-minute intervals for ten minutes and by stopping for over an hour in the middle of the journey to eat a midnight supper of canned ham and tea. At four o'clock in the morning we made camp near the remains of an old igloo built many years before by arctic Eskimos, over here for a hunt.

Camp consisted of a 10 by 11 foot rectangular canvas, sloping backward from a horizontal front ridgepole, held taut by other poles and ropes, and covering a patch of level ground where we laid spruce boughs. On the boughs we spread our sleeping bags. There was also ample space under the fly to place supplies we wanted to keep dry. Directly in front of the fly we built a fire of dry spruce and cottonwood. After a supper of macaroni and cheese, canned ham, bread and butter, and green tea, we retired for the "night" at the odd hour of seven in the morning and did not stir until four in the afternoon.

With this upside-down schedule the evening meal became breakfast, hence we had oatmeal, bacon, and coffee. It was shortly before eight when we started again. We followed the right bank of Glacier River for mile after mile of slow, plodding travel. It is hard to describe how slow and plodding it really seems when you are out of practice and there is no trail and you have a 55-pound pack tugging on your headstrap and shoulders. You have hardly gone five minutes when the muscles in your neck are so sore that you know every step for the next six or seven hours will be pain. You throw off the headstrap to rest the neck and the pack pulls so violently on your shoulders you imagine it is turning them inside out. You go back to the headstrap again, pushing against it for all you are worth, perspiring freely in spite of the hour of evening, swatting at fifty mosquitoes which have lighted on your forehead and your cheeks and your neck, letting down your black mosquito net which instantly makes the whole world dark, pulling it up again when you almost stifle in the sultry evening, noticing suddenly that your ankle is sore where the boot has rubbed off the skin, stumbling over sedge tussocks, forcing your way through thick willow brush, sliding along on uncertain side hills ankle deep with sphagnum moss, neck aching, shoulders aching, ankle aching, on, on, on.

But surprising things happen in the midst of such travel. Unexpectedly you notice a clump of lovely *Pyrola* you almost stepped on, with round, shiny leaves and with stalks topped by almost bell-shaped five-petaled white flowers. Now, under a clump of spruce, you discover those gayest of white flowers, the *Dryas*, fairly sparkling with their eight bright petals set off against the light green of the sphagnum moss.

Now your attention is drawn to fresh sheep or moose or bear tracks on the mud of the river bar or, on occasion, to tracks of wolves traveling together.

Then, as you get into the swing of it, the pack seems to bother less the farther you go. You no longer look at your watch every ten minutes to see how soon the end of the fifty-minute shift will come. You enjoy more and more the freshness and the freedom from trails and human signs in this remote country, and you realize that one incentive for setting out to climb Mount Doonerak is the satisfaction in conquering the seventy-five miles of back packing across untamed country, which is necessary to reach its base.

Around eleven at theoretical night it started to rain steadily, though not hard. This did not deter us from thirty-eight hearty back slaps at midnight as Harvey moved into his thirty-eighth birthday. A short time later, as we were starting up after midnight supper, something in Moose's swagger seemed to irritate White-eye, who was still virtually a stranger to him, and amid frightful snarls we had the one and only dog fight of our expedition.

We pitched camp at three in the morning directly under the great limestone tower of Chimney Mountain. It rose sheer on three sides for 300 to 400 feet, but on the fourth it sloped at an angle that could be climbed. The chimney was perched on top of a 1,500-foot mountain, and it was a stirring feeling to be camped directly underneath it. Weird and amazing, too, when I woke after hours of unbroken slumber, expecting to see the familiar alley back of an old stable converted into a garage which had greeted my eyes upon awaking all of a Washington winter, to find this wild chimney overhanging me. It took a while to connect with reality and convince myself that I was not dreaming.

The next night we traveled across the low pass between Glacier and Clear rivers with no adventures, but with the pleasing sight of a moose feeding along the marshy edge of a small lake in the middle of the pass. We made what proved to be an exceptionally comfortable three-day camp in the willows at the junction of Holmes Creek and Clear River.

Next evening it was overcast, but the clouds were high, so Harvey and I decided to seek out the never-visited source of Pinnyanaktuk Creek, one of ten large creeks flowing into that super-Yosemite of the North, the eight-mile glacial valley of upper Clear River. On the winter trip of March,

1931, I had named this creek with the Eskimo word meaning "superlatively rugged." Looking up into it was like looking into a great basin which instead of being hollow, was filled with sharply pointed peaks packed together closely.

We pushed our way across two and a half miles of sedge tussocks and soft moss and Labrador tea in full white blossom, to the point where Pinnyanaktuk flows into Clear River at the foot of the mountains. Within the first three miles of its boulder-filled course, two large forks plunged in from the right, and the view up each revealed many unknown crags. Shortly after passing the second fork, Harvey spied four sheep on the hillside to the left. As we needed fresh meat badly, he decided to go after them.

Meanwhile I continued up the valley. The main Pinnyanaktuk climbed rapidly, sometimes cutting through steep dirt banks, sometimes splashing over bedrock, often tearing its way through yet unmelted snowbanks. The bluish white of the anemone profusely speckled the sphagnum. Wherever I looked was the deep purple of phlox and shooting star. The heather was thick; its delicate white bells were lovely and filled the atmosphere with a delightful scent. The creek roaring in the rocky gorge below made stirring music, and every sense seemed satisfied except the sense of touch, which to my unpleasant surprise was just as much abused by mosquitoes above 3,000 feet, with the ground all excellently drained, as it had been in the boggy lowlands.

When I reached a bench along the uppermost forks of Pinnyanaktuk I could see the final divide between Clear River and North Fork less than two miles away. Shortly before, I had heard a shot echoing in the steep valley and felt confident that Harvey had got his sheep.

Although it was midnight, I snapped several pictures. In the middle of this occupation, I was startled by small rocks bounding down the hillside above me. I looked up in time to see four sheep beating a retreat across the slide rock.

When I rejoined Harvey he had a fine 90-pound ram. We cut him up and divided the load among ourselves and Moose. At the mouth of Pinnyanaktuk we left the meat on a gravel bar, and hiked briskly along the river bottom five miles up to the source branches of Clear River valley. The clouds had all vanished during the night and the air was crisp and clear. We enjoyed exciting views up St. Patrick's Creek (which runs parallel to Pinnyanaktuk) on our side of the Clear River and up a couple of deep, nameless creeks on the other. On the return journey the sun over the mountains kept lighting more and more of the valley and the great precipice walls which bounded it.

Back at the mouth of Pinnyanaktuk we picked up the sheep and strode into camp among the willows of the Holmes Creek–Clear River junction at four in the morning. Jesse and Nutirwik had caught a nice mess of grayling, so we were now plentifully supplied. That morning we enjoyed the first sheep meal, which as usual consisted of those choice morsels, heart, tongue, and liver.

When I awoke at two in the afternoon the sun was still shining so brightly that I rushed up on the hill back of camp to photograph everything in sight. The whole gay valley seemed to be white and green with millions of flowers and plants. Not the white and green of lifeless paintings, but living, vivid colors sparkling from miles of hillside in the crystal-clear atmosphere. So they had sparkled for many millenniums since the last ice sheet receded, without any purpose of being looked upon by man, but as just a part of great objective nature.

The fresh sheep plus my journey to upper Pinnyanaktuk Creek somewhat changed our plans. I got the notion that instead of reconnoitering Mount Doonerak from the mountains of upper Pyramid Creek, as we had originally planned, we could climb the wall at the head of Pinnyanaktuk Creek and see the south side of Mount Doonerak just as well from there. At the same time we could eat another day's worth of meat and thereby save packing that much extra load over Holmes Pass.

So Harvey and I set out again for Pinnyanaktuk Creek. The first miles to the upper forks were a repetition of the previous night's gay blossoms and jagged pinnacles. Above the upper forks we climbed over slide rock and snowbanks to the very source of Pinnyanaktuk, and then by easy grade to the 5,000-foot divide.

There, just ahead of us, was the great black bulk of Mount Doonerak, rising gigantically into the sky, directly in front of the sun. To our left was one of the steep mountains at the head of Pinnyanaktuk, and this peak we decided to climb in order to get a better picture of the lay of the land. The best possible picture was certainly needed, because the land, as seen from the top, did not look as we expected. We at first had thought that the deep creek behind which Mount Doonerak rose was Pyramid Creek; then, after checking the known topography, we realized this could not be right. Suddenly I discovered that Bombardment Creek, which we always supposed had its source only a few miles south of the North Fork (on the north side of Doonerak and Hanging Glacier Mountain), actually cut a deep gorge between the two peaks. Pyramid came nowhere near Mount Doonerak, and the fog-covered mountain at its head which Ernie and I had assumed was Mount Doonerak the previous summer, in reality was part of Hanging Glacier Mountain. Worst of all, while that mountain could be climbed from the south side, just as we reported, Mount Doonerak's south side was almost sheer for 6,000 feet and appeared utterly unscalable. The only possibility in the half of its circumference which we could see was a very steep ridge running toward lower Bombardment Creek. Even this possibility seemed highly remote, but at least we knew that Bombardment Creek and not Pyramid Creek, as we had thought, was the best site for our first base camp.

We spent more than an hour, equally distributed around midnight, on the summit, and called our peak Midnight Mountain. As if to celebrate the christening, at exactly midnight the sun suddenly illuminated the finger of Chimney Mountain, jutting into the sky a dozen miles southward. Twenty minutes after midnight the sun shot out from behind Mount Doonerak. Even the sun, however, did not make us warm and we had to pound each other frequently to stop shivering. Yet we savored the intimate view of hundreds of nearby, never-scaled pinnacles, blackly puncturing the midnight arctic sky.

Next evening we broke our comfortable three-day camp at the Holmes Creek junction and started the long uphill drag toward Holmes Pass, eight and a half miles to the northwest and 1,300 feet above us. First we stumbled over sedge tussock- and moss-covered hillsides for a couple of hours, scrambling through the dense brush of the dwarf birch, pushing for all we were worth against headstraps as we gained steep grades. A heavy rainstorm broke shortly after we started and soon had us soaked to the skin. We stopped for a lunch of tea and cold mutton chops at the last dry willows big enough to make a fire. Then we splashed along up Holmes Creek, sometimes on gravel bars, sometimes through willow brush, often right through the water. At one place the creek narrowed into a canyon not more than ten feet wide and half barricaded by a huge wall of yet unmelted ice. In order to get around this we had to climb a steep bank for several hundred feet and then descend again into the creek.

We reached the broad pass just before midnight. It was completely barren of woody growth, but profusely covered by many-colored flowers and the lovely greens and yellows of mosses and lichens. To the west was the familiar North Fork.

The steep descent into Pyramid Creek was almost as hard as the ascent to Holmes Pass had been. We had to be constantly on edge to keep from falling in as we stepped over the water-splashed boulders. Lower down, the creek became too deep to be forded comfortably, so we took to the side-hill moss. This was slippery, but not hard going except at half a dozen steep, brushy gulches. At one place the brush tore into the breeching on the pack of White-eye, and we had to repair it on the hillside.

It was nearly four in the morning when we made camp in ankle-deep sphagnum moss under a thrifty young spruce stand near the mouth of Pyramid Creek. The scene of last autumn's shipwreck was only four miles to the south, but none of us had any inclination to visit it. We had, however, a great desire to sleep, and after a huge supper of pea soup, sheep steak, and boiled dried apples, we retired at seven-thirty in the morning for ten hours of slumber.

Another night's hard scrambling through thick brush and along soft, slippery, moss-covered hillsides, with 65-pound packs tearing at our neck and shoulder muscles, brought us the nine and a half miles to our destination at the junction of Bombardment Creek and the upper North Fork. Here we set up base camp for our assault on Mount Doonerak.

It was a lovely location on a spruce flat between the two streams. The sphagnum moss covered the ground in great, dry mats, fifteen inches thick, which beat a feather bed for softness. The early morning sun, rising upriver, gave a sparkling brightness to a 200-foot waterfall tumbling off the side of Hanging Glacier Mountain, which loomed high over our camp.

When we awoke next evening, the bright sunlight had given way to an ominous sky. Just as we finished our oatmeal and mutton it started to rain hard. Nevertheless, we decided to spend an active night. Jesse and Nutirwik walked back eight miles to our cache of last year where we had left 44 pounds of food, and picked up some sugar, rice, butter, and dried apples. Harvey and I set out to explore the intriguing recesses of Bombardment Creek.

This little eight-mile creek had cut out a fabulous gorge between Hanging Glacier rising 4,000 feet above it to the west and Doonerak rising 6,000 feet directly to the east. Higher and higher, as we ascended the valley, the great rock crags of these two towering mountain masses rose. Loftier and loftier grew the sheer rock faces. At places waterfalls dropped over them, 100, 200, even 300 feet high.

With mosquitoes swarming about us all the time, we picked a route just below the base of the precipices, on unstable slide-rock slopes, lying at too steep an angle for repose. Every now and then we would start small avalanches. After three and a half miles we came to a sharp turn in the valley beyond which, we decided, it was not safe to go, with the rain making the rock so slippery and with frequent slides starting from the mountainside above. Even while we were discussing the return a small rock from far up the mountainside went bounding over Harvey's head.

The downhill route over the sliderock was much easier than the ascent. We reached Bombardment Creek just below its plunge over a 125-foot wall. We followed up the narrow gorge, crawled under a massive icebank which overhung for 10 feet, and stood in the spray at the base of the fall, which dropped through a narrow chute, rock on one side and ice pillar on the other. At one place the chute was not more than eighteen inches wide. The fall set up a strong breeze, which, together with the cold of the surrounding ice chased away the mosquitoes which had followed us all evening.

The two following nights were also stormy. Jesse and I spent the first in camp, while Harvey and Nutirwik went hunting—and came back empty-handed, because they would not shoot a ewe with a lamb. The second evening it rained only intermittently, so I decided to climb a gray foothill of Mount Doonerak about three miles west of camp from which I would get a better view of the north side of the mountain and look directly down on what the autumn before had appeared to be a glacier. Harvey and Nutirwik went out after sheep again.

The sky cleared to the north and west, and I climbed 3,000 feet through a garden of bright flowers, keeping pace with the setting sun as shadows rose ever higher on the mountain. Growing luxuriantly were the many-blossomed white heads of bear cabbage (*Veratrum*), the gold of the arctic poppy and the buttercup, the sparkling white of *Dryas octopetala* nodding above its fernlike leaves, the deep purple clumps of phlox.

Now I could look directly over to the black pinnacle of Mount Doonerak, jutting almost straight up for 4,000 feet. It seemed utterly unscalable from this side. At the lower edge of this wall was the glacier indeed, darkened by centuries of tumbling rocks which had mingled with the ice. It was half a mile away and 500 feet below me. There appeared to be no possible way of climbing to the glacier for measurements. I estimated it was 2,000 feet long and 800 feet wide, and the surface sloped at thirty degrees. The face must have been about 50 feet thick, and a large chunk had apparently broken off just a few days before, because it lay yet unmelted where it had tumbled into a hollow a thousand feet below.

At eleven-fifteen the sun finally dipped behind the mountains across the North Fork and I returned to Bombardment Creek camp. An hour later, Harvey, Nutirwik, and Moose trudged in under the load of a large sheep. Since we were all back in camp by one-thirty in the morning, we decided this would be a good time to change from night to day schedule, which would be better for climbing mountains.

In the later morning, after breakfast, our first job was to cut up the meat, set it on poles under willow shade, and protect it from flies by a mosquito tent. The sky was overcast, but the clouds were high and the top of Mount Doonerak clear, so we decided to make an attempt. Unfortunately we started up a ridge which ended in sheer limestone precipices only 3,000 feet above the valley. We were completely stopped for this day, but we could see that the next ridge to the south would permit us to rise higher, even though the summit now appeared impossible.

Next morning the sky was cloudlessly blue. Harvey, Nutirwik, and I set out at six-fifteen, Jesse remaining in camp as his one arm made steep rock work not feasible. We followed up the bench above Bombardment Creek for a mile and then started up a steep, green shoulder leading to the ridge we had, on the previous day, decided to follow. When we reached it we got a fine view into the upper gorge of Bombardment Creek where, to our amazement, we saw a half-mile-long lake which was still frozen on this July 5. Below it, Bombardment Creek spilled over a waterfall, 100 feet high.

As we followed the ridge on good footing we were suddenly face to face with Mount Doonerak. About half a mile away its northwesterly abutment rose straight up for 2,000 feet. Nowhere did we see a chance to scale it, and yet from a distance this had seemed the most feasible side. The only other remote possibility was some shoulder leading up from the northeast.

We continued climbing easily until we were nearly 6,000 feet high. Then we had precarious footing for a quarter of a mile over tumbling slide rocks toward the base of a rocky dome, a thousand feet high, to the north of Mount Doonerak itself, but sitting on the same massif. We called this dome North Doonerak and started to work our way up it in the hope that from there we would be able to see what the chances for a northeastern ascent of Doonerak might be. We proceeded with great caution, the rock being loose and crumbly.

We labored up almost vertical chimneys, crawled around the edges of great cliffs, took toe and finger holds, and pulled ourselves up ledges. By slow degrees we worked higher until finally, five hours after leaving camp, we reached a knife-edge ridge which dropped precipitously on one side toward the North Fork and on the other toward Bombardment Creek. It was a short and easy climb on the crest of this ridge to the summit of North Doonerak. Here was a most comfortable little flat, about 10 by 6 feet, covered with reindeer moss, *Dryas,* and heather. We sprawled out in comfort and leisure to enjoy mountains everywhere under the blue sky.

Dominating the scene, of course, was the great black face of old Doonerak, less than half a mile away and jutting straight up for nearly 2,000 feet. I did not believe that any climber, however expert, could make that face. The northeast shoulder which had been our one remaining hope, we could now see plainly. Some day, probably, people with years of rope-climbing experience will succeed in reaching the top by this route. We all knew that we never could.

There were other superb views. Northward we looked over the back crests of Inclined Mountain and Blackface Mountain toward those lofty gray lime summits where the Anaktuvuk originates, including Marshmallow Mountain, which next to Mount Doonerak is probably the highest mountain in the Brooks Range. Directly west, across Bombardment Creek, was Hanging Glacier Mountain, a great black wall against the sun, considerably higher than our 7,250 feet. In the far west, in the hazy distance, we could see the dome of Nahtuk, shaped like an owl's head, lying sixty-five miles away between the Alatna and John rivers in country I had not looked into since 1931. In all the vast panorama we could see on this clear day there probably was not a human being outside our party.

Time on the mountaintop passed quickly. First we just sat and enjoyed the view while munching our lunch. After a while we began to discuss and identify dubious geographic features. Then Harvey and I took still and moving pictures, got compass shots on more than thirty points, and measured the vertical angle to most of them by means of a Brunton pocket transit. Meanwhile Nutirwik scanned the panorama with field glasses to pick out sheep. For three and a half hours we stayed on North Doonerak, this superb observation point of the Arctic, before we returned to camp.

EDITOR'S AFTERWORD: *Thirteen years after Robert Marshall's second failed attempt on Doonerak, rock climbers George Beadle (then chairman of the California Institute of Technology's Division of Biology), Gunnar Bergman, and Alfred Tissieres completed the first ascent of the mountain. The team started at Wiseman, as Marshall had done, and, carrying seventy-pound packs, hiked on foot to Doonerak, a distance of about 130 miles round-trip. Seen from a distance, the peak "looked steep and dark and forbidding," Beadle later recounted in* The Living Wilderness. *But the climb itself proved easier than expected, and the trio reached Doonerak's summit on June 30, 1952.*

Shot Tower, Arrigetch

– David Roberts –

The Brooks Range is not a place that attracts many mountaineering expeditions. Running east-west across the state's arctic region, Alaska's northernmost chain is a subdued mountain kingdom, with wave upon wave of bare ridgelines and gentle peaks—most of them less than 6,000 feet high—that can be easily ascended in a day or less, with little or no technical-climbing expertise. But there are dramatic exceptions. And chief among those are the Arrigetch Peaks, a group of steep-sided and big-walled granite spires, 5,000 to 8,000 feet high, in the west-central Brooks Range.

Named by the region's Eskimo peoples—the English translation is "fingers of the hand outstretched"—the Arrigetch were explored (and later described) in the early 1900s by geologist Philip Smith. Two decades later, Robert Marshall and Ernie Johnson passed near "the bizarre fingers of the Arrigetch." But because "neither Ernie or I belonged to the human-fly category," Marshall writes in Alaska Wilderness, *"we did not try to climb the Arrigetch peaks." Not until the 1960s did a group of climbers, inspired by Marshall's descriptions, finally make the first attempt. Reporting on her expedition's successful ascent of seven granite peaks in 1965 in* The American

Alpine Journal, *Jeanne Bergen spoke of "[virgin] granite towers and spires with clean, sweeping faces—on the order of [Canada's] Bugaboos or Logan Mountains . . . a mountaineer's daydream."*

By the mid-1970s, all of the Arrigetch's major fingers had been ascended. Among those to complete several of the most difficult ascents were mountaineering authors David Roberts and Jon Krakauer (though on different expeditions, in different years). Both writers consider the Arrigetch Peaks to be among their favorite places—in fact, Krakauer's first published piece described an Arrigetch expedition—and Roberts has called this group of granitics "probably the finest mountains in arctic Alaska . . . a glimpse of the Perfect Place." Powerful words from a world-class climber who has participated in dozens of mountaineering expeditions around the globe, including many in Alaska. Though he's best known for his ascents, and stories, of Alaska Range peaks, Roberts has participated in—and written about—several milestone Brooks Range climbs.

David Roberts provides a glimpse of the Perfect Place in the essay "Shot Tower, Arrigetch," which first appeared in the 1972 American Alpine Journal *and later in his 1986 anthology,* Moments of Doubt *(published by The Mountaineers). He wrote of that 1971 ascent: "Shot Tower was the happiest climb of my life."*

ALREADY WE'RE MAKING EXCUSES. "You probably won't have to wait around too long," I tell my wife Sharon. "We may back off right at the beginning." Ed Ward voices similar doubts; the tower looks hard. The date is only June 22, but it's too warm—hot, almost, at six in the morning. In the last few days, we have run into mosquitoes as high as 6000 feet. And I am worried about lightning: even as far north as the Brooks Range, you can get it on a warm afternoon.

The peak itself: for Ed, a discovery of that summer. But I remember Chuck Loucks describing it, as he'd seen it in 1963; maybe the best peak in the Arrigetch, he had said. And I had glimpsed it, obscure but startling, from a plane in 1968, and again, from summits a few miles north, in 1969. Not an obsession yet; but something under the skin, part of my dream wilderness.

We take our time sorting hardware and food. Still down on our chances, we pretend to Sharon that we feel more casual about the peak than we do. At least I haven't had trouble sleeping the night before, as I have often in the last few years. And I feel good about going up there with Ed.

We get started. The first three pitches initiate us gently: clean, easy pitches on a sharp-edged spine. Old plates of granite, covered with scratchy black lichens; then fresh-cut blank plates of almost orange rock. Sharp cracks, good for nuts and pins alike. Gradually we get involved, as we discover the quality of the climb. "Pretty fine rock," says Ed. "Yeah, the best we've seen."

For me, this is what climbing has become: a question, always, of how much of myself to give to the mountain. As I get older, it becomes increasingly hard to give, to surrender to the novelty of risk and cold and tiredness. You can't really give to the mountain itself, of course, to unfeeling rock in the middle of an empty wilderness. So the giving you do, perhaps, is to your partner, and that too gets harder as you grow older. Instead you hedge with easier climbs, or talk yourself out of hard ones, or back off prudently. But now and then a mountain teases you into commitment.

On the fourth pitch things get hard. Ed leads it, and I can tell by how slowly he moves that it's tricky. "Not so bad," he shouts down. "It's neat." Above him, the rock stretches dully into the sky. Way up is the "Mushroom," the first crux, we guess.

I feel the first half-pleasant gnawings of fear. What if the next pitch doesn't go? What if I get psyched by all these left-hand flakes? And what if there's no good belay ledge? The sun is sliding around from the south. Soon we'll get it directly. My god, it's hot already—what will it be like then? To be sweltering here, north of the arctic circle—absurd!

The fifth pitch, my pitch, goes, but it is hard and devious. I overprotect it, and the rope drag makes me shaky. Standing on a skimpy ledge, I bring Ed up, and notice that my toes are starting to ache, my arms to feel tired.

The obverse of commitment—and this, too, I always feel—is doubt. About whether the whole thing is worth it. About why I have to do something artificial and dangerous to feel content. About whether I haven't used up the impulse—can anyone really go at it year after year, climb after climb, without deadening his openness to other things? And about the danger, pure and simple—I want to stay alive. I can't understand why I must eventually not exist: that makes no sense at all. But I can easily believe that I could fall and be killed.

Or that Ed could fall now, leading the sixth pitch. It looks as hard as mine. He pauses on an awkward move. A simple slip, a twelve-foot fall, a mere broken ankle . . . and then what do I do? Or if it happens higher, after we have gone farther into this labyrinth of inaccessibility—what could I do for him? And supposing I had to leave him? Is it all worth it, and why do we both feel it matters so much?

In the valley below us flowers are blooming, hillsides of tundra creeping out from under the nine-month smother of snow. There are birds reconnoitering the willow thickets, and butterflies, and bumblebees—a beautiful part of the earth, wild, and for a month, all ours. Why is it not sufficient?

The climb eases off. A bit of lunch, but we are mainly thirsty. Sips from the water bottle, then, from a cake deep in a crack, a few blessed chips of ice. We are both tired, and it's well into the afternoon. The clouds are building up in the southeast, over the Alatna valley; wasn't that thunder just now?

The climb gets hard again, harder than it looks, complicated. I lead the ninth pitch, all nuts in a left-handed crack. We're under the Mushroom, which looks especially rough. We talk about going straight over it—but a ceiling bulges ominously, and that new-cut rock on the right is sheer and frightening. Ed leads left. We've brought a single fixed rope. Here's the place for it; no hope to rappel the delicate traverse he's doing now.

Little things preoccupy me. How many shots left on my roll of film? Should I save some for the descent? Do we have enough hardware? Already—I curse our clumsiness—we've dropped two pins and had to leave one. If the lightning comes, could we get off quickly? Or better to hole up somewhere? My arms are tired; my knuckles have raw, scraped places on them. How should I string out the fixed rope?

I realize that I haven't thought for quite a while about Sharon waiting below. The climb has indeed teased me into commitment. For some time now I have been acutely aware of each crack in the plated granite, of the grain of the rock under my fingers—and of little else in the universe. On the one hand, it is all so familiar; on the other, utterly new. This is the way the Romantic poets saw the world, it seems to me; no wonder mountains were for them so primeval a presence, comparable only to the open sea.

But just as Keats could not see a nightingale without seeing a Dryad, so, on a climb, it is almost impossible for us to encounter nature directly.

We dare not descend to the simplicity, the banality of rock itself: we keep those touchstones of sanity safely packed in our minds—the awareness of time, and the abstract thread of a route. What becomes precious to us on a climb is not the mountain itself, in all its bewildering intricacy, but the things we bring to it, the cheese and the candy bars in our pack, the invaluable metal things dangling under our arms, the quarter-inch of rubber under our feet. More than fear, more than self-consciousness, it is thirty centuries of acquisitive, aesthetic Western culture that stand between us and any unfiltered contact with what is there.

Ed has done the pitch, bypassed the Mushroom. Seconding, stringing out the fixed rope behind me, I am absorbed by the delicacy of the pitch, the nicest yet. On the ridge Ed has found a platform. More lunch, a patch of ice to chop up and add to our water bottle. But above us the going, which we had thought would be easy, looks tough, and the vertical wall below the summit shines unrelenting in the afternoon sun.

Pitches eleven and twelve go slowly; meanwhile the lightning is flashing southeast of us. We're too high to get off fast now. If it hits us, we'll simply stop somewhere and wait it out. It's still hot, too hot, sweaty and weird. The thirteenth pitch uncovers an incredible "moat," a slash across the ridge, as deep as a chimney, with a long patch of ice for a floor. We suck greedy mouthfuls of water off its surface, while the thunderstorm passes just east of us. A friendly place, this moat.

Evening now. The real crux is just above us: a sixty-foot wall, quite smooth, overhanging by a degree or two. From below, a week before, I had thought I saw a bypass on the left, over the north face. Now it simply vanishes, was never there. Nor any hope on the right. A single shallow, crooked crack splits the wall. Ed's lead. He goes on aid, the first time we've had to. The pins are lousy, tied off, bottoming. He doesn't like it. I belay in a trance of tiredness. Halfway up, Ed says, "We just don't have the pins to do it." I know it, too, but I urge him to keep trying.

He climbs doggedly, nervily. Two tiny nuts in shallow rivulets of rock. A cliff-hanger, even, which he'd brought along as a kind of joke. A nut in an overhanging groove comes out; Ed falls three feet, catches himself on a lower stirrup. I'm not frightened any more; only afraid that we will fail.

Ed persists. Pins tied off, the wrong size, one wedged in a shallow hole. He edges toward the lip of the wall. At some point I realize he is going to make it. I feel almost matter-of-fact. "Way to go," I shout, but not with the enthusiasm of half a day before. It is approaching midnight. Sharon has gone back to base camp; we are alone. We have twenty-two pins and nuts; I use one for an anchor, Ed uses seventeen on the aid pitch, and three bad ones to anchor the top.

We are at the pole of inaccessibility of our climb; it is the day after the solstice, and the sun hovers low and smoky in the north. The world is empty, alien, and we have never been more alone nor more self-sufficient. "Really fine, Ed," I say. "An incredible lead."

Two pitches to the summit, almost walking. A big place, unspecial; yet special to us, cozy in its barrenness. The best rock climb of our lives, for both of us. We look at each other, shake hands, self-conscious for the first time, as if we had not really known how little we knew of each other. It is almost midnight.

And all the long descent. Our tiredness builds, we seem half-asleep. The sun wheels east again, the heat returns. As we go down, the mosquitoes wander up to find us. It is even hotter than the day before. We have lost the edge of excitement; in its place is only wariness, carefulness. Rappels, especially: I hate them, would rather down-climb almost anything.

The going passes from tedious to oppressive. Our hands have become raw from so much grasping and hammering. Our feet are painfully sore. The heat and mosquitoes conspire to make us miserable and, in our ragged fatigue, urge us to the edge of carelessness. As I belay Ed below me, two birds land on my ledge, mocking, in their unthinking grace, our whole enterprise. I want only to be down, off the climb, alive again. And it hits me now how indifferent the mountains are, and therefore, how valuable: for on them we cannot afford to be relativistic. The terms of our combat are theirs, and if we discover on them nothing we can take back to show others, still we discover the utter alienness of•the Not-Self, of the seemingly ordinary world all around us.

Running short on pins; we have used too many for anchors. The rappels now are just reaching, our single 180-foot rope forcing us to stop on ledges we hadn't found on the way up. We are so tired: all our conversation, all our thoughts, seem directed toward safety. We rehearse precautions as if they were lessons we had half-forgotten: check the anchor, check the clip-in, check the bottom of the rope. I want only to be off, free, able to walk around unroped. My arms, fingers, palms, toes ache.

The mosquitoes are everywhere, horrible. But we are getting down. It is full morning, another day: at base camp the others have slept and are waking to wonder about us. At least we have the luxury of knowing where we are. Down to seven or eight pins, we descend the easy first three pitches. Never too careful; take your time; don't think about the mosquitoes. Something about it is hectic and petty; something else seems tragically poignant. At last I step off Shot Tower onto real earth, and belay Ed down.

We're safe, and again it is over—the whole thing in the past already, though our arms ache and our fingertips are raw. We take off our kletter-shoes and wiggle our toes wantonly in the air, laughing as if we were drunk. Sharon has left us a full water bottle. We seem to be falling asleep with our eyes open, going off in short trances. Everything seems good, but the climb is over, and already I anticipate the long ordinary months stretching into our futures, the time to be lived through before life can become special and single-minded again.

Permissions

1. *The Ascent of Mount St. Elias* by Filippo de Filippi was originally published in 1900 by Frederick A. Stokes and Co. in New York. Copyright © 1900 is now held by Pia Passigli de Filippi. Chapters VII and VIII are reprinted with the permission of Pia Passigli de Filippi.

2. "First Up Mt. Blackburn" by Dora Keen was originally published in the November 1913 edition of *The World's Work*. It is now in the public domain.

3. "Ice-Cliff and Earthquake: Mount Fairweather" by Paddy Sherman was originally published in *Cloud Walkers: Six Climbs on Major Canadian Peaks* by St. Martin's Press, New York. Copyright © 1965 by Paddy Sherman. Reprinted by permission of the author.

4. "The Devils Thumb" by Jon Krakauer was originally published in *Eiger Dreams: Ventures Among Men and Mountains* by Lyons & Burford, New York. Copyright © 1990 by John Krakauer. Reprinted by permission of Lyons & Burford.

5. "The Ascent of Mt. St. Agnes" by Bradford Washburn was originally published in 1939 in *The American Alpine Journal* by The American Alpine Club, New York. Copyright © 1939 by Bradford Washburn. Reprinted by permission of the author.

6. "The Sourdough Expedition, 1910" by Bill Sherwonit was originally published in *To the Top of Denali: Climbing Adventures on North America's Highest Peak* by Alaska Northwest Books, Seattle. Copyright © 1990 by Bill Sherwonit.

7. *The Ascent of Denali* by Hudson Stuck was originally published by Charles Scribner's Sons, New York, in 1914, and reprinted in 1989 by the University of Nebraska Press (Bison Books), Lincoln, Nebraska. It is now in the public domain.

8. "The South Buttress of Mt. McKinley" by Riccardo Cassin was originally published in *Fifty Years of Alpinism* by The Mountaineers, Seattle. Copyright © 1981 by Riccardo Cassin. Reprinted by permission of the publisher.

9. *Minus 148°: The Winter Ascent of Mt. McKinley* by Art Davidson was originally published in 1969 by W. W. Norton Co., New York, and reprinted in 1986 by Cloudcap Press, Seattle. Copyright © 1969 by Art Davidson. Reprinted by permission of the author.

10. "Hunter and Foraker" by Michael Kennedy was originally published in 1978 in *The American Alpine Journal* by The American Alpine Club, New York. Copyright © 1978 by Michael Kennedy. Reprinted by permission of the author.

11. "Denali's Child—1954" by Fred Beckey was originally published in *Mount McKinley: Icy Crown of North America* by The Mountaineers, Seattle. Copyright © 1993 by Fred Beckey. Reprinted by permission of the author.

12. "Lone Wolf (The *Other* John Waterman)" by Jonathan Waterman was originally published in *In the Shadow of Denali: Life and Death on Alaska's Mount McKinley* by Dell Books, New York. Copyright © 1994 by Jon Waterman. Reprinted by permission of Dell Books, a division of Bantam Doubleday Dell.

13. "The Mountain of My Fear" by David Roberts was originally published in 1968 by Vanguard Press, New York, and then in *The Early Climbs: Deborah and the Mountain of My Fear* by The Mountaineers, Seattle. Copyright © 1968 by David Roberts. Reprinted by permission of the author.

14. "Californians in Alaska" by Royal Robbins was originally published in 1970 in *The American Alpine Journal* by The American Alpine Club, New York. Copyright © 1970 by Royal Robbins. Reprinted by permission of the author.

15. "East Face of the Moose's Tooth: The Dance of the Woo Li Masters" by James D. Bridwell was originally published in 1992 in *The American Alpine Journal* by the American Alpine Club, New York, and then in *Climbing Adventures: A Climber's Passion* by ICS Books, Merrillville, Indiana. Copyright © 1992 by James D. Bridwell. Reprinted by permission of the author.

16. "North Doonerak" by Robert Marshall was originally published in *Alaska Wilderness: Exploring the Central Brooks Range* by the University of California Press. Copyright © 1970 by the Regents of the University of California. Reprinted by permission of the University of California Press.

17. "Shot Tower, Arrigetch" by David Roberts was originally published in 1972 in *The American Alpine Journal* by The American Alpine Club, New York, and then in *Moments of Doubt and Other Mountaineering Writings*. Copyright © 1972 by David Roberts. Reprinted by permission of the author.

About the Editor

Outdoors and nature writer Bill Sherwonit has always loved the mountains and been intrigued by the people who climb them. Those interests led him, in 1987, to Denali, where he ascended the West Buttress on a guided expedition; it was, he says, a once-in-a-lifetime adventure. Three years later he wrote his first book, *To the Top of Denali: Climbing Adventures on North America's Highest Peak.* Bill continues to spend much of his time in Alaska's mountain ranges, hiking, scrambling, and observing the natural world.

Born in Bridgeport, Connecticut, in 1950, Sherwonit earned an MS degree in geology from the University of Arizona. Switching careers in the late 1970s while in California, he returned to school and entered the field of journalism. In 1982 he joined the now-defunct *Anchorage Times,* working first as a sports writer, then as the newspaper's outdoors writer. Now a full-time freelance writer and photographer in Anchorage, he contributes to a wide variety of publications, including *Alaska, Audubon, Climbing, National Parks, National Wildlife,* and *Summit.* He is also the author of *Iditarod: The Great Race to Nome* and *Alaska's Accessible Wilderness: A Traveler's Guide to Alaska's State Parks.* He has contributed to several Alaska guidebooks and teaches a wilderness writing class at the University of Alaska Anchorage.

Index

Recommended Reading

Beckey, Fred. *Mount McKinley: Icy Crown of North America*. Seattle: The Mountaineers, 1993.

Bridwell, James D., with Keith Peall. *Climbing Adventures: A Climber's Passion*. Merrillville, Ind.: ICS Books, 1992.

Browne, Belmore. *The Conquest of McKinley*. (1913. Reprint, Boston: Houghton Mifflin, 1956.)

Cassin, Riccardo. *Fifty Years of Alpinism*. Seattle: The Mountaineers, 1981.

Cook, Frederick A. *To the Top of the Continent*. London: Hodder & Stoughton, 1909.

Davidson, Art. *Minus 148°: The Winter Ascent of Mt. McKinley*. Seattle: Cloudcap Press, 1986.

Dunn, Robert. *Shameless Diary of an Explorer*. New York: The Outing Publishing Co., 1907.

Filippi, Filippo de. *The Ascent of Mount St. Elias*. New York: Frederick A. Stokes and Co., 1900.

Krakauer, Jon. *Eiger Dreams: Ventures Among Men and Mountains*. New York: Lyons & Burford, 1990.

Marshall, Robert. *Alaska Wilderness: Exploring the Central Brooks Range*. Berkeley: University of California Press, 1970.

Moore, Terris. *Mt. McKinley's Pioneer Climbs*. Seattle: The Mountaineers, 1981.

Randall, Glenn. *Breaking Point*. Denver: Chockstone Press, 1984.

Roberts, David. *Moments of Doubt and Other Mountaineering Writings*. Seattle: The Mountaineers, 1986.

———. *The Early Climbs: Deborah and the Mountain of My Fear*. Seattle: The Mountaineers, 1991.

Roper, Steve, and Allen Steck. *Fifty Classic Climbs of North America*. San Francisco: Sierra Club Books, 1979.

Sherman, Paddy. *Cloud Walkers: Six Climbs on Major Canadian Peaks*. New York: St. Martin's Press, 1965.

Sherwonit, Bill. *To the Top of Denali: Climbing Adventures on North America's Highest Peak*. Seattle: Alaska Northwest Books, 1990.

Snyder, Howard. *The Hall of the Mountain King*. New York: Charles Scribner's Sons, 1973.

Stuck, Hudson. *The Ascent of Denali (Mount McKinley): A Narrative of the First Complete Ascent of the Highest Peak in North America*. 1914. (Reprint, Lincoln: University of Nebraska Press, 1989.)

Washburn, Bradford, and David Roberts. *Mount McKinley: The Conquest of Denali*. New York: Harry N. Abrams, 1991.

Waterman, Jonathan. *Surviving Denali: A Study of Accidents on Mount McKinley 1910–1982*. New York: The American Alpine Club, 1983.

———. *High Alaska: A Historical Guide to Denali, Mount Foraker, and Mount Hunter*. New York: The American Alpine Club, 1988.

———. *In the Shadow of Denali: Life and Death on Alaska's Mount McKinley*. New York: Dell Books, 1994.

Wilcox, Joseph. *White Winds*. Los Alamitos, Calif.: Hwong Publishing Co., 1981.